ROUTLEDGE LIBRARY EDITIONS: ART AND CULTURE IN THE NINETEENTH CENTURY

Volume 7

VINCENZO BELLINI AND THE AESTHETICS OF EARLY NINETEENTH-CENTURY ITALIAN OPERA

VINCENZO BELLINI AND THE AESTHETICS OF EARLY NINETEENTH-CENTURY ITALIAN OPERA

SIMON MAGUIRE

Taylor & Francis Group

LONDON AND NEW YORK

First published in 1989 by Garland Publishing, Inc.

This edition first published in 2019
by Routledge
2 Park Square, Milton Park, Abingdon, Oxon OX14 4RN

and by Routledge
711 Third Avenue, New York, NY 10017

Routledge is an imprint of the Taylor & Francis Group, an informa business

© 1989 Simon Maguire

All rights reserved. No part of this book may be reprinted or reproduced or utilised in any form or by any electronic, mechanical, or other means, now known or hereafter invented, including photocopying and recording, or in any information storage or retrieval system, without permission in writing from the publishers.

Trademark notice: Product or corporate names may be trademarks or registered trademarks, and are used only for identification and explanation without intent to infringe.

British Library Cataloguing in Publication Data
A catalogue record for this book is available from the British Library

ISBN: 978-1-138-35894-2 (Set)
ISBN: 978-0-429-42671-1 (Set) (ebk)
ISBN: 978-1-138-36598-8 (Volume 7) (hbk)
ISBN: 978-1-138-36601-5 (Volume 7) (pbk)
ISBN: 978-0-429-43051-0 (Volume 7) (ebk)

Publisher's Note
The publisher has gone to great lengths to ensure the quality of this reprint but points out that some imperfections in the original copies may be apparent.

Disclaimer
The publisher has made every effort to trace copyright holders and would welcome correspondence from those they have been unable to trace.

Vincenzo Bellini and the Aesthetics of Early Nineteenth-Century Italian Opera

Simon Maguire

Garland Publishing, Inc.
New York & London 1989

Copyright © 1989 by Simon Maguire.

Library of Congress Cataloging-in-Publication Data

Maguire, Simon.
Vincenzo Bellini and the aesthetics of early nineteenth-century Italian opera / Simon Maguire.
  p. cm. — (Outstanding dissertations in music from British universities)
Originally presented as the author's thesis (Ph. D.)—Worcester College, Oxford University, 1984.
Bibliography: p.
Includes index.
ISBN 0-8240-2344-7 (alk. paper)
1. Bellini, Vincenzo, 1801–1835—Criticism and interpretation. 2. Opera—Italy—19th century. 3. Music—Italy—19th century—Philosophy and aesthetics. I. Title. II. Series.
ML410.B44M3 1989
782.1'092—dc20   89-31439

Designed by Valerie Mergentime

Printed on acid-free, 250-year-life paper.
Manufactured in the United States of America

Preface
Italian Attitudes To Music At The Close Of The Bel Canto Era

This thesis is a first attempt to study the Italian attitudes to opera current while Bellini was studying and composing. It draws mainly on Italian critical and aesthetic writing dating from the end of an era that was still dominated by the Italian *bel canto*. The last part examines *bel canto* itself in more detail. Many of the writers considered are unfamiliar today, and occasionally their attitudes seem impossibly dated, but they express the accepted views on music, opera, and singing that still dominated a particularly insular tradition. Consequently, more progressive figures like Mazzini are not featured in the following exploration of Italian aesthetics of opera, as they represent ideas that grew after the period considered here.

Since 1985, I have worked more on Bellini's music than on the ideas it springs from. However, before knowing that the thesis itself might be published, I did prepare an essay concentrating more specifically on Italian reservations concerning the particular expressive powers of music during the pre-Romantic period. As a preface to the thesis, I thought that it might be helpful to place Italian attitudes more clearly into the broader context of European musical aesthetics.

Considering the historical importance of Italian opera, the attitudes that form part of its tradition still seem to have evaded critical attention remarkably successfully, even though there is a growing literature on musical thought during the period 1750–1835.[1] One recent book is that by E. Fubini; this shows that perhaps the area will not forever remain critically obscure.[2] However, Fubini does not explore the attitudes peculiar to Italians in much detail, so the written tradition considered here is hardly touched upon. In fact, these preconceptions had dominated

Italian writing on music for about as long as *bel canto* had existed, and touch on the question of just how much Italians expected the actual musical part of their operas to contribute to the whole.

It is worth making clear at the outset what Italians thought the effects of music were, because it seems to have since been assumed by everyone that their opera was a purely musical affair. Carl Dahlhaus, for example, claims that the texts of eighteenth-century Italian operas were "aesthetically secondary" to the music, even though they preceded it.[3] Although this might be regarded by some as a valid judgement on their actual dramatic quality, it is not an explanation of the nature of opera that would have been acceptable to contemporaries of the works themselves. Italians do not appear to have believed that music dominated opera, nor even expected it to have the power to do so; and, before the advent of Verdian opera and the eventual encounter with Romantic symphonism, there was no musical tradition to suggest it. The assumption, partly inherited from Wagner, that the earlier Italian opera was, at heart, a purely musical form, seems to be born of the conviction that it was certainly not a dramatic one, rather than from any faith in the Italian appreciation of music.

Musical thought in other countries evolved from, and gradually grew out of, traditional theories of imitation, a complex process recently described in detail by John Neubauer.[4] Although this theme can also be traced in Italy, it was less influential than was the actual operatic repertory itself. In fact, Italian attitudes to music were largely determined by the example of *opera seria* and by the inevitable search for its origins. Nearly all studies of music began with an account of the origins of opera in the pre-dramatic poetry of Ancient Greece and its subsequent flowering in the theater as described by Aristotle. An increased feeling for the prestige of Greek culture was reflected by the appearance of Winckelmann's writings in Italian editions of 1779 and 1783. French texts seem to have been particularly influential: for example, Jean Jacques Barthélemy's *Entretiens sur l'état de la musique grecque vers le milieu du quatrième siècle avant l'ère vulgaire* (Paris, 1777), whose opinions and phrases regularly appear in Italian speculations on the subject. Typical of the writers referred to in the chapters that follow is G. B. Gennaro Grossi, for whom poetry and music were quite inseparable.[5]

In fact, Italians of the late eighteenth and early nineteenth centuries wrote as if "the arts" embraced most aspects of human life, even involving fields like philosophy and law-giving. This approach is not as peculiar as it might seem, and can be traced to earlier English and French texts. The most comprehensive eighteenth-century exposition on the theme was provided in *A Dissertation on the Rise, Union and Power, the Progressions, Separations, and Corruptions of Poetry and Music* (London, 1763) by the Reverend John Brown (1715–1766); this book was published in Italian in 1772. There were many similar, if briefer, accounts to draw on from the great classicist Gravina, from Rousseau, Barthélemy, and the Spanish Jesuit, Arteaga.[6] Such an approach seems to have lasted a very long time: it can still be found with Bellini's classically-minded librettist, Felice Romani, who described the first lyric poets as "high priests of the divinities, legislators of the people, and inspirers of good moral character."[7]

These writers considered that arts like poetry, gesture, and singing, which had such an important bearing on the health of society, were summed up in the great art-form of opera, and their descriptions of Ancient Greek tragedy were cast in the same mold. The stance taken by Grossi in 1820 therefore comes at the end of a long series of standard works on the subject: Padre Martini's history of music (1781), Calsabigi's "Dissertazione" on Metastasio (1755), Metastasio's own *Estratto dell' Arte Poetica d'Aristotile* (which probably dates from the 1770s), and the writings of another Spanish Jesuit, Eximeno.[8] They concocted a history of the birth of opera from texts by Aristotle, Horace, and Athenaeus, and focused on a singer-poet exerting his skills in music, poetry, costume, design, dance, and acting.[9] Italians believed that these arts had been unified in ancient drama just as they should be in contemporary opera.

It was remarkable that nearly all Italians asserted that the ancient dramas had been sung throughout. Such a claim is associated primarily with the scholars and musicians of the

Florentine *Camerata*, although they had stressed the idea perhaps to give prestige to their musico-dramatic productions, rather than out of ignorance of the classics.[10]

The sixteenth century had in fact seen the high-water mark of Italian classical scholarship, and such a misconceived view of the Ancients had never been widely held.[11] Indeed, it seems to have been generally accepted that only the choruses had actually been sung, and the later abandonment of this position represents a rejection of the achievements of Renaissance scholarship. It is illuminating to discover that eighteenth- and early nineteenth-century Italians felt the need to stress the links between opera and Greek drama much more strongly and more often than had earlier writers. In fact, the theory that the ancients had sung their dramas throughout was accepted almost universally by the later eighteenth century, attracting men like Rousseau and Charles Burney as well as the majority of Italians. By 1826, we find Lichtenthal asserting, in what was the most authoritative Italian musical dictionary yet compiled, that the poets and actors of ancient drama had been the same, and that music had been part of its essential nature. He concluded, as had Rousseau, that Greek tragedy was "sung throughout in the manner of our recitatives, and accompanied by instruments."[12] Indeed, Carlo Ritorni accepted this as the authorized standpoint as late as 1841.[13]

Metastasio had dwelt at great length on this issue in his *Estratto*, adducing passages in Aristotle, Livy, and other mostly Roman sources in support. This list by then constituted something of a litany that had been ritually brought out to link opera with Greek drama ever since the days of Girolamo Mei and Vincenzo Galilei—though Metastasio's immediate source would have been his mentor, Gravina.[14] However, what underlay his continued commitment to the traditional arguments was his belief in the essential unity of poetry and music. He argued that the result of dramatic declamation to a large audience was, inevitably, an elevated type of speech, and the need to move the hearts and stir the minds of so many spectators required the organization of this speech into song. The consistency of the Italian tradition can be judged by the fact that his arguments were precisely the same as those put forward by Bernardo Segni in 1549, in what was perhaps the first description of a completely sung ancient drama.[15]

The extent to which Italian writers adhered to this idealized Greek opera, and the extent to which they elaborated it with precise details, can be seen as a measure of their commitment to the traditional association of music and words. Therefore, their speculations about origins should not be regarded as the cause of their other theories about opera, but rather as a remarkable manifestation of them. For example, Eximeno gave elaborate details about Greek opera, openly modeling them on those of his own time. Such was the weight of opinion, that a scholar as diligent as Padre Martini declared himself unable to decide whether the dialogues, rather than just the choruses, had been sung—a measure of how clouded the issue had become since the sixteenth century.[16] Calsabigi assumed that it was by now "the received opinion of everyone" that the dialogues were also sung, "with a type of singing such as that which we have invented for our recitatives, that is to say faster and less encumbered with the trappings of harmony."[17] It is salutary to reflect that Rinuccini would have been more justified in claiming that it was "the opinion of many" that Greek tragedy was sung throughout, if he had written in 1800 rather than 1600.

The conclusion that Italian writers drew was that their opera was directly descended from Greek drama and that, like the Greeks, they should preserve the balance of the arts that was the basis of its success.[18] Consequently they regarded any weakness in the opera of their own times as the inevitable consequence of the separation of the arts. Composers themselves rarely showed any interest in such aesthetic theories, but in the first third of the nineteenth century it became a commonplace to refer to the *filosofia* of composers, by which was meant a proper regard for the balance of individual elements within opera. Bellini was always praised for his *filosofia* because his operas seemed to put these ideals into practice, rather than being taken up with the mysterious technicalities of harmony, counterpoint, or instrumentation that were beyond the comprehension of most such writers. For his contemporaries, Bellini's *filosofia* lay in the close relationship between poetry and music.[19] Yet we would seriously misunderstand contemporary aesthetics of opera were we to assume that an aria such as "Casta Diva," in *Norma*, was regarded as expressing the text in a modern sense. Italians seem to have concluded that music gained its expressive content from its association with poetry, rather than having it inherently. Such an aria might be praised for encapsulating the ideal enunciation of the verses, but hardly for their musical expression.

Since it was accepted that music was not originally a complete art form in itself, there was a wide-spread assumption that it was not actually capable of expressive power—at least not unless it was combined with words. This conclusion was reinforced by the traditional explanations of the nature of art that had been derived ultimately from Plato and Aristotle. For example, according to theories of imitation, music without a text was open to the objection that it was "very difficult to know what is intended and which of the worthwhile imitations are being imitated.... [A]ll those creations which depend on speed, dexterity and beastlike cries, which lead to the employment of aulos and kithara without dance and song, must be considered completely uncouth."[20] This passage from Plato, referred to by Barthélemy and by Italian writers, would not have been out of place in early nineteenth-century writings on music in opera. The theory of imitation, which literary men in Italy still clung to, was understood to imply an injunction against music without poetry.

There does not seem to have been any Italian literature of musical speculation, comparable to Mattheson's *Affektenlehre* or Rameau's attempts at a Cartesian methodology, that might have prompted a study of the particular powers of music. This partly explains the survival of the literary approach derived from classical teaching. The need for music to be appropriate to the sentiments of the text had been occasionally mentioned, but only in the vaguest of terms. Even professional musicians seem to have accepted that music, by itself, was unable to arouse emotions satisfactorily without the help of words.[21] Calsabigi had therefore attributed the power, variety, and beauty of contemporary opera to the excellence of Metastasio's poetry, concluding that a good opera would be inconceivable without a fine poetic text.[22] This conflicts with more modern views that consider a poetic libretto to be transformed by its musical setting, no longer exerting any independent effect. Until the mid-nineteenth century, Italian aesthetics assumed music to be incapable of such a feat and continued to assess the poetic value of the words.

It is worth putting this attitude to music into a broader European context. Of course, Italian aestheticians were not alone in approaching music from a literary standpoint; Dahlhaus has shown that men like Kant and Hegel regarded music without poetry as more entertainment than culture. Yet, there are some areas where the lack of an Italian tradition in musical speculation prevented the adoption of newer opinions that were beginning to be found abroad. For example, there is no obvious parallel in Italian musical aesthetics to the consideration of music's particular expressive power, such as Herbert Schueller discerns amongst British empiricists like Avison and Webb, who compared the effects of music with those exerted by kindred art forms.[23] Even Burney, although he shared many of the Italians' convictions about Greek "opera," differed from them in seeing considerable virtue in the separation of the arts, as it led to a "degree of cultivation" that "increased the power of each of them."[24] This conclusion is directly opposed to that reached by practically all Italian writers, who remained sceptical about the value of spoken drama or independent instrumental music.

It was really only with the writings of Mazzini that a contrasting view of opera began to be heard from within Italy, although Romanticism had already begun to permeate literary criticism. Mazzini wrote eloquently in favor of a Romantic opera that would turn away from the *ancien regime* that the Metastasian tradition represented. Perhaps best known is his call for a drama that transcended current formal conventions. His enthusiasm for Donizetti's *Anna Bolena* reflected his desire for a drama based on historical realities rather than on idealized classical figures; his appreciation of the piece suggests he thought that music might be the principal agent of the drama.[25] Certainly, his *Filosofia della musica* (1836) bears little relationship to the notions of *filosofia* discussed in this thesis; not surprisingly, he had little more enthusiasm for Romani and Bellini than he had for Metastasio.[26] Yet even Mazzini shared the traditional views about the separation of the arts, and seems to have limited his sights to opera. His writings still reflect the Italocentric outlook of his predecessors and he looked askance at the instrumental developments in music by men like Berlioz.

It is perhaps not surprising that Italians were slow to pick up these new ideas. Even in a European context, E.T.A Hoffmann's eulogy of Beethoven's symphonies—precisely because they scorned "every aid, every admixture of another art (the art of poetry)"—marked a new departure in 1810, and Italians were not to be exposed to such a repertory until very much later. During the early nineteenth century, the Italians were left increasingly alone in their commitment to the old aesthetic values, and northern visitors grew dissatisfied with the operatic culture that had been such a delight to men like Rousseau and Burney. Spohr, Weber, Berlioz, and Mendelssohn found themselves alienated from a tradition that was championed only by Stendhal. Professional musicians had little time for the musical restraints that were demanded in the name of *filosofia*.

Many features of early nineteenth-century Italian music show the extent of this difference of viewpoint; some have a direct relevance for Bellini's operatic style. Firstly, and perhaps most obviously, there was a marked lack of enthusiasm for instrumental music, whether in an operatic context or not. Italians treated instrumental music as if it were detrimental to the balance of different contributions to the *melodramma*, because it seemed to threaten the primacy, not so much of the singers, as of the poetry. In fact, Italian instrumental music had declined considerably from the prominence it had enjoyed during the late Baroque era and, by the early nineteenth century, composers wrote orchestral works either as student exercises or as accompaniments to church services. Concert life was inexorably eclipsed by opera and largely disappeared. Even in Milan, where Bellini made his name, there had been no follow-up to the achievements of Sammartini's day, and, by the time he was writing his greatest successes there, the decline was more or less complete.[27] Yet aestheticians continued to warn of the damage too much instrumental music would inflict on opera, as if they feared the vitality of the symphonic repertory that had developed abroad. The instrumental continuo bass was likened to a pedestal on which the singer stood, but any other instrumental lines tended to be viewed as merely serving the vanity of professional composers. This explains the peculiar constitution of their opera orchestras, which always strongly emphasized the bass lines at the expense of inner parts. This feature continues to be observed in literature, but scholars do not look to Italians themselves for contemporary explanations of their outlook.[28]

It was held that ancient music had owed its unrivalled power to its simplicity and avoidance of unnecessary complications like counterpoint and had thereby "assured the triumph of the poetry."[29] As this appealed to their literary approach, Italians like Antonio Planelli and Francesco Milizia had always urged composers to show similar restraint: "because music that is too full of notes, whether they come simultaneously or successively, is incapable of expression."[30] Although this seems curious, such a standpoint has echoes of the familiar arguments used in the disputes over French and Italian opera during the 1750s and 1770s. As was true of these later Italian writers, the *Encyclopédistes* (for example, Rousseau) retained a classical approach to opera, and had no faith in the individual power of sound. Music had to restrict itself to serving the poetry, rather than indulging in the mysterious complexities of musical craftsmanship. Otherwise, the composer would create what was contemptuously called *contrappunto* rather than music. *Contrappunto* was the term used to denigrate complex, unpoetic music that for some reason appealed greatly to northern composers.

Just as they remained suspicious of music independent of poetry, so the same classical approach had naturally turned Italians away from creating a repertory of pure literary drama (without music); it had only started to appear with Alfieri's plays. Drama was reckoned to benefit from its association with the rhythms of music, and, as late as 1870, Francesco de Sanctis argued that music had simplified literary style, "forcing it to abbreviate its sentences, curbing its pomposity and solemnity... its futile academicism, and causing it to acquire fluency and succinctness."[31] A simple, limpid style was demanded of operatic poetry, over and above any consideration of the actual subject matter, and Calsabigi singled out Metastasio's dramas in this respect. Metastasio's style was disdained by the champions of the new theater, such as Bettinelli, Alfieri, and later even by Calsabigi; but, for more traditionally minded writers, it remained the model for librettists well into the nineteenth century.[32] The same classical convictions also limited subject matter. The Italian resistance to Shakespeare's "barbarisms" was remarkable, even in plots to operas like *Otello* and *I Capuleti e i Montecchi*, where the plays were either brought into conformity with Aristotelean rules, or ignored completely.

An operatic tradition dominated by poetry rather than drama naturally relied on the singer more than on the orchestra. In the early nineteenth century, Italians still looked to the Greeks for their model and to the *bel canto* singer as the modern representative of that ancient eloquence, even down to the details of vocal ornamentation.[33] In fact, the Italian art of *bel canto* encapsulated many of the qualities that writers looked for in opera. Inevitably, it was regarded more as a poetic art than a musical one, since music itself was held to have little or no expressive power. As music depended on poetry for its artistic content, singing required the most noble and elegant delivery of the words, rather than their interpretation. Not surprisingly therefore, *bel canto* treatises stressed the importance of a natural style of pronunciation more strongly than considerations of expressivity, in order to achieve what Crescentini called "un imitazione del discorso."[34]

The subject of *bel canto* is explored at the end of the thesis. Modern writers still tend to treat the tradition with suspicion. Apart from Duey's book mentioned in the text, the only recent work is that by Rodolfo Celletti, which considers the technical aspects of *bel canto* in impressive detail. His comments on the growing power of music evinced by Rossini's writing are particularly relevant to the themes developed in the thesis. However, Celletti is evidently not interested in those contemporary attitudes to musical aesthetics considered here. Bellini's music is obviously much more Romantic in tone and technique than is the music Celletti is primarily concerned with; but it seems extraordinary that Rossini's music should be featured so prominently, and Bellini's music so little, in a work treating Italian *bel canto*.[35] Rossini's vocal writing certainly uses some techniques of *bel canto*, at least those concerned with *agilità*; but such an approach ignores the importance Italians attached to the *canto spianato*, which reflected traditional concerns for poetry. That contemporaries saw in Bellini the return to values that Rossini had neglected, suggests that there may be more to *bel canto* than Celletti offers us.

The neglect of the aesthetics of classical Italian opera has harmed not just the reputation of *bel canto*. Elvidio Surian pointed out that the whole field of Italian opera studies has suffered from the application of assumptions and criteria derived solely from German Romanticism.[36] Operas based on principles of poetic song have been assessed according to concepts of musical drama dependent on symphonic continuity. Most of the features of Italian opera discussed in the thesis illustrate that its character was considered more from a literary point of view.

The presumption that Italian opera was dominated by musical considerations, besides being at variance with contemporary thought, is not supported by the musical evidence either. One of the most obvious features of eighteenth- and early nineteenth-century operas, compared with later works, is the extent to which they are supported by great tracts of recitative, where it could hardly be maintained that music is the main issue. Current studies of opera discount the importance of recitative almost entirely, precisely because scholars search for dramatic action generated by musical continuity, just as they would when considering the works of Verdi or Wagner. Italians considered recitative, particularly accompanied declamation, to be the "foundation of opera," and they frequently studied its poetry in detail.[37] The recitative styles of Donizetti and Bellini represent the final flowering of this tradition: operatic trends from 1750 to 1850 show a radical switch from poetic to musical domination, and such recitative was pruned fairly ruthlessly in Verdi's operas of the 1840s.

The thesis follows through some of these themes in more detail, paying particular regard to the time just before and during Bellini's actual career. It must be admitted, however, that Bellini's music is not treated systematically and no attempt is made to account for the effect of his operas. On the other hand, the subject is not, strictly speaking, that of aesthetics. I tried to clarify my aims in a motto from A. J. Ayer, the context of which was his remark that there is "no possibility of arguing about questions of value in aesthetics, but only about questions of fact. A scientific treatment of aesthetics would show us what in general were the causes of aesthetic feeling, why various societies produced and admired the works of art they did."[38]

We can certainly illuminate criticism of Italian opera if we place tradition in some aesthetic context, where attitudes to instrumental music, poetry, and singing show themselves to follow a coherent approach. We should perhaps beware of concluding that Italian opera at the close of the *bel canto* era was simply a product of contemporary aesthetic preconceptions. Sometimes the literature was conditioned by the musical tradition, and not *vice versa*, not least in its speculations on Greek "opera" and its judgments on the expressive power of instrumental music. Nevertheless, Italian views already had an impressive pedigree by the early nineteenth century, drawing not only on English and French writing, but also on their own perennial classicizing tendency, that had been displayed by men like Galilei, Doni, Gravina, and Metastasio. This overwhelming inheritance could hardly fail to exert a considerable effect, and our understanding of Italian opera requires a greater breadth of cultural perspective than musicians are often prepared to consider: both the aesthetic literature and the musical repertory form complimentary facets of a distinct tradition.

Simon Maguire
April, 1989

Notes

1. For example, Italian writers before Mazzini do not figure much in Peter le Huray and James Day, *Music and Aesthetics in the Eighteenth and Early Nineteenth Centuries* (Cambridge, 1981).
2. E. Fubini, *Musica e cultura nel settecento europeo* (Turin, 1986).
3. Carl Dahlhaus, *Richard Wagner's Music Dramas*, translated by Mary Whittall (Cambridge, 1979), p. 54
4. John Neubauer, *The Emancipation of Music from Language. Departure from Mimesis in Eighteenth-Century Aesthetics* (New Haven and London, 1986).
5. See Chapter 1, notes 4 to 8.
6. Some of the key writings can be found in Gianvincenzo Gravina, *Della tragedia*, in *Scritti critici e teorici*, edited by Amedeo Quondam, Scrittori d'Italia 255 (Bari, 1973), p. 507; Rousseau, *Essai sur les origines des langues*, translation in Le Huray and Day, p. 92; Barthélemy, pp. 64–67; Stefano Arteaga, *Le rivoluzioni del teatro musicale italiana dalla sua origine fino al presente*, second edition, 3 vols. (Venice, 1785), II, 179.
7. Felice Romani, "La poesia lirica in Italia," in Romani, *Critica letteraria*, edited by Emilia Branca, 2 vols (Milan, 1883), I, 56: "i primi poeti lirici furono sacerdoti della divinità, legislatori dei popoli, ispiratori dei miti costumi." The assertion that the original laws were sung was derived ultimately from Aristotle's almost wholly spurious *Problems* 919^b36 (no.28); and Plato's *Laws* 700 b, and 799 e.
8. Grossi, I, 3; I, 66; Giambattista Martini, *Storia della musica*, 3 vols. (Bologna, 1757–1781), III, 104–109; Ranieri de' Calsabigi, "Dissertazione su le poesie drammatiche del Signore Abate Pietro Metastasio," in *Poesie del Signor Abate Pietro Metastasio*, 9 vols. (Paris, 1755), I, xxxiv–xxxv; Metastasio, *Estratto dell' Arte Poetica d' Aristotile e considerazioni su la medesima*, in Metastasio, *Opere*, 12 vols. (Paris, 1780–1782), XII, 203–204;

Antonio Eximeno, *Dell' origine e delle regole della musica, colla storia del suo progresso, decadenza e rinnovazione* (Rome, 1774), pp. 332–333.

9. Frequently quoted or referred to were: Aristotle, *Poetics*, 1449^a 15; Aristotle, *Rhetoric*, 1403^b 20; Horace, *Ars Poetica*, 275–280; Athenaeus, *The Deipnosophists*, I, 21 d-e.

10. On this question see Barbara Hanning, "Apologia pro Ottavio Rinuccini," in the *Journal of the American Musicological Society*, XXVI (1973), 240–262.

11. Even Castelvetro, widely regarded as the most radical Renaissance commentator on Aristotle's *Poetics*, had concluded that the singing and the acting had been performed by different people at different points in the drama (Ludovico Castelvetro, *Poetica d'Aristotele vulgarizzata et sposta*, second edition (Basle, 1576, pp. 114–115).

12. P. Lichtenthal, *Dizionario e bibliographia della musica*, 4 vols (Milan, 1826), I, 313: "da una gran quantità di testimonianze degli antichi scrittori si può argomentare che le tragedie fossero del tutto cantate a guisa de' nostri recitativi, ed accompagnate con istrumenti." Compare Rousseau, *Dictionnaire de musique*, 2 vols. (Amsterdam, 1769), II, 39.

13. C. Ritorni, *Ammaestramenti alla composizione d'ogni poema e d'ogni opera appartnenente alla musica* (Milan, 1841), pp. 8–9.

14. Metastasio, pp. 47–53; Galilei, *Dialogo della musica antica e moderna* (Florence, 1602), p. 145; Gravina, pp. 556–559. A fine adumbration of Metastasio's thesis is in Piero Weiss's "Metastasio, Aristotle, and the *Opera Seria*," in the *Journal of Musicology*, I (1982), 385–394; however, it is important to appreciate that Metastasio's views were by no means unusual at the time.

15. Metastasio, pp. 45–46; compare Bernardo Segni, *Rettorica et poetica d'Aristotele* (Florence, 1549), pp. 294–295.

16. Martini, III, 175–176.

17. Calsabigi, p. xxxi: "È opinione ormai da tutti ricevuta che ... il recitativo delle antiche Tragedie cantato fosse, ma con una spezie di canto qual'è quello che noi per i recitativi nostri ab-

biamo immaginato, cioè più corrente e meno caricato de' vezzi dell'armonia."

18. Metastasio was not alone in claiming a classical pedigree for his dramas; Calsabigi described them as "perfette Tragedie lavorate sulle vere leggi che dagli antichi si sono prescritte" (p. clxxxvii).

19. F. Lippmann, *Vincenzo Bellini und die italienische Opera Seria seiner Zeit, Analecta Musicologica VI* (Cologne and Vienna, 1969), p. 251, notes this use of *filosofia*. However, Bellini's attitude to poetic values confirms his links with traditional outlooks on opera, rather than showing him to prefigure more celebrated composers in the manner Lippmann suggests.

20. Plato, *Laws*, 669 e–670 a, in *The Laws of Plato*, translated by Thomas L. Pangle (New York, 1980), pp. 51–52. Compare Barthélemy, p. 98; F. M. Colle, *Dissertazione sopra il quaesito dimostrare, che cosa fosse, e quanta parte avesse la musica nell' educazione de' Greci* (Mantua, 1775), p. 7.

21. Marcello Perrino, *Osservazioni sul canto*, first edition (Naples, 1810), p. 51–52.

22. Calsabigi, p. clxxxviii.

23. Herbert M. Schueller, "Correspondences between Music and the Sister Arts According to 18th Century Aesthetic Theory" in the *Journal of Aesthetics and Art Criticism*. XI(1953), 334–359.

24. Charles Burney, *A General History of Music*, 2 vols., edited by Frank Mercer (London, 1935), p. 145.

25. G. Mazzini, *Filosofia della musica*, in *Scritti editi ed inediti di Giuseppe Mazzini*, 94 vols. (Imola, 1906–43), VIII, 160–162. On p. 126 he describes music as "un'armonia del creato, un eco del mondo invisibile."

26. Mazzini, VIII, 129n. and 158n. As Gary Tomlinson observes, his remarks about Bellini are very perceptive, at least in as much as the operas reflect reservations about Romanticism ("Italian Romanticism and Italian Opera: an Essay on Their Affinities," in *19th Century Music*, X [1986], pp. 43–60 [p. 54]). Yet Mazzini's negative tone does not allow for the possibility that Bellini might have had other artistic aims.

27. R. Parker, "'Classical' Music in Milan during Verdi's

Formative Years," in *Studi musicali*, XIII (1984), 259–273.

28.   Gregory W. Harwood, "Verdi's Reform of the Italian Opera Orchestra," in *19th Century Music*, X (1986), 108–134. Harwood makes the interesting point that Italian orchestral directors were placed in a central position, rather than at the side as was the practice in France and Germany. This reflects the different process that led to conducting in Italian theatres, which is related to Italian attitudes to the orchestra in Chapter 5, below (Harwood, p. 121).

29.   Barthélemy, p. 73: "La simplicité des moyens employés par la musique, assuroit le triomphe de la poésie." This theory can be traced right back to Galilei's *Dialogo* of 1581.

30.   A. Planelli, *Dell' opera in musica* (Naples, 1772), p. 124: *"Lo stile della Musica Teatrale vuol poche note.* Perciocchè una Musica troppo rinzeppata di note, sieno simultanee, o successive, è incapace di patetico." Similar opinions can be found in F. Milizia, *Trattato completo, formale e materiale del teatro* (Venice, 1794), p. 57; and in Ferro, I, 201.

31.   Francesco de Sanctis, *Storia della letteratura italiana*, edited by Benedetto Croce, 2 vols. (Bari, 1925), II, 336: "costringendola ad abbreviare i suoi periodi, a sopprimere il suo cerimoniale e la sua solennità, i suoi aggettivi, i suoi ripieni, le sue perifrasi, i suoi sinonimi, i suoi parallelismi, le sue trasposizioni, tutte le sue dotte inutilità, e a prendere un'aria più spedita e andante." De Sanctis thought Metastasio's style was the last to be influenced by a classical language already permeated by music, in contrast with the abrupt theatrical language of Alfieri (II, 317–319; 366–367).

32.   See, for example, Milizia, p. 44, and *Giornale delle due Sicilie* (Naples, 13 June 1826) specifically urging Bellini and Gilardoni to follow his example.

33.   The Italians had long pointed out references to "ornamentation" in Quintilian and Cicero (see, for example, Donatella Restani, "Martini studioso di musica greca." in *Padre Martini, Musica e cultura nel Settecento europeo*, Quaderni della Rivista italiana di musicologia 12, [Florence, 1987], p. 35). A later example is Andrea Majer in 1821 (see below, Chapter 2 note 21).

34. Crescentini, *Raccolta di essercizi per il canto all' uso del vocalizzo* (Paris, 1811), p. 4.

35. Rodolfo Celletti, *Storia del belcanto* (Fiesole, 1983), p. 190–192.

36. Elvidio Surian, "Musical Historiography and Histories of Italian Opera," in *Current Musicology*, XXXVI (1983). 167–175.

37. See, for example, Milizia, p. 53; Calsabigi, pp. clxi–clxiv; Stendhal, *Lives of Haydn, Mozart and Metastasio*, translated by R. N. Coe (London, 1972), pp. 214–220.

38. A. J. Ayer, *Language, Truth and Logic*, second edition (London, 1946), p. 113.

ACKNOWLEDGEMENTS

No doubt every doctoral thesis is dependent, to a greater or lesser degree, on the qualities and experience of the writer's supervisor; but, in this case, special thanks should go to Professor Denis Arnold, without whose constantly shrewd advice and endless perseverance the thesis would never have been completed at all. Indeed it was his rare enthusiasm for the Italian repertory that suggested research into it might be possible in the first place. Many libraries have afforded me help with my studies: including the staff at the Bodleian Library, the Museo Belliniano at Catania, the Conservatorio di San Pietro a Majella, Biblioteca Nazionale and Archivio di Stato at Naples, and the British Library. I am particularly indebted to Albi Rosenthal for the loan of material otherwise difficult of access; and to Julian Budden and Fred Sternfeld for pertinent advice. Special help in the final completion of the thesis came from my parents, Helen de Bray, Dilwyn and Helen Marple-Horvat, and Gloria Gaiba, who kindly checked all the Italian translations. The debt I owe to my typist, Margaret Smith, is only too evident on the pages that follow. For the contents, I have no excuse but Pilate's: "What I have written, I have written".

"A scientific treatment of aesthetics would show us what in general were the causes of aesthetic feeling, why various societies produced and admired the works of art they did."

            A.J. AYER

CONTENTS

	Page
Chapter 1: Introduction	1
Chapter 2: The aesthetic roots of Italian opera in the early nineteenth century	13
Chapter 3: The role of the singer on the stage	42
Chapter 4: Poetry and drama in the libretto	71
Chapter 5: The constitution of the orchestra and its place in the melodramma	107
Chapter 6: The heritage of the bel canto	148
Bibliography	190
Index	203

CHAPTER 1

INTRODUCTION

This study deals with the aesthetics of Italian opera, not the analysis of its scores. This is to say that it is less concerned with the operas of Bellini and his contemporaries than with the ideas behind them; the ideas and attitudes that caused them to be the way they are. This has been undertaken in the belief that the understanding of opera, and indeed music generally, should be done in the light of an adequate knowledge of the culture from which it springs; in particular some acquaintance with what contemporary listeners expected from it. This has, so far as it has been possible to discover, never been done before. This is not in fact because the field in general has been neglected; indeed there have been a very large number of writings on the music of Bellini. One bibliography compiled in 1923 lists no fewer than eight hundred and eighty-eight items;[1] and nearly all the significant contributions to Bellinian studies have come since that date. However, it has to be said that a great many of such writings have been of the nature of Italian omaggi, designed to venerate the composer, rather than to study his music and his context.

This has been often done rather on the defensive, aware that a general consensus of opinion existed that Italian opera was rather trivial. Hanslick's view, after all, was that one only had to look at any theme of Italian opera and it would "without the need of further examination, convince us that the music is fit only for low music halls".[2] Most writers have been aware that they would inevitably be read by the concert-goer who, like Sydney Smith when confronted with the prospect of sitting through Semiramide, had a horror of the

---

1. Orazio Viola, Bibliografia belliniana, second edition (Catania, 1923).
2. Eduard Hanslick, The Beautiful in Music, translated by Gustav Cohen (Indianapolis and New York, 1957), p.125.

Italian opera; or else accepted without further thought that, as in The Portrait of a Lady, it would be "bare, familiar and trivial", and that even "Verdi's music did little to comfort him".

But the most severe strictures were reserved for the operas of the era before Verdi, which Alfred Einstein called "internally even more poverty stricken, if possible, than before."[3] As a result most writers have tried to present Bellini as rising above that "dead level" and beginning to create serious operas worthy of the attention and study of musicologists. Foremost in this has been the work of Friedrich Lippmann in his pioneering study Vincenzo Bellini und die italienische Opera seria seiner Zeit.[4] In this work, Bellini is seen as a great advance on Rossini and early Donizetti, and a precursor of Verdi in his concern for dramatic values; failing to achieve Verdi's consistent portrayal of character, but displaying a more intensive and consistent consideration of the text than the more frivolous Rossini, with more precise declamation of the words than his predecessor.[5] In Dr. Lippmann's view, Bellini is the first Italian composer to achieve a seriously dramatic style of opera; progressing from the somewhat inconsequential works of composers before him, and leading the way to the greater composer who took on this line of development to create works such as Otello and Falstaff.

Apart from the fact that there is the obvious spectre of an evolutionary approach to music history behind much of this, there is also the problem that it views Bellini with a particular historical

---

3. Alfred Einstein, A Short History of Music, fourth American edition (New York, 1969), p.208.
4. Friedrich Lippmann, Vincenzo Bellini und die italienische Opera seria seiner Zeit, Analecta Musicologica VI (Cologne and Vienna, 1969).
5. Lippmann, Vincenzo Bellini, p.341. "Die Abkehr von Rossini äussert sich sehr spürbar im intensiveren, konsequenteren Eingehen auf den Text, angefangen bei genauerer Text-Deklamation (falsche Wortbetonungen werden selten) - und geendet, leider, vor der Verwirklichung einer strikten Personencharakteristik."

perspective. That is to say that it judges Bellini according to what came after him rather than trying to understand what Bellini grew from. We have to decide whether the values that we gain from the experience of later opera, where the dramatic power is generated through the orchestra, are appropriate to the proper understanding of works written at a time when these means were not available. Dr. Lippmann's approach makes the assumption that before Bellini, little attention was given to the text. How true is this? The impression that the book gives is that the later opera is unquestionably better than the more primitive types of opera that were prevalent before. Because the more mature Romantic opera is a repertory that we know well, we are very well acquainted with the values and aesthetic purposes that govern it. It is too easy to see earlier opera as being less sophisticated and therefore bereft of as many aesthetic considerations. Instead of assuming that earlier traditions mostly lack the sense of artistic purpose of the later opera, it might be possible to discover that they had a different conception of what opera was, and therefore different priorities.

Assumption that Italian opera of the first third of the nineteenth century is trivial may lead to some surprise when we discover not only that they wrote about it a great deal, but also that they took its history and traditions very seriously. Through such writings we can find out just what Italians thought of the dramatic element of the opera. Dr. Lippmann's thesis presupposes that opera should develop consistent drama and characterization. In trying to emphasize how Bellini progressed in this respect towards the style of Verdi, it is easy to fall into the danger of assuming that Bellini shared these ideals. To just what extent did Italians look for drama, or were they more interested in the poetic quality of individual static situations? To find this out it is necessary to ask Bellini and his contemporaries. So far little has been done in this respect, and so the present study will devote much time to investigations that will be of the nature of a voyage of discovery into the aesthetic world of early nineteenth century opera, the territory from which Bellinian opera springs. This has been undertaken in the belief that these ideas should be properly considered before sympathetic analysis of the precise nature of particular operas can be attempted.

The music of Bellini seems particularly likely to benefit from an approach of this nature, as he seems so naturally to spring from Italian operatic traditions. Bellini came to Naples from Catania in 1819, and up to that time his musical experience and instruction was largely in the hands of his grandfather, Vincenzo Tobia Bellini (1744-1829).[6] Vincenzo Tobia had attended the Conservatorio di Sant'Onofrio a Capuana in Naples from 1755 onwards, and had moved to Catania in 1767-1768. Thus the teaching that he passed on to Bellini would have been based on the mid-eighteenth century traditions of the Neapolitan School. A list of his own works is dominated by liturgical music but also includes some azioni sacre.[7] The music for these has not survived, but the librettos[8] show texts of arias in a Metastasian style, cast in the form of double quatrains. One can well imagine that, on his arrival in Naples, Bellini's style was more likely to be old-fashioned than progressive.

The city that he arrived at was one that was extraordinarily proud of its musical past. In the 1770s Eximeno, whose writings will

---

6. Maria Rosaria Adamo, 'Vincenzo Bellini, biografia', in Adamo and F. Lippmann, Vincenzo Bellini (Turin, 1981), p.18.
7. Orazio Viola, 'Vincenzo Bellini seniore', in Rivista del commune di Catania Anno II (Catania, 1930), p.3.
8. A collection of the librettos of seven of these azioni sacre, dating from Il trasporto delle reliquie di S. Agata of 1797 to his La vittoria di Gedeone of 1808, all produced in Catania, is held at: Naples, Conservatorio di S. Pietro a Majella, 5. 12. 24.

be referred to more in the next chapter, was convinced that music had reached its peak of perfection in that century, particularly with the work of Pergolesi. It had, he thought, "renewed ... qualities of expression not felt since the times of the Greeks".[9] In the next chapter we shall explain more of the links that Italians saw with the culture of ancient Greece, but here we would like to emphasize how Naples regarded its own contribution to this. Still in Bellini's day, much emphasis was put on the Neapolitan tradition in historical writing. An article in the *Rivista teatrale* in 1824 by "nostro correspondente di Sicilia" shows the extent to which perspectives of music history were limited by local pride. He refers to Pergolesi as "il primo codice del vero gusto" particularly in his setting of Metastasio's *Olimpiade* (1735). The other composers that he mentions in the development of opera are Sarri, Feo, Vinci, Leo, Jommelli, Piccinni, Sacchini, Traetta and Anfossi. Later he mentions Paisiello, Cimarosa, Zingarelli, Mayer and Paër. All but the last two are connected in some sense with the conservatories at Naples.

Italians tended to assume that they had taught music to other nations and, for that reason, were very slow to accept that there was anything worth listening to in operas from abroad. Their interest in non-operatic music was even less enthusiastic, as Berlioz noted in Rome in 1831, where "the names Weber and Beethoven are virtually unknown".[10] The anecdote of Spohr in Naples meeting Bellini's teacher Niccolo Zingarelli (1752-1837) is well known. Zingarelli

---

9. Antonio Eximeno, *Dell' origine e delle regole della musica, colla storia del suo progresso, decadenza e rinnovazione* (Rome, 1774), p.273: "La Musica à rinnovata in questo secolo l'espressione non mai sentita dopo i Greci". See also p.334: "Oggi però che la Musica è giunta alla somma perfezione". See also p.443: "Ora figuriamoci uno spettacolo, quale si sarebbe potuto rappresentare in questo secolo, cioè l'Olimpiade del Metastasio posta in Musica dal Pergolesi, cantata da Farinelli, Raff, Cafarello".
10. *The Memoirs of Hector Berlioz*, translated and edited by David Cairns (London, 1969), p.186.

proved to have some "very erroneous notions" on German music and considered that Mozart "was not deficient in talent, but [that] he lived too short a time to cultivate it in a proper manner".[11] Any enthusiasm for German music in particular was greeted with much scepticism. Commenting on an account of German opera in a Viennese music journal, the Neapolitan Rivista teatrale notes sourly that the Viennese enthusiasm for Gluck, Haydn and Mozart resulted in hyperbole, and that "the glory of these great composers still reflects more on Italy than on Germany, Italians having been their teachers and Italian their traditions".[12] This goes some way to explaining the dearth of foreign works to be seen in Italian opera houses. Mozart's operas were not quite unknown,[13] but tended to be given in adapted and mutilated versions:[14] Even with Mozart it was sometimes complained that he appealed "più all' intelletto che al cuore".[15] As we shall see later, this was no little complaint since the primary duty of music was seen as affecting the heart. As late as 1834 one newspaper described Don Giovanni Tenorio as "a nauseous and bitter pill".[16] No doubt the mutilations did not help.

Lacking outside influences, Italians tended to be rather inward

---

11. Louis Spohr, Autobiography, 2 vols. (London, 1865), II, 17.
12. Rivista teatrale, Naples, 1 May 1824: "la gloria di questi grandi compositori appartiene più ancora all' Italia che non alla Germania, italiani essendo stati i loro maestri, ed italiana la scuola loro".
13. Friedrich Lippmann, 'Mozart Aufführungen des frühen Ottocento in Neapel', in Analecta Musicologica VII (Cologne and Vienna, 1969), pp.164-179. Dr. Lippmann lists a number of performances during the period 1809-1816, and a very few later ones.
14. Rivista teatrale, 21 February 1824: "Erano preperati pel carnevale questi altri spettacoli: ... Le Nozze di Figaro e D. Giovanni Tenorio del Mozart". The productions were eventually abandoned through illnesses, but an actual performance of a much mutilated Don Giovanni at the Teatro Nuovo is reported in Rivista teatrale, 12 June 1824.
15. Monitore delle due Sicilie, Naples, 28 June 1813.
16. Il Veritiero, Giornale periodico ameno-letterario, Naples, 11 July 1834: "una nauseosa e rancida pillola, qual'è D. Giovanni Tenorio del Mozart".

looking, and depended on their own proud traditions. In the eighteenth century Naples was regarded more or less as the capital of the musical world, even by foreign travellers, as noted by Michael Robinson.[17] The introductory summary of musical history provided in Choron and Fayolle's Dictionnaire historique des musiciens of 1810 laments that Italian music was no longer what it had been in the preceding centuries. However, it adds to this: "but it also has to be said that, despite this very obvious decline, we believe that Italy still retains a superiority over all the other nations in Europe ... Besides which, the schools [of music] there are still excellent even though public education is weak, and there are still a large number of learned masters."[18] Burney's famous report on the Neapolitan conservatories rather contradicts this; but it would seem that most European musicians expected standards to be good in Italy, even if, like Berlioz, they turned out to be disappointed once they got there.

Italians themselves, especially composers brought up under the traditional schooling, seem to have had no doubts. Hucke has charted the decline of the Neapolitan conservatories during the later eighteenth century,[19] but this remained a fact that Neapolitans tended to gloss over, whilst emphasizing the length of their traditions. In 1867, Saverio Mercadante (1795-1870), then principal of the Neapolitan conservatory, where he had studied as a contemporary of Bellini, wrote

---

17. Michael F. Robinson, Naples and Neapolitan Opera (Oxford, 1972), p.1.
18. A. Choron and F. Fayolle, Dictionnaire historique des musiciens (Paris, 1810), p.lxxii: "mais ce que nous devons dire aussi, c'est que, malgré cette décadence très sensible, nous croyons que l'Italie garde toujours la supériorité sur les autres nations de l'Europe ... Outre cela, l'école y est toujours excellente quoique l'instruction publique y soit faible, on y trouve encore un grande nombre de savans maîtres".
19. Helmut Hucke, 'Verfassung und Entwicklung der alten neapolitanischen Konservatorien', in Festschrift Helmut Osthoff, edited by L. Hoffmann-Erbrecht and H. Hucke (Tutzung, 1961), pp.139-154.

an account of opera in the preceding century, which is almost wholly devoted to a listing of composers of the Neapolitan school. He states that during the eighteenth century "music discovered forms more appropriate to benefit from inspiration, particularly in dramatic music. Two great men personify this great advance, Pergolesi and Cimarosa".[20] This tendency to see the whole history of eighteenth century opera in terms of Naples reaches a height in Mercadante's assertion that Paisiello was responsible for the development in writing for wind instruments, quite ignoring the activities of more obviously symphonic writers further north. "Hayden, Mozart e Beethoven" are referred to briefly as composers that made use of harmonic developments in theatrical music, very much a backhanded compliment in terms of Italian aesthetics.[21]

The Neapolitan conviction that their musical traditions were still intact led them to continue to treat with reverence certain works by these old composers, even at a time when operas generally had a short life expectancy. Thus there continued to be performed in Naples works by Paisiello and Cimarosa well into the 1820s. As the Neapolitan paper Il Galiani commented, "works of true inspiration, like the scores of the greatest masters, need not fear aging. Let the proof of this be the number of our works that are still staged in Naples and elsewhere, such as il matrimonio segreto [1792] by Cimarosa ... Paolo e Virginia [1817] by the younger Guglielmi [1763-1817] ... la modista

20. Saverio Mercadante, 'Breve cenno storico sulla musica teatrale da Pergolesi a Cimarosa', in Atti della Reale Accademia di Archeologia, Lettere e Belle Arti III (Naples, 1867), pp.33-37 (p.33): "Nello scorso secolo, più che ne' precedenti, l'arte musicale trovò forme più acconce all' inspirazione, in special modo nella Musica teatrale. Due grandi uomini personificarono il suo incremento, il Pergolesi, il Cimarosa".
21. Mercadante, pp.36-37.

raggiratrice, [1787] and the magical Nina [1789] by Paisiello ..."[22]

Newspaper reviews give us a chance to trace the performances of many operas long after their early productions. It is true, as John Rosselli[23] states, that newspapers tended to be venal in the most literal sense and often displayed a lack of acquaintance with a broad repertory of music; but on factual matters they are often helpful in noting performances of operas that do not appear in theatrical chronologies, devoted for the most part to detailing first performances. We therefore can find evidence of the continuing survival of Cimarosa's Gli Orazi ed i Curiazi (1796) as well as Il matrimonio segreto,[24] and also of many works by Paisiello such as his Nina pazza per amore (1789), and his La serva padrona (1781).[25] Other works that received regular performances were operas by Mayr and Paër, especially Agnese di Fitzhenry (1809).[26] Of all these operas none was more common, however, than Spontini's La Vestale (1807) which seems to have been given continuously from 1811 through the 1820s. The seven hundred and eighty-ninth performance was reported in Naples in 1824.[27] Spontini was always regarded as a native composer, since he had studied in Naples (although he had long since gone to France) and

---

22. Il Galiani, Giornale di amena letteratura, Naples, 20 June 1824: "I parti di genio de' sommi maestri, le produzioni di vera ispirazione, non temono vecchiezza. Prova ne sieno parecchie del nostri primi lavori che son sempre in possesso delle cittadine e straniere scene, come il matrimonio segreto del Cimarosa, ... il Paolo e Virginia di Guglielmi figlio, ... la modista raggatrice, ... la magica Nina di Paisiello".
23. John Rosselli, 'Agenti teatrali nel mondo dell' opera lirica italiana dell' Ottocento', in Rivista italiana di musicologia XVII (1982), pp.134-154 (p.146).
24. Rivista teatrale, 10 April 1824.
25. L'Omnibus, 14 June 1834.
26. Rivista teatrale, 21 February 1824.
27. Rivista teatrale, 7 July 1824: "La sera de' 24 avevamo avuta la settecentottantesimanova rappresentazione della Vestale". See also Rivista teatrale, 21 February 1824, 16 June 1824, 23 June 1824, 12 January 1825.

Bellini owned a score of the opera.

As we have noted, however, it was Pergolesi who represented for Italians, as also for Stendhal, the perfection that music could attain. This was in some ways a veneration that limited itself to theory, since few operatic performances are traceable. The emphasis moreover was not on the Serva Padrona (1733), so famous today, as his opera seria L'Olimpiade (1735) and his church music, particularly the Stabat mater (1736). It is these works that are emphasized by Villarosa in his biographical essay of 1831.[28]

Bellini's education in this tradition was in the hands of Zingarelli, a man that he seems to have always retained a great respect for. Despite the failings that Zingarelli as a composer might have for us, and the cultural provincialism that he displayed to Spohr, Zingarelli appears continuously as a father-figure in Bellini's letters. In one letter he describes to his lifelong friend Francesco Florimo (1800-1888) how he is studying Zingarelli's scores, although by that time he was well launched into his own career.[29] Zingarelli's role was quite clear in the Neapolitan tradition: it was what the Monitore delle due Sicilie wrote in 1813 that he was perfectly suited to: "to inculcate into the students the Italian taste in melody and singing".[30]

We know also that Zingarelli took a particular care in guiding Bellini through this type of education, emphasizing the importance of melody over the technical accomplishments of harmony, double counter-

---

28. Marchese di Villarosa, Lettera biografica intorno alla patria ed alla vita di Gio. Battista Pergolese (Naples, 1831), p.25.
29. Vincenzo Bellini, Epistolario, edited by Luisa Cambi (Verona, 1943), p.99 (24 May 1828).
30. Monitore delle due Sicilie, 21 August 1813: "Zingarelli: Questo valente maestro ... è attissimo ad infondere negli allievi il gusto del canto e della melodia italiana".

point, fugues and canons.[31]

A great deal of this study will have taken the form of assimilating the music of the all-pervading Neapolitan tradition. The internal regulations for the Conservatory of San Sebastiano are quite strict, and lay down that "during the period of concerts, the student composers will occupy themselves in reading and studying the music of the classical authors, which at their request will be provided them by the Archivist".[32] Not long after Bellini's departure, that post was given to Florimo. Bearing in mind the Neapolitan outlook on music, there should be no doubt as to what was meant by the classical authors. The archive was enriched by the order of 1795 that laid down that a copy of the score of every opera performed in Naples should be deposited in the Conservatory library.[33]

We know that Bellini profited from such studies because of the accounts of Florimo, who tells us that "among the great masters of the Neapolitan school he loved more than the others Jommelli and the melodious Paisiello; but his favourite was Pergolesi, with whom he felt a special personal affinity".[34] Later we find in his letters references to the works of Paisiello and Pergolesi.

It should not be thought that the present study intends to show that Bellini was another composer in the Neapolitan tradition. Although

---

31. Adamo, p.32.
32. Stabilmenti per l'interno regolamento del Real Conservatorio di musica San Sebastiano in Napoli (Naples, 1809), p.10: "Durante il tempo de' concerti gli Alunni compositori si occuperanno nell' Archivio a leggere, e studiare le musiche de' classici Autori, che a loro richiesta le saranno consegnate dall' Archivario". According to Florimo, La scuola musicale di Napoli, 4 vols (Naples, 1881-1882), II, 39, these regulations remained in force until 1848.
33. Francesco Florimo, La scuola musicale di Napoli, 4 vols (Naples, 1881-1882), II, 124.
34. Florimo, Bellini, memorie e lettere (Florence, 1882), pp.6-7: "Tra i sommi della Scuola napolitana egli amava, più che altri, il Jommelli ed il melodico Paisiello; ma il Pergolesi era l'autore di sua predilezione, col quale il suo cuore simpatizzava compiutamente".

he was frequently regarded by contemporaries as showing a preference for the style of the old Italian school,[35] in many ways he shows musical traits that place him apart from his Neapolitan predecessors. In this respect it should be pointed out that the present writer agrees with, and values highly, the magisterial work of Dr. Lippmann. No one has done more to further the study of Bellini's music. But because the materials used here are so different from those relevant to Dr. Lippmann's work, some new conclusions are arrived at. These should not necessarily be looked on as contradicting the analyses of Bellini provided by Dr. Lippmann. It is more that the present study seeks to do something rather different; that is, to analyse the musical culture from which the masterworks that Dr. Lippmann deals with ultimately spring. In that respect, it is to be hoped that the foregoing introduction will have shown that these traditions are not totally irrelevant to the music of Bellini. Bellini was not a student of the fine arts or a musical aesthetician; but there are aspects of his work that are more easily understood from the perspective of the traditions and practices in Naples of his time, than by accepting modern assumptions. To this extent, it is more a case of showing the other side of the coin than of rejecting the conclusions of Dr. Lippmann. But it is to be hoped that analysis will be able to take on board these aesthetic considerations, and that future studies of Bellini can be made that benefit from a similar interest in what caused Italians to write the way that they did.

---

35. See *I teatri*, Milan, 19 March 1829; quoted after *Vincenzo Bellini, Epistolario*, edited by Luisa Cambi (Verona, 1943), p.206. See also the report from the *Gazzetta privilegiata di Milano*, referred to in Herbert Weinstock, *Vincenzo Bellini, his Life and his Operas* (London, 1972), p.66.

CHAPTER 2

THE AESTHETIC ROOTS OF ITALIAN OPERA
IN THE EARLY NINETEENTH CENTURY

In his essay 'The Antigone of Sophocles' (1846), Thomas De Quincey writes:

> "The first elementary idea of a Greek tragedy is to be sought in a serious Italian opera. The Greek dialogue is represented by the recitative, and the tumultuous lyrical parts assigned chiefly, though not exclusively, to the chorus on the Greek stage, are represented by the impassioned airs, duos, trios, choruses, etc., on the Italian." (1)

Whether or not this is actually meant to be more than general praise of Italian opera, De Quincey touched on something that was very dear to all Italian writers on the subject of opera. There is hardly to be found a single book that does not begin its consideration of the nature of opera with a lengthy section on the theatre of the Greeks. This is not to say that all writers knew the subject in great depth but such is the consistency of their views that it suggests a tradition of approach passed on from one writer to the next. Most of the writers are in some sense best regarded as <u>dilettanti</u> and, as we shall see, much of their information and attitudes stem from the views of the French Encyclopedists. This is not to be regarded as necessarily a weakness since it gives notice of a broad cultural perspective and is part of an honourable tradition of such writing that includes such men as Rousseau and lasts well into the nineteenth century with men such as Stendhal.

The view that music was rooted in Greek drama can be seen through a wide variety of Italian books and journalistic writing during the eighteenth and early nineteenth centuries. Here we shall look at some of these views from

---

1. Thomas De Quincey, <u>Works</u>, second edition, 17 vols (Edinburgh) 1862-1878), XIII, 208.

writers that are particularly explicit, including some with special connexions with Naples. One writer on the subject is significant, for example, in that it is obvious from his book that he had strong connexions with the educational traditions of the Naples Conservatories where Bellini, and before him his grandfather, studied.

The "avvocato G. B. Gennaro Grossi" describes himself as an associate of the Reale Academia Ercolanese and addresses himself directly "Ai signori Alunni del Collegio Reale di Musica in Napoli".[2] Listing a number of his contributions to the Allgemeine Musikalische Zeitung on the state of music and the conservatories in Italy, Piero Lichtenthal describes him in his great Dizionario e bibliografia della musica of 1826 as "wishing to revive the ancient music of Italy, and showing himself to be an enemy to mere noise".[3] In his book Le belle arti Grossi gives extensive consideration to the music of the Greeks and, almost at once, makes reference to one point that has considerable implications for the proper understanding of the Italian opera.

> "Music gave life to the poetry of Homer, Hesiod, Archilocus, Terpander, Simonides, Pindar, Anacreon and Sappho. Poetry was quite inseparable from it and both lent themselves to a reciprocal exchange of their graces." (4)

It is this idea of the joining of music with the verses so that one is inseparable from the other, that provides a thread that runs throughout the writings of the period on this subject. Music as one part of a greater cultural entity is to be regarded according to the tradition of the times as the property of sages and filosofi, or as

---

2. G. B. Gennaro Grossi, Le belle arti, 2 vols (Naples, 1820), I, v.
3. P. Lichtenthal, Dizionario e bibliografia della musica, 4 vols (Milan, 1826), III, 169. The Italian text reads: "l'Autore vuol ricondurre l'antica musica italiana, e si mostra nemico del fracasso". Besides the articles in AMZ, Gennaro Grossi wrote Richerche su' l'origine, su i progressi, e sul decadimento delle arti dipendenti dal disegno (Napoli, 1821).
4. Gennaro Grossi, I, 2: "La musica diede l'anima ai versi di Omero, di Esiodo, di Archilao, di Terpandro, di Simonide, di Pindaro, di Anacreonte e di Saffo. Essa era inseparabile la poesia, e l'una e l'altra s'imprestavano a vicenda le loro dolcezze".

Grossi puts it,

> "These musician-poets were held to be sacred by the people, and came to be known as bards. They knew the art of exercising the full power of music and poetry over the hearts of the people of their city, and ensured that their influence served to inflame them with patriotic pride and motivate them to glorious deeds". (5)

The idea that music and words were born together and should remain unified is a more complicated matter than at first might seem likely; and as we shall see at the end of this chapter, involved the participation of more arts than just poetry and music. Confining ourselves for the present just to this idea, however, we can see that the unification of the two arts was regarded as an absolute prerequisite for music that meant anything at all. Gennaro Grossi saw absolute disaster following music's separation from words, and connected it with the decline of the philosophical culture of the ancient Greeks and the growth of internal civil strife. In other words, the great theatrical works of classical Greece came from an underlying philosophical healthiness, and the separation of words and music was a symptom of the decline in society as a whole. Music, it should be remembered, was properly the province of _filosofi_, and its decline went hand in hand with the fall of such philosophers.

> "Such marvellous products of the human mind began to decline at the time of Alexander the Great, but crumbled away completely during the occupation of the area made by the Romans. Aristoxenus and Plutarch attribute this to the innovations, effeminacies and barbarities introduced into the theatres. It seems to me that other internal causes were also contributing to this fatal decline. During the time that Greece was able to maintain its freedom, those sublime geniuses cultivated all such arts as one, as the very foundations of public education ... but as soon as music was no longer in the hands of philosophers, as soon as Greece was for many years torn apart by brutal civil strife; ... then the two divine sister arts, frightened

---

5. Gennaro Grossi, I, 2-3: "I musici poeti eran tenuti per sacri dal popolo, e venivan chiamati col nome di VATI. Essi avean l'arte di esercitare tutto il potere della musica poetica sul cuore dei cittadini, e facean servire la sua influenza per inflammarli all'amor di patria, e alle azioni gloriose".

by the horrors of war ... disappeared completely with
the arrival of the ambitious and ferocious Romans". (6)

Grossi sees the two sister arts as being held together by the sublime Greek genius; standing as a monument to the integrity of the Greek state. With its fall, brought about by internal decline, the two arts fell apart with the arrival of the Romans, who were no philosophers. The impression is that both the artistic decline and the civil strife are symptoms of the unhealthiness of the state. "As soon as music was no longer in the hands of the philosophers" then Greece was in decline.

Gennaro Grossi also gives us some idea as to what contemporary writers understood of the historical developments of Greek drama, and the connexions that, within its framework, music had with the other arts; a topic dealt with more fully by other writers as well. It is obvious that Gennaro Grossi sees this as something that had its roots in the earliest classical models of drama that they were acquainted with, involving the earliest bards in both music and words.

> "the music for the theatre was always inseparable from the poetry and the same actors provided both the musicians and the poets. Creators of comic drama such as Eupolis, Cratinus and Aristophanes were deeply knowledgeable about harmony and melody. Thespis, the inventor of tragedy, sung his extraordinary tales upon a movable stage to the sound of his own lyre. Aeschylus, who moved Thespis's stage into

---

6. Gennaro Grossi, I, 77: "Queste amabile produzioni dello spirito umano cominciarono a declinare ai tempi del grande Alessandro, ma caddero intieramente nella occupazione di quei luoghi fatta dai romani. Aristosseno, e Plutarco ne attribuscono la cagione alle morbidezze, e alle barbarie introdotte nei teatri. A noi sembra che altre intrinseche cagioni fossero ancora concorse a questo fatale decadimento. Finché la Grecia si mantenne nella sua libertà, quei Genj sublimi coltivarono tali arti unite, come fondamento della pubblica educazione ... Ma subitoche la musica non fu più trattata da filosofi: subitoche rimase seperata dalla poesia, subitoche la Grecia fu dilaniata per molti anni da ferale guerra intestina; ... allora le divine sorelle spaventate dagli orrori della guerra ... disparvero totalmente all' apparire delle armi degli ambiziosi e feroci romani".

the theatre, Sophocles, and Euripides, all did the same". (7)

Later Gennaro Grossi stresses the importance of Aeschylus in establishing the permanent theatre in a form more easily recognizable by his own contemporaries. But for Gennaro Grossi, Aeschylus was obviously much more than a reforming playwright since his control extended over the composition, rehearsal and performance in person of the poetry and music.

> "Aeschylus, who followed him, transformed Thespis's stage into a fixed theatre. To it he added a contrasting character and the chorus. He made use of masks, the buskin, and costumes that corresponded to the subject of the play. He introduced the use of perspective in the scenery, and other decorations as well as the dances. He himself wrote the play, set it to music, rehearsed his actors and sang his own part, as later did all his followers". (8)

The writer then goes on to describe the use of the music involved in this drama to excite particular passions in the audience through "modulazioni sublimi" and "ritmi impetuosi", and the part that instruments had in this process. Aeschylus's contribution to this dramatic offering can be broken down into a number of different arts, such as music, poetry, costume, design, dance and acting. One might indeed say that already we have here all the constituent elements of opera required by contemporary writers, as we shall see, for consideration in theatrical composition of their own time. At such a happy golden age as that of Aeschylus, however, all these arts are seen as being

---

7. Gennaro Grossi, I, 3: "la musica teatrale fu sempre unita alla poesia, e gli stessi attori eran musici e poeti. I comici <u>Eupoli</u>, <u>Cratino</u>, ed <u>Aristofane</u> furono profundi conoscitori dell'armonia, e della melodia. <u>Tespi</u> inventor della tragedia, al suono della sua lira, cantava su di un palco mobile le avventure staordinarie. <u>Eschilo</u> che trasformò in teatro il palco di <u>Tespi</u>, <u>Sofocle</u>, e <u>Euripide</u> fecero lo stesso".
8. Gennaro Grossi, I, 66: "<u>Eschilo</u>, che venne dopo, trasforma in teatro fisso il palco di <u>Tespi</u>. Vi aggiunge un altro personaggio ed il <u>Coro</u>. Fa uso della maschera, del coturno, e di abiti corrispondenti al soggetto. Introduce la prospettiva nelle scene, ed altre decorazioni, e la danza. Egli stesso compone il dramma, lo mette in musica, esercita i suoi attori e canta la sua parte, siccome poi fecero tutti gli attori suoi successori".

inconceivable as separate.

Another writer on this subject who had particular connexions with the Naples Conservatories was the Ferro who in 1808 wrote <u>Dissertazioni sulle belle arti</u>. According to Lichtenthal,(9) he was also the author of the anonymous <u>Stabilmenti per l'interno regolamento del Reale Conservatorio di musica San Sebastiano in Napoli</u> (1809) which laid down the conditions under which Bellini trained from 1819 to 1827. His treatise on the fine arts gives considerable attention to the musical theatre of the Greeks and stresses another point that colours the consideration of Italian opera. This is the idea that the theatre should have some elevating purpose, since it is to be seen as part of the most solemn ceremony of the state.

> "The Greeks stayed in silence when in the theatre, they listened and were edified, and left it full of feeling and admiration. Their music and their poetry did not only tickle the ear, but struck their very hearts; it did not just express the words but the feelings". (10)

In the same way, the most often quoted of all the writers on Italian opera, the exiled Spanish Jesuit Stefano Arteaga (1747-1799), stresses the uplifting nature of the drama as a whole and the poetry in particular:

> "The Poet has three objectives: to move, to depict and to instruct ... He instructs, seeking by means of the appreciation of intellectual and physical Beauty, to carry men forward to the appreciation and to the love of moral Beauty." (11)

---

9. Lichtenthal, III, 168.
10. Cavaliere di Ferro, e Ferro, <u>Delle belle arti, dissertazioni</u>, 2 vols (Palermo, 1807-1808), I, 197: "I Greci stavano al Teatro in silenzio, ascoltavano, apprendevano, e ne uscivano pieni di centimento e di ammirazione. La loro Poesia, e la loro Musica, non solleticava solo l'orecchio, ma feriva il cuore; non esprimeva le sole parole, ma i sentimenti".
11. Stefano Arteaga, <u>Le rivoluzioni del teatro musicale italiano, dalla sua origine fino al presente</u>, seconda edizione, accresciuta, variata e corretta dall'Autore, 3 vols (Venice, 1785), I, 5-7: "Il poeta ha per oggetto tre cose: commuovere, dipingere, ed istruire ... Istruisce cercando per mezzo della cognizione del Bello intelletuale, e del Bello fisico portare gli uomini alla cognizione e all' amore del Bello morale".

It is in this context of moral edification that we should understand references to filosofi, who through the combination of arts moved the heart and edified at the same time. It is perhaps not without significance therefore that critics of the 1830s were particularly liable to refer to Bellini's filosofia, as in an article on La straniera appearing in I teatri of Milan which referred to "la scienza e filosofia musicale di chi la compose".[12] References to Bellini of this nature are by no means uncommon. It was through appropriate regard for the diverse elements contributing to an opera that a philosophical approach to the work as a whole could be arrived at, and an edifying cultural art work could be produced.

What is particularly important is to see the extent to which Italian writers consider the vital position of Greek drama to society as a whole. Grossi mentions how the decline and separation of the arts led to internal strife. Not many writers went that far, but all saw it as having a central position. The view percolates down from books on fine arts into the general understanding of what the true theatre should be in the musical press.

Thus we find in one Neapolitan newspaper of 1831 an article on the role of singing in opera and its Greek roots:

> "In their ancient wisdom, our ancestors used music during the most solemn ceremonies; that is, when they sang hymns to their gods, and when they immolated sacrificial victims, and other offerings ... Their singing was the language of impassioned souls ... its mysterious and magical power standing wholly in its ravishing melody". (13)

We perhaps can recognize in this idea of the divinely impassioned

---

12. I teatri, Milan, 25 February 1829; quoted after Vincenzo Bellini, Epistolario, edited by Luisa Cambi (Milan, 1943), p.203.
13. La farfalla, Giornale di letteratura, d'invenzione, scienza ed arti, Naples, 7 May 1831: "L'antichissima sapienza degli avi nostri usò musica nelle più solenni circostanze: quando cioè si cantavano inni agli Dei, quando s'immolavano vittime, e si offrivano sacrifizi ... Il canto fu il linguaggio delle anime appassionate ... e la sua misteriosa e magica eloquenza sta tutta nella sua soavissima melodia".

singer some of the descriptions of Bellini's singers who were thereby to instil passions in the hearts of the audience, and certainly contemporary writers were very emphatic on the need to stir hearts through the power of melody; but what is significant is that the position of this type of music is seen historically to be part of the most important workings of society. This goes a long way to explain the formal and stylized nature of so much of the eighteenth century opera seria.

Writers were usually interested in seeing the links between such ancient uses of music and their own. This involves much consideration of the actual theory and practice of music in ancient times about which they seem to have known very little.

The musicographer and theorist Andrea Majer (1765-1837) who wrote a number of works on the history of Italian music and its roots in ancient theory, naturally enough begins his <u>Discorso sulla origine, progressi e stato attuale della musica italiana</u>, with the warning that "In the first part, I have begun with some observations on the music of the Ancients, from which our own music is directly descended".[14]

When we look for precise details as to how writers thought Greek music sounded, it is usually much more difficult to find information, perhaps due to the fact that many of the writers were 'students of the fine arts' rather than trained musicians. A sometimes controversial writer and, like Arteaga, an exiled Spanish Jesuit, Antonio Eximeno (1729-1808) writes that "The Greeks and the Romans wrote out

---

14. Andrea Majer, <u>Discorso sulla origine, progressi, e stato attuale della musica italiana</u> (Padua, 1821), p.13: "nella prima [parte] ho premesse alcune osservazioni sulla Musica degli antichi, da cui è direttamente derivata la nostra". Other works by Majer include his <u>Discorso intorno alle vicende della musica italiana</u> (Rome, 1819); and an article, 'Sulla conoscenza che avevano gl' antichi del contrappunto ossia dell' armonia equitemporanea', in <u>Nuova raccolta di scelte opere italiane e straniere di scienze, lettere, e arti</u>, III (Venice, 1822).

their theatrical declamations in musical notation, and very often recited them with the help of instruments".[15] Later he tells us how Greek, like Italian, is naturally musical because of the predominance of vowels[16] and how music became an essential part of education.[17] No doubt Eximeno had in mind Rousseau's famous strictures on the inadequacy of the French vowel system for musical setting in his *Lettre sur la musique française* (1753). As with other writers, we learn from Eximeno that "Music was born and perfected amongst the Greeks inseparable from poetry".[18] We also learn more from Eximeno on what Greek music actually sounded like, and here there is an obvious attempt to emphasize its similarities to contemporary Italian music, thus confusing the Greek word for a scale with harmony:

> "Therefore the comedies could be sung in the manner of our own burlettas; at least they were recited in a tone of voice that was clear and musical enough to be accompanied by instruments. In particular, the orchestra interpolated concertos or sinfonias adapted to the subject of the comedy". (19)

> "Their poetic compositions brought to life the variety and vivacity of their passions, which could not be expressed in music without a corresponding richness of modulations and melody. I do not mean to suggest by this that Greek music was exactly the same as our own ... what I do mean is that Greek music was full of harmony, and variety of

---

15. Antonio Eximeno, *Dell'origine e delle regole della musica, colla storia del sua progresso, decadenza e rinnovazione* (Rome, 1774), p.146: "I Greci ed i Romani notavono come con note di Musica le declamazioni teatrali, e le recitavano spesse volte accompagnandole con qualche strumento".
16. Eximeno, p.323.
17. Eximeno, p.330.
18. Eximeno, p.332: "La Musica nacque e si perfezionò tra i Greci unitamente colla poesia".
19. Eximeno, p.333: "Poterono dunque le Commedie cantarsi a guisa delle nostre burlette: almeno la loro recita si facea con un tono di voce così chiaro e sonoro, che potea essere sostenuta degli strumenti. Sopratutto l'orchestra interponeva qualche concerto o sinfonia addattata al Soggetto della commedia".

modulations, and that the whole experience was such as to give pleasure to a cultured soul". (20)

Andrea Majer refers directly to Cicero to try to give us rather more startling revelations concerning the actual singing of the Ancients. He tells us that "the Ancients used to decorate their singing ... <u>Flexiones atque falsae voculae</u> is the elegant term used by Cicero to describe volatinas, appoggiaturas, gorgheggi, trills, mordents and other similar graces of our own singing".(21)

What is fascinating here is not so much to consider how much or how little a contemporary writer knew about ancient music as the extent to which their own music was thought to be a natural descendant of it. Here we are given by Eximeno and Majer a picture of an orchestrally accompanied musical drama in which different arts combined to give an edifying whole, and in which even the <u>bel canto</u> traditions of vocal embellishment have their place.

In the transmission of this ancient culture Italy,was assumed to have an important place. For Gennaro Grossi, it was of course Naples that as a "colony of Athens carried forward from that cultured city its mode of speech, its customs, and its finest culture. She was always naturally attracted to the charms of Poetry and abandoned herself with delight to those of music".(22)

From this point Grossi jumps straight through musical history to

---

20. Eximeno, p.339: "I loro componimenti poetici ci rappresentano al vivo la varietà e vivacità delle loro passioni, quali non si possono esprimere in Musica senza la corrispondente varietà di modulazioni e melodie. Non pretendo per questo che la Musica greca sia stata onninamente come la nostra ... Quello che intendo dire si è che la Musica greca era piena di armonia, e composta di varietà di modulazioni, che la sperienza ci mostra essere attissime a dar piacere ad un animo culto".
21. Majer, p.32: "gli antichi usassero d'infiorare il loro canto ... <u>Flexiones atque falsae voculae</u> vengono elegantemente da Cicerone chiamate le <u>volatine</u>, le <u>appoggiature</u>, i <u>gorghetti</u>, i <u>trilli</u>, i <u>mordenti</u> ed altri simili vezzi del nostro canto".
22. Gennaro Grossi, I, 3: "Napoli colonia di Atene trasse da quella colta metropoli il suo linguaggio, il costume, e le più belle istruzioni. Ella fu sempre per genio attaccata alle grazie della poesia, e si abbandonò con trasporto alle delizie della musica".

the beginnings of what was assumed to be the Neapolitan opera school with Alessandro Scarlatti "nato a Napoli nel 1650", whom Grossi credits with being "the first man to succeed in perfecting the grammatical rules of music";[23] and then to "Pergolesi, who was like Raphael ... and who led dramatic music to its highest point of perfection, and who creates that magical effect which so moves and ravishes the heart of the listener".[24] This linking of the names of Raphael and Pergolesi as models of natural and unaffected beauty was in fact a commonplace of writing at the time.

To almost all writers Pergolesi remained the paragon to which all composers should aspire, and the finest composer of the school that leads, according to Grossi, to Hasse, Haydn, Mozart and Spontini (Grossi, pp.12, 17). Similarly, Ferro notes "Italy, which after Greece was the handmaiden of nature, has become pre-eminent over all the other modern nations in this respect".[25]

One of the most prolific and influential writers was Pietro Napoli-Signorelli (1731-1815), whose <u>Storia critica de teatri musicali italiani</u> was widely used in its several expanding editions until brought out in ten volumes in 1813. His more modest <u>Vicende della coltura nelle due Sicilie</u>, in only eight volumes (1810-1811), deals in its first volume particularly with the transmission of the ancient cultures of Magna Graecia into Modern Italian art forms.

> "The neighbouring Etruscans and their Greek counterparts were greatly enamoured of games, festivals, gymnastic shows and musicians or poets, and such practices gave

---

23. Gennaro Grossi, I, 8: "il primo che riuscì a perfezionare la grammatica della musica".
24. Gennaro Grossi, I, 10: "<u>Pergolesi</u> simile al <u>Raffaello</u> ... riduce la musica teatrale al sommo e perfetto, e produce quell' incanto che il cuore seduce e rapisce".
25. Ferro, I, 157: "Italia che dopo la Grecia è stata la confidente della natura, si è sollevata in questa facoltà sopra tutte le moderni nazioni".

rise amongst us to gymnasiums, circuses, amphitheatres and theatres". (26)

"... with regard to these musical and poetic games of the Ancients, we have reminders of them in the various famous theatres in Sicily". (27)

For Napoli-Signorelli, the presence of the old Roman and Greek theatres throughout the Kingdom of the Two Sicilies was a great influence in the development of the theatre in Italy, and in particular around Naples. In his *Del gusto e del bello* he proudly states that through this influence the Neapolitan tradition assimilated not only

> "most of the musical value emanating from men such as Timotheus and Terpander in handling emotional expression, but every benefit concerning aesthetics over and above what the Greek Aristoxenus was able to teach its [the Neapolitan] composers Scarlati, Vinci, Leo, Buranelli [Galuppi], Logroscino, Pergolese, and then Durante and La-Sala and their pupils Jommelli, Finaroli, Piccinni, Sacchini, Guglielmi, Paisiello, Cimarosa ... Italy who was without rivals in teaching the fine arts, perfected in this manner, to countries north of the Alps, added to it its own wonders". (28)

It should be pointed out that all of the above composers, with the sole exception of Galuppi, were regarded as being of the Neapolitan school. Particularly where writers are from the south themselves, this general emphasis on the Neapolitan tradition is strong; but it is only fair to add that at least three-quarters of the

---

26. Pietro Napoli-Signorelli, *Vicende della coltura nelle Due Sicilie, dalla venuta delle colonie straniere sino a' nostri giorni*, second edition, 8 vols (Naples, 1810-1811), I, 237: "I vicini Etruschi e gli affini Greci amavano eccedentemente i giuochi, le feste, gli spettacoli ginnici e poeti ossiano musici, e queste cose fecero elevare fra noi ginnasii, circhi, anfiteatri e teatri".
27. Napoli-Signorelli, *Vicende*, I, 245-246: "Quanto a' giuochi musici ossia poetici gli antichi ci hanno conservata memoria di varii famosi teatri della Sicilia".
28. Napoli-Signorelli, *Del gusto e del bello*, edizione napolitana (Naples, 1807), p.130: "buona parte del merito musicale emminente de' *Timotei* e dei *Terpandri* nel maneggiare il patetico, ma ogni vantaggio poi per la parte estetica sopra quanto potè insegnare il Greco Aristossseno ne' suoi maestri *Scarlati*, *Vinci*, *Leo*, *Buranelli*, *Logroscino*, *Pergolese*, e quindi *Durante*, e *La-Sala*, e ne' loro sommi alunni, *Jommelli*, Finaroli, *Piccinni*, *Sacchini*, *Guglielmi*, *Paisiello*, *Cimarosa* ... L'Italia che senza contrasto trasmise agli oltremontani le belle arti così perfezionate ... ne addita le proprie meraviglie".

composers that achieved any eminence during the eighteenth and early nineteenth centuries had strong Neapolitan connexions, either being born there or having studied there, and often teaching there as well. The sense of the continuity of tradition is what strikes the researcher most strongly in investigating these composers.

It is perhaps only to be expected, since contemporary writers saw their musico-dramatic traditions as being rooted in the theatre of the Greeks, that what were considered as the important values of the Greek drama should be emphasized as consistently as they are. What we are given is a comprehensive picture of the opera as an encyclopedic synthesis of the arts that strikingly anticipates the theories of Wagner in this respect. Just as the Greek theatre was regarded as the most solemn platform for the expression of the culture of a society, involving far more than just the combination of words and music, though this was perhaps the most important aspect to be considered, and the one that is most obvious to modern musicians; so was the Italian opera regarded as the summit of cultural achievement for the society within which it thrived for so long.

To contemporaries it was far more than a drama set to music, and indeed such a concept was alien to writers of that time who talked of 'poesia' and 'musica', and of the 'poeta' and 'musicista'; it was the only large scale musical form that could be taken seriously by Italians to whom 'music' meant 'opera'. Perhaps because to us opera is only one musical form amongst many, we run the risk of seriously underestimating the cultural significance that opera held for the contemporary Italian theatre-goer, and therefore misunderstanding the reasons for its formal and stylized nature.

Perhaps the most prestigious of all the aesthetic works on the Italian opera, Arteaga's <u>Le rivoluzioni del teatro musicale italiano</u>, opens thus:

> "What is to be understood by this word <u>Opera</u> is not one thing but many, that is to say an aggregate of poetry, music, decoration and pantomime; all of which, but principally the first three, are so closely bound up with each other that one cannot consider one without the others, nor understand the nature of opera without considering the union of all its parts ... In any other poetic composition, poetry is the absolute mistress of the other arts, to which they all defer; in opera she is not the mistress, but the companion of the other two, rather overall one judges it good or bad, according to the measure that it is adapted to the nature of the music and the decoration". (29)

An earlier though highly esteemed writer was Count Francesco Algarotti (1712-1764). His <u>Saggio sopra l'opera in musica</u> (1755) gained wide currency through translation, including into English. He was a widely travelled and cultured man, acquainted with the views of the encyclopedists, and perhaps the first to be partly influenced by them. He, like Arteaga after him, stresses the combination of the arts that constitutes opera.

> "It may with reason be affirmed, that the most powerful charms of music, of the mimic art, of dancing, and of painting, are in operatical performance all happily combined, that they may conspire in a friendly manner to refine our sentiments, to soothe the heart, and subdue the stubbornness of reason, that cannot help surrounding itself to so pleasing a fascination". (30)

The same picture strikes a foreign visitor in John Brown,

---

29. Arteaga, I, 1: "Qualora sentesi nominare questa parola <u>Opera</u> non s'intende una cosa sola ma molte, vale a dire, un aggregato di poesia, di musica, di decorazione, e di pantomima, le quali, ma principalmente le tre prime, sono fra loro così strettamente unite, che non può considerarsene una senza considerarne le altre, ne' comprendersi bene la natura del melodramma senza l'unione di tutte ... In qualsivoglia altro componimento poetico la poesia è la padrona assoluta, a cui referisce il restante; nell'Opera non è la padrona, ma la compagna delle altre due, anzi in tutto se dice buona, o cattiva, in quanto più, o meno si adatta al genio della musica, e della decorazione".
30. Francesco Algarotti, <u>An Essay on the Opera</u>, anonymous English translation (London, 1767), pp.1-2. Excerpts from this translation appear in Oliver Strunk, <u>Source Readings in Music History</u> (London, 1952), pp.657-672. These pages correspond to pp.10-49 of the edition of 1767.

painter (1752-1787):

> "... the serious Italian opera, ...
> as it is acted in Rome, though it may not be so
> perfect as it formerly was, is still the most perfect
> junction of Poetry, Music and Action (or Dancing as the
> ancients called it, which amongst them was an Art of
> Imitation, as well as Poetry and Music), the three
> finest of the Fine Arts, that is now to be found in the
> world, and such as only can give us any idea of <u>Attic
> Tragedies, of statliest and most Regal Argument</u> (to use
> an expression of Milton), with which that learned and
> elegant people were so much delighted, and upon the
> Representation of which they bestowed the greatest part
> of the revenue of their state". (31)

Ferro, however, places Poetry over all the other arts (unlike Arteaga)

> "Poetry, Music and Dance present us with depictions of
> Man's emotions, Architecture, Sculpture and Painting
> embellish the scene, the location and the Spectacle:
> but it is only Poetry that should prevail, and the other
> arts should all help and be subservient to it". (32)

This last point was soon to become a commonplace, particularly where Rossini and, later, Verdi were to make the music more complex so that it usurped, according to the values of contemporaries, the place of poetry. This gave rise to complicated results as will be dealt with in greater detail.

Perhaps the most succinct adumbration of the ideals of the Italian opera appeared in a splendid Neapolitan journal, the <u>Rivista teatrale e giornale di mode</u>. In Number 77 dated 22 December 1824, an article entitled 'Dell'opera in musica' was begun. The writer explains that "one is dealing in opera with an ideal over and above that to

---

31. John Brown, <u>Letters upon the Poetry and Music of the Italian Opera</u> (Edinburgh, 1789), p.ix. There is also, by a different man, another book in English on this subject: Dr. John Brown, <u>A Dissertation on the Rise, Union, and Power, the Progressions, Separations, and Corruptions of Poetry and Music</u> (London, 1763).
32. Ferro, II, 87-88: "Accade sovente, che si uniscano più arti a darci lo spettacolo (1)"; note 1: "Ciò accade benissimo in teatro; la Poesia, la Musica, la Danza ci rappresentano l' immagine delle passioni dell' Uomo, l'Architettura, la Scoltura, la Pittura, apparecchiano il luogo, la Scena, lo Spettacolo: ma la sola Poesia deve regnare, ed il resto delle arti tutte devono servirla, ed ajutarla".

which we should be carried by tragedy which is merely spoken". (33) Later in the article he adds that "All the fine arts are united in producing the Opera in music". (34)

A final example will show that this view of opera was still prevalent until the middle of the century. It sums up well the moral aspect of this art and its values as edification. Giuseppe Mastriani's <u>Il teatro e gli artisti</u> (1849) sets out a consciously Platonic view of the Moral Dignity of Art in general and <u>il teatro</u> in particular. His chapter headings include 'Dignità delle Arti', 'Scopo morale', 'Educazione morale e civile'. His thesis is that through music, and opera in particular, one can hope to benefit society at large, and so therefore it is necessary that all the artistic achievements of that society should be involved.

> "The ultimate purpose of art one can generalize as the moral perfection of mankind ... it seems to me a reasonable proposition to derive the whole dignity of art from this principle. And therefore we find contributing to theatrical productions, poetry, music, acting, painting, decoration, architecture, etc. It is certainly reasonable enough to maintain that those artists involved in the theatre should consider themselves second to none in being worthy of public esteem". (35)

The views of all these writers are remarkably consistent; so much so as to suggest the reference to the earlier standard works on the part of the later writers. There is no doubt as to how the ideals

---

33. <u>Rivista teatrale e giornale di mode</u>, Naples, 22 December 1824: "Nell' opera in musica si tratta di un ideale anche al di là di quello al quale dee trasportarci la tragedia semplicemente declamata".
34. <u>Rivista teatrale</u>, 24 December 1824: "Nell' opera in Musica concorrono tutte le belle arti riunite".
35. Giuseppe Mastriani, <u>Il teatro e gli artisti</u> (Naples, 1849), p.14: "alle arte vuolsi generalmente porre per iscopo ultimo il perfezionamento morale dell' uomo ... parmi ragionevol cosa da siffatto principio derivare la dignità delle arti. E poichè alle rappresentazioni teatrali concorrono la poesia, la musica, la mimica, la pittura, la decorazione, l'architettura ec. Si può certamente con ragione sostenere che gli artisti di Teatro non abbiansi a tenere meno degli altri degni della pubblica stima".

of the opera were seen, and the direction in which creators of opera ought to aspire. This seems to have been the built-in basis to the consideration of what was important in an opera, particularly around Naples, if only because the city was more than usually conscious of its traditions. This naturally does not mean that the ideals were always realized, and indeed all writers seem to have had a habit of complaining that standards were not what they once were. It is noticeable that this trend is seen much more in the later writers, such as Grossi and Ferro and many of the journals, than in the earlier works by Algarotti, Eximeno, or John Brown.

The reasons for the decline in standards where it appears are strictly logically explained in terms of the general philosophy of opera at that time. At the heart of the classical ideal of opera we have the theory of the combination of all the arts, as mentioned time and time again by contemporary writers. At the basis of this we have the fusion of the poetry and the music; and at the time of the purest manifestation of this type of culture, of the poet and the musician. It is most interesting for its future ramifications, therefore, that the decline of the arts should be seen as coming from the breakdown of this union. A key feature is the lack of *filosofia*. Therefore Arteaga writes:

> "in the resurgence of the arts in Italy, as all over Europe, the fine arts were produced only as an imitation of the ancients. One can see this in the origins of tragedy and comedy, and we have seen it most clearly in those of drama. ... the duties of poet, musician, singer, legislator, singer and philosopher were in Greece for many centuries united in one sole person ... The principal [reason for the decline of the arts] is that amongst us for a long time, philosophy, legislation, poetry and music have become separated, and that, thus divided,

their individual influence has become much diminished". (36)

More specifically, he calls one of his chapters: "Cap. XIII. Cause particolari della decadenza attuale dell' opera. Prima causa. Mancanza di filosofia nei Compositori".(37) Arteaga makes it clear that by this he means that composers have become too complicated in their approach; that is to say, that they have become involved with musical effects for their own sake rather than composing with a correct balance of all the different elements of opera, as was required by a proper philosophical approach.

> "the first and most grievous defect of the theatrical music of today is that it is too sophisticated and not philosophically considered, designed solely with the intention of gratifying the ear, rather than affecting the heart; besides which it ignores the sense of the words which should be the one and only duty of music for theatrical production ... the works of the great composers of the bygone age are no longer studied or followed". (38)

Later he criticizes singers for no longer being "as in the olden days, musicians, poets and philosophers at the same time".(39) Similarly, Gennaro Grossi, as we have seen, explains the decline in opera

---

36. Arteaga, II, 178-180: "nel risorgimento delle lettere in Italia, come in tutta Europa, le belle arti non furono che un prodotto della imitazion degli antichi. Ciò si vede nell' origine della tragedia, e della commedia, e l'abbiam più chiaramente veduto in quello del dramma ... Gli uffizj di poeta, di musico, di cantore, di legislatore, e di filosofo si videro nella Grecia per molti secoli riuniti in una sola persona ... La prima è che essendo fra noi da gran tempo seperate la filosofia, la legislazione, la poesia e la musica, la loro individuale influenza ha devuto esser minore perchè divisa".
37. Arteaga, II, 251.
38. Arteaga, II, 254: "il primo e capitale difetto dell' odierna musica teatrale è quello di essere troppo raffinata e poco filosofica proponendosi solamente per fine di grattar l' orecchio, e non di muovere il cuore, nè di rendere il senso delle parole, come pur dovrebbe essere il principale ed unico uffizio della musica rappresentativa ... non si studiano, non si imitano le opere dei sommi compositori della trascorsa età".
39. Arteaga, III, 4: "come in altri tempi musici, poeti, e filosofi insieme".

as being due to the fact that "music was no longer in the hands of philosophers".(40) The idea therefore was that if composers ignored the broad cultural approach of _filosofi_, and in its place devoted themselves to the technical mysteries of harmony and counterpoint, they could never hope to create again the balanced masterpieces that all writers saw in the model of musical Greek theatre and the great composers of bygone ages of Italian opera, particularly Pergolesi. The precise nature of this problem, and the reasons why it causes unsatisfactory works, is explained in the **Rivista teatrale** article referred to earlier:

> "If we are to trust in the ancient traditions, at one time poet and musician were one and the same person ... It would seem to us therefore that, divorced from music, poetry necessarily declined into prose ... and on the other hand, music by itself just made prodigious advances in harmony and counterpoint, and in melody and construction ... Since these are the results of letting music and versification develop by themselves, it is obvious what must happen to them if we wish them to be united in creating a coherent effect ... for the combination of these two arts to produce a unified effect it is necessary for each of them to be reined by the needs of the other. Thus it is only poetry that can be declaimed musically: and it is only the singer that can invest the complete expression of the poetic conceit with the expressive effect of music in all the richness of its magical power". (41)

The contemporary view was thus that it was only through the connexion with the rhythms and charms of music that words took the form

---

40. Gennaro Grossi, I, 77: "la musica non fu trattata da filosofi".
41. **Rivista teatrale**, 24 December 1824: "Se vogliam credere alle vecchie tradizioni, una volta poeta e musico erano una persona sola ... Parea che distaccata dalla musica, la poesia dovesse declinar nella prosa ... Dall' altro canto, la musica da per sè sola fece anch'essa prodigiosi passi nell' _armonia_, nella _melodia_, ne' periodi ... Essendo queste le condizioni necessarie de' progressi della versificazione e della musica seperate tra loro, è facile il veder quale esser deggia la loro condizione nel volerli riunire insieme per farli concorre ad un effetto unico ... per la combinazione di queste due arti a produrre un effetto ragionevole è necessario che ognuna di esse retroceda ... e allora soltanto la poesia può essere musicalmente declamata: allora soltanto l'esecutore vocale a tutta l'espressione del concetto poetico accoppiar può tutta l'espressione dell' incanto musicale in tutta quanta l'ampiezza della sua magica prepotenza".

of poetry with its metrical vitality and variety; otherwise it would decline into mere prose. As far as the music was concerned, it had to be tied to the words of the poetry or it would become distracted by its own technicalities and degenerate into a sort of musical prose, a complex aural effect that would tickle the ear rather than have some poetic purpose that might affect the heart. Of course this should be seen in the context of an Italian operatic culture that had not experienced the development of musical expression independent of poetry. For Italians, until quite late in the nineteenth century, music had to be linked to poetry to be properly regarded as a viable art form. Pure music that elsewhere might be heard in orchestral or chamber concerts, was simply music that was unpoetic. The simple corollary of this was that only to a limited extent were Italians of Bellini's time- and Bellini was only just on the eve of producing his first student opera, <u>Adelson e Salvini</u>, when the article in the Neapolitan <u>Rivista teatrale</u> appeared- interested in music for its own sake.

To take this last point immediately, though it will be expanded on much more fully later on, this meant that, as we are only too well aware, music in Italy had to be vocal music; not just because Italians liked voices, but because it was only the singer that could fuse the poetic conceit with the magic power of music, to paraphrase the end of the passage from the <u>Rivista teatrale</u>. In terms of musical texture as we think of it today, this meant that the chordal principles that lie at the basis of our harmonic approach to music meant nothing to Italians in as much as they dealt with matters unconnected with the poetry. For most of the listeners and writers on Italian opera this was increased by their essentially <u>dilettante</u> approach, and as far as they were concerned, that part of the music was in the hands of curious craftsmen; musicians who studied what was known as "contrappunto". They were regarded as artists when they brought this technical expertise to the service of the words, at which point they might begin to qualify as "filosofi".

Since the vocal line was necessarily pre-eminent rather than merely the top line of a chordally conceived texture, it would appear that Italians still thought of their music initially in terms of the two outer parts. As with its guiding aesthetic philosophy, this seems to have been a relic of the days of baroque opera. Manfred Bukofzer writes of the polarity between harmonic support and the melody dependent on such support as the essence of the monodic style. "The outermost voices acquired, in baroque music, a domineering position: bass and soprano furnished the skeleton of the composition. This structural contour was the essential part of the music, the rest could be filled in at the discretion of the improvising continuo player".[41a] By the early nineteenth century, the harmonies were no longer dependent on the improvised accompaniment of the continuo player, but now appeared in the score. Yet despite this, the initial conception of the music does not seem to have changed very much, although it should be added that this did not preclude harmonic richness any more than it had for baroque harmony. In later chapters some consideration will be given to the way in which this led to an emphasis on the outer parts of the orchestral textures, and to an emphasis in the arias on the bass line in opposition to the voice. The extent to which Italians avoided any elaboration in the working out of the inner parts can be seen as a barometer of their awareness of the value of musical elements independent of their poetical origins. The instrumental bass, distinct from the vocal part above it, was an essential pedestal upon which the singer stood, to quote a contemporary metaphor; but any other accompanying instrumental lines did not at first seem to serve any artistic purpose beyond that of occupying the hands of the composer. Ferro complains "nowadays composers want to become all powerful ... instead of emphasizing the basses more, which are the shades of Music, they unphilosophically fill out the accompaniment with upper parts, dazzling [the audience] and covering the

---

41a. Manfred Bukofzer, Music in the Baroque Era (London, 1948), p.11.

voice, which is the very one that should be brought out".[42]

The implications of such a new approach to composition are far reaching and will of course be dealt with more fully later. What is immediately important is to see such a process in the terms in which contemporary theory saw it; that is, as a product of the separation of the arts.

The classical opera, seen in the light of these writers' consciousness of its ancient roots, was a remarkable aesthetic concept. With the increase in the complexity of one of its parts, that is to say music, the delicate balances upon which it based its whole survival, could only become threatened. Before it passed into the Romantic *melodramma* that we see brought to its perfection in the later works of Donizetti and particularly Verdi, it produced some remarkable works of its own which are only too easily seen and judged according to how much they approach the later work and not in the light of their own aesthetic concepts.

The ideals of classical opera have much similarity with those of the Wagnerian *Gesamtkunstwerk* and the common traditions in Greek theatre that their champions assumed that they inherited. Indeed in some ways Wagner lost one important branch of the arts so combined when he darkened his auditorium. Both the architecture of the theatre and its illumination was considered very much part of the spectacle in the Italian opera. In Naples, as in some other places, it also had another element, most clearly concentrated on the prominent royal box. The visit of a

---

42. Ferro, II, 88, note 2: "Eppure i compositori d' oggi giorno volendo far da despotici ... essi invece di far lavorare maggiormente i bassi, che sono gli scuri della Musica, accrescono con poco filosofia l' accompagnamento coi sprani, abbagliando, e cuoprendo la voce, che dovrebbe essere la sola a figurare".

monarch was naturally a major social occasion, often celebrated by a Grande illuminazione. Wagner definitely cut the audience out of his concept of the total art-work.

Italians of the period under study here, however, considered that a representation of society should be present at opera. This must in part be understood as a desire to enjoy opera as a social meeting place, but it is mistaken to completely ignore the fact that for them it represented the fusion of all the finest cultural achievements of their society. One should perhaps resist cynicism here and remember the links that writers on aesthetics saw between the opera as properly directed by filosofi, and the healthiness of the society from which it sprang. For this reason, even the most highminded of writers on the aesthetics of opera, like Algarotti, argued for an opera house designed so that all the spectators could see not only the drama in question, but also the auditorium as well. This should be remembered in connexion with the magnificence of the decoration of the auditorium and the emphasis put on its illumination.

> "the architect's principal care, should be to leave no article unremedied that might any way tend to impede the view: and at the same time, to let no gaping chasm appear, by any space remaining unoccupied, and lost to every serviceable purpose. Let him also contrive, that the audience may appear to form a part of the spectacle to each other". (43)

The magnificence of the design of the interior was usually regarded as being of sufficient importance as to merit its inclusion in the libretto crediting contributions to the spettacolo. At the San Carlo Opera House in Naples these were the work of Antonio Niccolini who was called the architetto although his responsibilities were really concerned with the interior and the facade, restored after a fire in 1816. Niccolini writes about his purpose in decorating the

---

43. Algarotti, p.104.

auditorium, making it plain that although it somewhat distracts attention from the stage, the illumination is important in order to promote the social purpose of the theatre to greatest effect.

> "It is no doubt true that the total combination of a hundred torches flickering amidst the spectators, does impede vision, and destroy some of the illusion of the scenes, causing the effect of daylight to lose its splendour, and night its darkness; but such not inconsiderable defects are balanced by the gaiety that is acquired by the auditorium thanks to its brilliance, and the clarity by which the spectators can be seen in all parts of it". (44)

The magnificence of the auditorium was obviously something to be highly prized. Its effect at the San Carlo was evidently dazzling, particularly when the theatre was graced by royalty; at which point the royal box stood as one stage balanced by the palco scenico directly opposite it. Niccolini makes special reference to "il gran Palco de' Sovrani".[45] Socially speaking, this was the zenith of magnificence attainable by the theatre. The atmosphere of such an occasion is described by many contemporary writers, but here is the judgement of a distinguished foreign traveller, the German dramatist August von Kotzebue (1761-1819), speaking of the San Carlo of a decade earlier:

> "The theatre San Carlo is the first in Naples, and the largest in Europe. I have seen it once only, but it was then in its full splendour. It was on the festival of the saint who has given it his name. The royal family sat there in state: the princesses glittering with diamonds. All the boxes were adorned with fashionable ladies, who had lavished jewels on their persons for this occasion. Here also the supreme enjoyment of the females in being seen, was attainable, in the highest degree; for the front of every box had a gilt chandelier with three torches (I will not call them merely lights) flaming in it. As the house

---

44. Antonio Niccolini, Sulla nuova decorazione del Real Teatro S. Carlo (Naples, n.d. (c.1817)), p.viii: "Egli è fuor di dubbio che la riunione di cento fiaccole scintillanti in mezzo agli Spettatori offende la vista, e distrugge l' illusione della Scena facendo che il giorno vi comparisce senza splendore, e la notte priva d' oscurità, ma tali non lievi torti son bilanciati dalla giocondità che, mercè la sua luce, acquista la Sala, e dalla distinzione con cui in ogni parte di essa si vedono gli Spettatori". Also by Niccolini is his essay, Del Real Teatro di San Carlo, cenno storico (Naples, 1817), 29 pp.
45. Niccolini, Sulla nuova decorazione, p.vii.

has in each of the six tiers ninety-eight boxes, it may
be easily conceived that so many wax torches besides the
candles, &c. would produce a very bright artificial day". (46)

Even allowing for some exaggeration on Kotzebue's part, one can easily see that this account shows much the same attitude to the auditorium as do those of Algarotti and Niccolini. No doubt this will come as no surprise to students of baroque opera but it is sobering to realize that the same situation still obtained at the start of the nineteenth century. For one thing it means that the social element of opera was still carried forward; for another it means that a proper understanding of opera in Naples at the time of the emergence of Bellini has to include consideration of the visual element, both on and off the stage. The dimming of the auditorium lights at the Teatro alla Scala in Milan is described by Stendhal in his Rome Naples et Florence en 1817 as an innovation of great interest, but it is clear that this did not preclude traditional social activities.

"There is not a single chandelier in the whole of the
auditorium; all the illumination there is comes from the
fan of light reflected from the stage ... In spite of
the almost total darkness in the auditorium, I managed
perfectly well to pick out different people as they made
their way into the pit. It is quite customary to give
and acknowledge greetings from box to box across the
theatre; I have a footing now in seven or eight different
boxes, in each of which there may be five or six persons,
and conversation firmly established, as in a salon". (47)

In the great majority of theatres there seems to have been no such attempt to darken the auditorium. This may have been partly due to the technical difficulties involved; but the traditional outlook that emphasized the importance of the auditorium in contributing to the spettacolo should not be ignored either. Therefore architecture and the social context are still important features that are too

---

46. August von Kotzebue, Travels through Italy in the years 1804 and 1805, 4 vols (London, 1806), II, 189-190.
47. Stendhal, Rome, Naples and Florence, translated by Richard N. Coe (London, 1959), p.8. The entry is dated 26 September 1816.

easily forgotten when writing about opera of Bellini's time. These considerations should, however, be understood in terms of the unification of all the arts that Italians of the early nineteenth century still believed their opera to be. When we read that they feared the disintegration of the opera and the separation of the arts, we should remember that here we have one example of a parameter of operatic criticism that we have undoubtedly lost. Of Arteaga's listing of the four elements of opera, he emphasized particularly poetry, music and decoration. Of these only music retains the importance it once had, indeed it has increased it; poetry has been much overshadowed by the demands of drama, as we shall see, and decoration today would be regarded as by a long way secondary to music and drama. For reasons of its social purpose and historical roots, Italians of Bellini's time still regarded it as of great importance in the context of the combination of cultural elements that they believed their opera to be.

In conclusion, some consideration must be given to placing the Italian view of opera into some historical context. This is of course not the occasion for a history of aesthetics, but no doubt the reader will have thought of some of the similarities that exist between these views that opera was born from Greek drama and the writings of the Florentine <u>camerata</u> of the late sixteenth century. It is possible that writings of this type can be found covering the period from 1600 until that under consideration here. However, it seems more reasonable to believe that the principal influence on our Italian writers comes from the Encyclopedists. If they are not directly responsible for the views held in Italy at this time, then, certainly, they gave them considerable reinforcement.

The Encyclopédie,[48] which had great influence on almost every aspect of cultural thought in the second half of the eighteenth century, devoted a great deal of space to the subject of music, and many of its views find some echo in those under study here. D'Alembert makes some illuminating remarks in the 'Discours preliminaire' found in the first volume of 1751 where he considers music's capabilities for expression. He concludes that absolute music, as composed at that time, is necessarily to be regarded as mere noise; just as, later, Italians felt there was no point in music for its own sake, that did not express words. D'Alembert writes: "Music that portrays nothing is merely noise, and would be scarcely more pleasurable than a succession of sonorous words lacking proper order and inter-connection".[49]

That the Encyclopédie was widely known and influential in Italy should hardly need stressing, but as it happens, this very passage is quoted by Francesco Algarotti in his Saggio sopra l'opera in musica of 1755,[50] to which reference has already been made (see note 30). It is equally possible to find amongst other French writers, the source and even many of the turns of phrase of ideas in the Italians. In Charles Batteux's Les beaux-arts reduits à un même principe (Paris, 1746), for example we read that "It is poetry, music and dance that present to us the image of actions and human passions. But it is architecture, painting and sculpture that set the scene for the drama".[51] Batteux maintains that though "poetry, music and dance are sometimes separated to satisfy the tastes and desires of men",[52] the three arts are more powerful when united. Another influential

---

48. Encyclopédie, ou dictionnaire raisonné des sciences, des arts et des metiers, edited by J. le R. d'Alembert and D. Diderot, 28 vols (Paris, 1751-1772).
49. Peter le Huray and James Day, Music and Aesthetics in the Eighteenth and Early-Nineteenth Centuries (Cambridge, 1981), p.59.
50. Oliver Strunk, Source Readings in Music History (London, 1952), p.670n.
51. Le Huray and Day, p.55. Compare Ferro in note 32.
52. Le Huray and Day, p.53.

writer referred to by Italians was Jean Jacques Barthélemy, in whose
<u>Entretiens sur l'état de la musique grecque au quatrième siècle</u> (Paris,
1777) we read that music "enlivened the verse of Hesiod, Homer,
Archilochus, Terpander, Simonides and Pindar. It was inseparable from
poetry".[53] Another work that dealt with the subject of the fall and
separation of the arts was Dr. John Brown's <u>Dissertation on the Rise,
Union and Power, the Progressions, Separations and Corruptions of
Poetry and Music</u> (London, 1763). The authority most often actually
referred to by Italians was Rousseau, particularly with regard to his
<u>Dictionnaire de musique</u> (Geneva, 1767), no doubt partly because he was
so impassioned an Italophile. His <u>Essai sur les origines des langues</u>
(1764) was another work that provided a source for the view that
"Poetry song and speech have a common origin" and that "the first
stories were told in verse and that the first laws were sung".[54]
Later Rousseau tells us how music declined because "whilst melody had
begun by being closely modelled on speech, it gradually took on a
separate existence, and music became increasingly independent of
words".[55]

The philosopher Rousseau was nevertheless a layman in terms of
music, and his view that music independent of words was suspect was
to be found quite commonly in similar philosophical writings in music.
Carl Dahlhaus has shown how even at the beginning of the nineteenth
century, such philosophers as Hegel and Kant tended to view musicians
with some suspicion that they were somewhat limited in culture.[56]
Kant in particular regarded music in itself as "more entertainment
than culture" and that it only attained the status of a fine art when

---

53. Le Huray and Day, p.167. Compare Gennaro Grossi in note 4.
54. Le Huray and Day, p.92.
55. Le Huray and Day, p.104.
56. Carl Dahlhaus, <u>Esthetics of Music</u>, translated by William W. Austin (Cambridge, 1982), p.29.

it served as a vehicle for poetry.[57] This supports the contention, made earlier, that at this time many people did not see music by itself as an art of any great consequence. Even in Germany, it would seem that only trained musicians were likely to regard it as such. For their part, Italians therefore had little use for instrumental music since it was devoid of poetry. To this extent they were following in a rich tradition of thought that viewed with regret the separation and independence of arts.

---

57. Dahlhaus, pp.31-32. See also page 47 on Hegel's contention that absolute music is concerned merely with the specifically musical features of composition and its skill; details that are of interest to connoisseurs only.

CHAPTER 3

THE ROLE OF THE SINGER ON THE STAGE

"In prehistorical times, exactly when we will not concern ourselves with here, singing was not regarded as an art in itself: it was not a distinct discipline so completely independent of poetry as it is now; where the poets have ceased to be also the singers, and the latter have also stopped composing the music, and, instead, are called on to execute that already written by the composer". (1)

This passage taken from Luigi Celentano's <u>Intorno all' arte del cantare in Italia nel secolo decimonono</u>, which was published in Naples as late as 1867, highlights one of the problems of studying individual aspects of opera from this period. We can see that strikingly late in the century, critics still saw opera as an art form in which all the arts were united; and naturally this has an obvious connexion with the concept of the Greek musician-poet that was referred to earlier. In other words, just as Aeschylus organized and set to music his own drama, so did he deliver it on the stage; "canta sua parte". (2)

It is necessary to understand the role of the libretto in early nineteenth-century opera in terms of the singer on the stage, since it was he who realized in music the poetry of the original inspiration. This is the reason why it is the singer that is central to this type of opera; the orchestral part, which is emphasized so often as the positive and progressive element in opera, can have no place in the realization of the poetry. This gives some clue to a later consideration of the relationship between this older idea of opera as a fusion of poetry and music and the growing

---

1. Luigi Celentano, <u>Intorno all' arte del cantare in Italia nel secolo decimonono</u> (Naples, 1867), p.7: "Nei tempi primitivi, che non accade qui determinare, il canto non era come <u>arte da sè</u>: e non era una disciplina tanto seperata e distinta dalla poesia, che i poeti cessassero di essere i cantori, e questi, senza nè anche inventar le note, fossero chiamati a far quelle già formate dal compositore".
2. Compare Chapter 2, note 8.

concept of opera as 'opera and drama'. As an essential part of dramatic opera, the orchestra grew in importance to act as a spur to the dramatic action; and for us this is a valued element in its stageworthiness. For the bel canto observer, however, it became a threat to the singer; and for that reason a threat to what was central to this type of opera, the poetry itself.

This goes hand in hand with the traditional view of instrumental music as a degenerate form which through the separation of the arts has lost its poetic element. In his interesting Trattato completo, formale e materiale del teatro, Francesco Milizia (1725-1798) states the view, universally accepted, that "music for the voice must have preceded that for instruments".[3] Later he explains this by saying that "all these instruments are nothing else than different voices so far as they strike the ear. They are so many artificial devices designed to produce sounds where there are no voices available",[4] a view clearly supported by the Spanish jesuit, Eximeno: "Instruments are a means of imitating singing artificially".[5] Lichtenthal's authoritative dictionary of 1826 defines a musical instrument as "an artificial device which can produce and vary sounds in imitation of the human voice".[6]

In other words, musical instruments have their place, but are to be regarded as secondary to the human voice because they cannot deal with the poetry. For this reason they cannot express the poetic

---

3. Francesco Milizia, Trattato completo, formale e materiale del teatro (Venice, 1794), p.45: "la Musica Vocale ha dovuto precedere la Strumentale". Further references will be made to this edition. The original version was Del Teatro (Rome, 1771). Also by Milizia is a Dizionario delle belle arti del disegno, 2 vols (Bassano, 1797).
4. Milizia, p.46: "Tutti questi strumenti non sono altro che voci differenti, per le quali si parla agli orecchi. Sono tante macchine inventate e disposte con arte per esprimere i suoni in mancanza della voce".
5. Eximeno, p.313: "Gli strumenti sono un artifiziosa imitazione del canto".
6. Lichtenthal, I, 351: "Corpo artifiziale, il quale puo rendere e variare i suoni ad imitazione della voce umana".

quality of the original inspiration of the composer. Of course this follows naturally from the consideration given in the previous chapter to the difficulty contemporary Italians had coming to terms with pure music that was independent of words.

Since it was just this capacity that the human voice had over musical instruments, it can be seen that the principal duty of the singer revolved around the idea of singing poetry. It will be remembered that this role was seen historically in terms of the singer declaiming poetry upon the stage as a combination of arts. It will cause no surprise therefore to discover that it is just this concept of singing that informs the didactic manuals of what is normally known as the era of the bel canto. The actual meaning of the term bel canto and its period of influence must await a later chapter, but it will be sufficient here to say that it is intended to be understood to refer to the traditions of that type of singing that was taught in Italy during the periods dominated by the castrato singers. This has now become synonymous with the cultivation of the purest techniques of singing without regard to ideas of expression. This is not a view that would have been accepted by Italians in the early nineteenth century, though it might be argued that it is a measure of the extent to which their acceptance of the idea of "expression in music" differed from our own.

If we accept the Italian idea of singing as part of a greater combination of the arts, and itself a fusion of music and poetry, then we are in a better position to understand the traditional view of Italian writers. One of the most famous of these was Pier Francesco Tosi (c. 1653-1732) whose Opinioni de cantori antichi e moderni dates from 1723, but who influenced Italian singing theses for many years afterwards; and through translation and imitation, conditioned much of the training in France, England and Germany. According to Tosi the poetic basis of singing should be brought out and the words therefore emphasized, since it is only this that distinguishes the voice from mere instrumental imitations of it.

> "If they are not heard, the singer deprives the listener of the greatest part of the delight that song derives from their effect, and if they are not heard then the singer devoids art of truth: and finally, if the words are not heard then there is no difference between the human voice and a Cornetto or Haut-bois. This is a defect which although one of the most grievous, is nowadays little short of universal". (7)

The consistency of the views expressed in Italian singing theses has been well shown in Duey's Bel Canto in its Golden Age (1951) to extend throughout the eighteenth century. What is interesting, however, is the extent to which this view of the voice was continued after that, especially in Naples. Again we have the concept, as an extension of the idea of poetry and music being born together, of the words being unseparable from the singer himself. Thus Girolamo Crescentini (1762-1846), who was one of the last of the great Castrati and the performer of many of the operas of Niccolò Zingarelli (1752-1837), and who taught Bellini himself at the Conservatory of San Sebastiano of Naples, writes in his preface to his Raccolta di essercizi (1811) that "Il canto deve essere un imitazione del discorso", and concludes that "Good taste in singing lies solely in the expression of the words, and in those appropriate inflexions that are mentioned in paragraph 8". (8)

---

7. Pier Francesco Tosi, Opinioni de' cantori antichi e moderni, o sieno osservazioni sopra il canto figurato (Bologna, 1723), p.35: "se non si sentono, chi canta priva gli ascoltanti d' una gran parte di quel diletto, che il Canto riceve dalla loro forza: Se non si sentono, quel Cantore esclude la verità dall' artificio: E se finalmente non si sentono, non si distingue la voce umana d' un Cornetto, o d' un Haut-bois. Questo difetto benché massimo in oggi è poco men che commune". Reference will be made to this edition generally, but a contemporary English translation, with "explanatory annotations", is sometimes referred to as well: Tosi, Observations on the Florid Song: or, Sentiments on the Ancient and Modern Singers, translated by Mr. Galliard (London, 1743).
8. Girolamo Crescentini, Raccolta di esservizi per il canto all' uso del vocalizzo (Paris, 1811), 'Discorso preliminare dell' autore', section 5 and section 12: "Il buon gusto nel canto non è altro che l'espressione della parola, e quelle inflessioni convenevoli come è stato detto nel paragrafo 8".

These inflexions or "inflessioni convenevoli" that he mentions as proper to a true delivery of the words include the ornaments such as "una <u>Volantina</u>, un <u>Gruppetto</u>, un <u>Trillo</u>", which were referred to earlier as being rooted in the oratorical traditions of the ancients.[9] Interestingly enough, Crescentini himself goes on to say that with study, the singer himself can produce those effects unknown to us but so much valued by the ancient Greeks.[10] Part of Crescentini's fame rested on his attention to the words and also his acting. Duey refers to Schopenhauer's praise of him in his <u>Reisetagbücher</u> of 1804 and to Fetis's judgement "Never was song and dramatic art carried to such heights".[11] It is certainly likely that Bellini's oft-praised attention to the words was influenced considerably by this <u>bel canto</u> tradition of song and dramatic art.

Another man that carried on this view of singing into the nineteenth century was Marcello Perrino (born 1765). His opera <u>Ulisse nell' isola di Circe</u> was first produced at the Teatro San Carlo in Naples exactly a week after Bellini's arrival there in June 1819.[12] More important for our study, however, is the fact that he became Rector of the Neapolitan Conservatory of San Sebastiano where Bellini studied. We learn from Francesco Florimo, the lifelong friend of Bellini, that he became <u>direttore economico</u> in 1806,[13] and that he was responsible for ameliorating the treatment of pupils. He also provided compositional examples and a "metodo di canto",[14] in which he is described as rector and administrator of the conservatory.[15] It seems that the

---

9. Crescentini, section 8. Compare Majer's reference to Cicero's "flexiones atque falsae voculae"; see Chapter 2, note 21.
10. Crescentini, section 6.
11. P. A. Duey, <u>Bel Canto in its Golden Age</u> (New York, 1951), p.56.
12. Felice de Filippis and R. Arnese, <u>Cronache del teatro di San Carlo</u>, 2 vols (Naples, 1959), I, 59.
13. Francesco Florimo, <u>La scuola musicale di Napoli</u>, 4 vols (Naples, 1881-1882), II, 37.
14. Florimo, <u>La scuola</u>, II, 41.
15. Marcello Perrino, <u>Osservazioni sul canto</u> (Naples, 1810), title-page: "scritte da Marcello Perrino, rettore ed amministratore del real conservatorio di musica di S. Sebastiano in Napoli".

book also had the sanction of Bellini's mentor Zingarelli who, Perrino claims, "asked by me for his opinions concerning the work called <u>Osservazioni sul canto</u>, reported that he found it excellent, and meriting publishing in order to revive the old schools of song".(16)

There seems always to have been a conscious desire to revive the old schools of singing: even at a time when vocal art was at its peak there seems to have been a yearning for a 'Golden Age' of bygone days. Tosi, who must be regarded as writing at the time of the classical era of <u>bel canto</u>, is already talking of grievous defects of his time compared with his predecessors, as in the extract given. Thus the talk of the old schools must sometimes be seen as a hankering after an unrealized ideal in singing, rather than necessarily as evidence of a continual decline. In Tosi's case, it could well be argued that the following generation of Pacchierotti (1740-1821) and his contemporaries represented the zenith of the <u>bel canto</u> tradition. This is the generation of singing represented in Giovanni Battista Mancini's <u>Pensieri e riflessioni pratiche sopra il canto figurato</u> of 1774, to which Perrino himself makes allusion in his own treatise. Perrino's work therefore stands in a long tradition and so it is only to be expected that he voices again the importance of poetry to singing:

> "The purpose of singing is to express such melodies, and to externalize those feelings which are all part of the sentiment of the musical composition and its text". (17)

There is no room for doubt that such expression of the words required music in a symbiotic combination "music by itself being neither

---

16. Perrino, p.3: "richiesta da me del suo parere intorno all' opera intitolata 'Osservazioni sul canto'; ha riferito di averla trovata eccellente, e che merita di esser pubblicata colle stampe per far rivivere l' antica scuola di canto".
17. Perrino, p.9: "L' oggetto del canto della voce umana è di esprimere quelle melodie, ed estrinsecare quell' affetto, cui è attaccato il sentimento della composizione musicale e delle parole".

able to arouse, nor depict with the necessary power, the emotions within the mind without the help of words".[18] There are definite echoes in this of the convictions referred to in the previous chapter that music required words to fix the precise emotions depicted, and that failing this, music portrayed nothing specific.[19] Perrino continues that, as the other side to this coin, "Music serves to give the words a greater power of expression"[20] which we might understand as saying that singing was a heightened form of declamation. This might be a commonplace, except that in contemporary terms it is to be seen as saying that this is music's sole purpose. Arteaga's famous thesis explains to us in terms similar to those of d'Alembert in his 'Discours preliminaire'[21] that music can deal with the emotional effects of sounds but not concrete ideas, but that in singing music and ideas are combined.

> "music is poorer than poetry, limiting itself to affecting the heart ... On the other hand music is more expressive than poetry, because it imitates the inarticulated signs that constitute natural language, which is therefore more vigorous, and imitates it through sounds, ... Thus it is that a simple melody will always move the heart much more than ever will a fine piece of poetry". (22)

Arteaga's idea that there is a natural, and therefore vigorous, language of inarticulated sounds must be seen as stemming ultimately from Rousseau's idea of a primeval language of natural beauty from which music derives, expressed in his <u>Essai sur l'origine des langues</u> of 1764,[23] a slightly different explanation for the origin of music from

---

18. Perrino, pp.51-52: "La musica da per se sola non potendo interamente nè suscitare nè dipingere con la dovuta forza le interne passioni dell' animo senza l' ajuto delle parole".
19. Compare Chapter 2, notes 56 and 57.
20. Perrino, p.52: "la Musica serve per dare alle parole una maggiore forza di espressione".
21. See Le Huray and Day, p.59.
22. Arteaga, I, 14: "La musica è più povera della poesia, limitandosi quella al cuore ... In contraccambio la musica è piu espressiva della poesia, perchè imita i segni inarticolati, che sono il linguaggio naturale, e per conseguenza il più energico, e gli imita col mezzo de' suoni ... Quindi è, che una melodia semplice commuove universalmente assai più che non faccia un bel componimento poetico".
23. See Le Huray and Day, p.92. Also see Dalhaus, p.21.

those contained in the aesthetic writings mentioned in the last chapter. Few theses tried to investigate the mechanism of the way music serves to heighten poetry in this manner, though it always seems to have been supposed that this was the true function of the singer upon the stage, so that well into the nineteenth century we find Léon Escudier saying that "song is a means of expressing more nobly what we say".[24]

The idea that ennobling poetry meant singing it is connected with the idea that the theatre should have some edifying purpose, mentioned previously. Francesco Milizia writes that "Pleasure and Usefulness, forever unified, and bound up with each other, constitute the purpose of the Theatre. Principal objective; which consists in presenting moral virtues in a pleasing way in order to draw out and inflame virtue in the spectators ... True Drama is thus a school of virtue".[25]

The manner in which the singer was to provide this edifying utterance of the poetry is naturally also discussed. It is important to understand the concept as a whole, since it gives some clue to the nature of the combination of the arts that was the <u>bel canto</u> opera. The singer and the poet were, as Celentano puts it, once the same person; so in opera the singer had the responsibility of expressing his own ideas. Milizia writes that "men have three means of expressing their ideas and feelings. The first is by words, the second by the tone of voice, and the third by gesture which consists of exterior movements and the postures of the body".[26]

---

24. Léon Escudier, Études biographiques (Paris, 1840), p.11.
25. Milizia, pp.9-14: "Piacere ed Utile, uniti sempre, ed amalgamati insieme, formano l' oggetto del Teatro. Oggetto massimo; che consiste <u>nella Morale posta piacevolmente in azione per iscuotere ed animare gli spettatori alla virtù</u> ... Il vero Dramma dunque è una scuola di virtù".
26. Milizia, p.59: "tre maniere hanno gli uomini d' esprimere le loro idee, e i loro sentimenti. L' una è la parola, l' altra il tuono della voce, e la terza il gesto, il quale consiste ne' movimenti esterni, e nelle attitudini del corpo".

Poetry and gesture are therefore the most important resources that a singer has at his disposal. Milizia is here referring directly to the singer himself in a chapter with the title "Degli attori". There are echoes of this, of course, in Crescentini's idea of singing as "un imitazione del discorso", and the effects achieved by the ancients; so the reader should not be too surprised at finding that Milizia too refers to an ancient oratorical model as his authority.

> "With Demosthenes, the whole force of oratorical art was centred on Action, that is on the tone of the voice and on the gestures. And perhaps because of this, the eloquence of the Ancients was so superior to our own". (27)

This type of oratorical gesture is important to bear in mind as it has considerable influence on the type of acting that was expected of a singer at this time. One might say that where we expect drama so they looked for poetry; and that on the other hand, where we expect the motions of the actor in a singer so they looked for oratorical gesture.

Because of the combination of the arts that was seen as being inherent in operatic singing, it is not surprising that the poetic and gesticulatory elements are much emphasized by all writers on the art of singing. This is certainly not how bel canto traditions are viewed today, when it is presumed that interest was centred solely on the production of a beautiful tone. The type of tone that was expected before the rise of the Verdian 'tenore di forza' will be dealt with later; but for now, considering singing in terms of its position within the spettacolo as a whole, it is worthwhile pointing out that, according to P. A. Duey, no scientific approach to training particular muscles or techniques in the mechanics of voice production seems ever to have been attempted or pretended in the period of the famous bel canto singing

---

27. Milizia, p.59: "Dimostene faceva consistere tutta la forza dell' arte oratoria nell' Azione, cioè nel tuono della voce, e nel gesto. E forse per questo l' Eloquenza antica era tanto superiore alla moderna".

schools, of which Naples had always been one of the foremost centres.[28]

In an age where the main means of vocal expression was not that of vocal force, which became necessary later when singing over much more extensive orchestral resources; one of the main elements emphasized for the treatment of the music's essential poetic basis was a natural style of pronunciation. Presumably the fact that contemporaries were not yet used to forced pronunciations, brought about by pressures exerted on vocal technique in an age which was to emphasize the drama rather than the poetry, meant that they were not prepared to accept unnatural types of pronunciation that were to develop later. However, the 'natural' aspect of the theatrical experience was also a curiously important consideration: curious because opera itself was in many ways an artificial mode of expression. Milizia, for example, writes that "Poetry is the imitation of Nature expressed in metrical speech with the purpose of both edifying and delighting".[29] It seems that Nature itself was taken as a model for edification and delectation.

In the standard late eighteenth century thesis by Mancini, we read how this natural pronunciation is tied up with the full realization of the poetic intent, so that "an actor will never be able to express these feelings naturally, nor make their effect clearly felt in the spectators, unless he understands the full force of the words".[30] Elsewhere he emphasizes the importance of naturalness in pronunciation and reciting, and in expression in acting.[31] Following Mancini, we find the sometime Rector at San Sebastiano, Marcello Perrino, saying

---

28. Duey, p.154.
29. Milizia, p.9: "La Poesia è l' Imitazione della bella Natura espressa con discorso misurato a fine d' istruire e di dilettare".
30. Mancini, Pensieri e riflessioni pratiche sopra il canto figurato, third edition (Milan, 1777), p.218: "Ora un attore non potrà mai con naturalezza esprimere questi affetti, nè con chiarezza farne conoscere agli spettatori gli effetti, s' egli non comprende la forza delle parole".
31. Mancini, p.240.

that since music serves to increase the expressive power of the words, "it is therefore the words that should above all be understood".(32) For this purpose he expects that the singer has to study the words themselves, explaining that "in order to carry out properly an objective of such importance, the singer should never commit himself to singing a piece of vocal music without having carefully read the text first".(33)

This is an idea extended by Andrea Majer by mentioning the connexion between the true expression of the words and their oratorical embellishment. Behind this we can find echoes of his reference to Cicero's *flexiones atque falsae voculae*.(34) He begins by remarking that "if the principal object of singing is to touch emotions, how can the singer achieve this without pronouncing the words in a manner that they can be appreciated by the listeners?".(35) In line with his conviction that Cicero's inflexions are oratorical devices that contributed so much to the eloquence of the ancients, Majer recommends to singing teachers the adoption of certain types of vocal exercises "training his disciples to produce, reinforce, fade, spin out, vibrate, draw up again the voice, to take breath imperceptibly, and to smooth the passage from one tone to the next with enharmonic commas and to open the mouth gracefully, which is the primary element of good pronunciation".(36)

---

32. Perrino, p.52: "sono dunque le parole, che sopra tutto debbono essere intese".
33. Perrino, p.52: "Dovrà quindi il Cantante, per non equivocare in un oggetto di tanta importanza, non esporsi giammai a cantare un pezzo vocale di musica, se prima non ne abbia ben lette le parole".
34. See Chapter 2, note 21.
35. Majer, p.145: "se il primario uffizio del cantare è quello di muovere gli affetti, come potrà egli riuscirvi senza pronunziare le parole in modo che vengano comprese dagli uditori".
36. Majer, p.145: "ammaestrando i discepoli a *fermare, rinforzare, smorzare, filare, vibrare, raccogliere* la voce a *prendere* impercettibilmente il fiato, ad *ammorbidire* i *passaggi* da un *tuono* all' altro con *comme enarmoniche*, ed a tenere aperta con grazia la bocca, primo *elemento* della buona pronunzia".

In other words what to us seem to be purely vocal exercises, that lead to types of vocal embellishment, are to be seen as necessary prerequisites of good pronunciation. Therefore, it can be argued that almost all of the tenets of the <u>bel canto</u> tradition mentioned here are still really the consequence of seeing music's primary role as the servant of the poetry; the desire to deliver the words in the clearest and noblest manner possible.

This seems not to have been a matter of interpretation of the words so much as their most elegant enunciation. Here we come to the crux of the issue of musical expression. We look to vocal music to express the words in the sense of their emotional interpretation, which presupposes the acceptance of the idea that music itself has interpretative and expressive powers which it brings to the poetry. In the thought of contemporary Italians, music gained that power from its association with the words rather than having it inherently. It was created from the combination of the arts in which music's first duty was the noblest presentation of the poetry. Therefore the moving of the affections in song came through the careful pronunciation and oratorical delivery of the words rather than in their interpretation in the manner of Romantic music.

We may look for more obvious signs of vocal interpretation of the poetry in the manner of later opera, but this should not blind us to the fact that Italians of Bellini's time were in their way as concerned for the words as were later generations. Their way was different and stemmed from an approach of its own with aims of its own, but its interest in poetic enunciation in place of musical interpretation does not mean that all that was required by <u>bel canto</u> was a fine vocal tone and technique; it merely means that Italians understood the word <u>esprimere</u> in a different way.

To some extent one can even see that the Romantic idea of interpreting a text was eventually in conflict with the bel canto ideal of its noble and elegant pronunciation. The attempt at forceful expression through variations in vocal timbre sometimes had the effect of cutting across the niceties that Majer is recommending as late as 1821. Looking back from 1867, Luigi Celantano, whose thoughts on singing opened this chapter, was able to see in what ways singing had changed when singers were urged to express the words more forcefully.

> "It is this forcefulness itself which is incompatible with the choice of the most beautiful sound, that stands in the way of the other fine virtues of good singing; flexibility, suppleness and mellowness, without which there cannot be any variety of tone, nor is it possible to have clear and natural pronunciation". (37)

In fact it could be said that our view of bel canto as being interested in a pleasing sound to the exclusion of expression is incorrect: Celentano sees that sound as being a prerequisite of clear and natural pronunciation. The emphasis on vocal flexibility will be dealt with in another chapter, but it is worth noting that Crescentini lists it as one of the three most important facets of good singing and interprets it in a similar way to Celentano as "that elasticity, suppleness and undulating" of the voice.(38) Thus it was that the pronunciation was often mentioned in assessing the virtues of a singer. Here is an example where it is set off against the other important elements of bel canto (This is incidentally a very early use of the expression which became more common when looking back at this period from a later perspective).

"The editor of the paper in Genoa ... concludes by praising the

---

37. Celentano, pp.27-28: "E quello sforzo istesso, essendo inconciliabile con la scelta del più bel suono, impedisce l' acquisto di altre doti del canto, la flessibilità, la morbidezza, la pastosità, senza di cui non si ha modulazione, nè riesce possibile aver chiara e facile sillabazione".
38. Crescentini, section 3: "quella Elasticità, morbidezza e ondeggiamento".

tenor Binaghi highly, whom however he taunts with having a pronunciation that is hardly precise, and with deficiencies in the refinements of the art of bel canto".[39] In other words, whatever the virtues of a singer generally, they can be ruined by his insufficient attention to delivery of the words which can be regarded as one of his most vital concerns. That this is the contemporary understanding of "expressing the words" can be seen in the following assessment of the tenor Winter in the role of Idreno in Rossini's Semiramide, carried in the Neapolitan paper Il caffè del molo, "Forcefulness in expression, expressiveness in the emotions, and above all, a fine and clear pronunciation".[40]

Celentano's complaints, however, were based on the idea that powerful singing that sought to express words was something that ruined bel canto specifically harming the pronunciation. We can see this now in terms of the aesthetic thought of Italians at the time. It is wrong to see the desire to care for the expression of the words as something new to Celentano's generation. The use of force in singing came to be deplored not because it put a higher value on expressivity than on beauty of tone, as is usually supposed, but because it struck at the roots of operatic singing as they were seen to be at the time; the poetry and its correct and elegant delivery. This can only be understood when it is appreciated that bel canto was not limited to a rather over-refined attention to classical beauty, but that it saw expressivity differently. What Italians meant by declamation was not something that endangered bel canto, but stood as its guiding principle.

---

39. Rivista teatrale, 15 January 1825: "L' estensore del foglio di Genova ... finisce con far grandi elogi del tenore Binaghi, a cui però rinfaccia una pronunzia poco esatta e mancanza di perfezione nei raffinamenti dell' arte del bel canto".
40. Il caffè del molo, Giornale critico-letterario, number 28 (Naples, 1830), p.4: "forza nell' espressioni, espressione nei sentimenti, e più di tutto, buona e chiara pronunzia".

The new style attacked declamation, instead of promoting it, in the eyes of Celentano, through over-straining the voice.

> "These methods ... have carried in triumph stress, exertion and shouting; a great insult to the true declamatory style, in which it is certainly not sufficient to have a rough and harsh sound in order to express every single gradation of emotion, and that at the expense of even the most basic and noble virtues of <u>bel canto</u>". (41)

Contemporaries tried to determine what were the precise problems that were being created in putting a greater emphasis on loudness in singing. This can be seen in a fascinating passage from a Neapolitan newspaper <u>L'Omnibus</u> which sought, under the influence of Garcia, to assess the differences between the "cantanti della scuola del 1820 e quelli del 1840".

> "It is in fact that modification of character or vocal <u>timbre</u>, as we would also like to call it, which occurs whenever the singer seeks to give volume to his voice, and it is achieved by raising up the palate to the point where it cuts off the opening of the nasal channel, and by furrowing the tongue, which is held rigid at its base in the larynx, which in this timbre remains permanently immobile and somewhat lower than normally. The form obtained by the pharynx from all this is the cause of the greater volume and fullness of vocal sound. This arrangement can only be achieved perfectly with the closed <u>e</u> and <u>o</u> and the vowel <u>u</u>. It is impossible to keep the above-mentioned positions of the vocal organs while singing the other vowels".

<u>L'Omnibus</u> then gives examples of this in practice when the tenor Donzelli sang in Mercadante's <u>Il bravo</u>, showing how the line

> "Trascorso è un giorno eterno" became
>
> "Trosuorso è un giuoreno etereno"

and other examples follow. The critic concludes, by noting the dangers that this has for the poetic basis of opera: "Anyone will be able to infer from the observation of these few words, what new forms will be

---

41. Celentano, p.32: "Quei mezzi ... han messo in trionfo e gridi, e sforzi, e conati, in oltraggio del vero stile <u>declamato</u>, cui certo non basta una <u>sola</u> aspra e ruvida tinta a dar tutte le gradazioni a tutti <u>gli</u> affetti, ed a scapito eziandio de' più nobili e radicali pregi del bel canto".

imposed on the expressions of the poets".[42]

It might be added that few things were more universally condemned in Italian theatrical reviews than singing that was too loud. One might say that the true meaning of this was that the new dramatically expressive vocal style of the 1840s, as L'Omnibus defines it, and the bel canto concept of clear and noble poetic declamation were mutually exclusive.

There is one final point that neatly encapsulates the bel canto idea of the singer and his poetry; which is that it was very common to use the word dire instead of cantare for singing, especially for the rendering of a particular aria. For example, of Guglielmo's opera Paolo e Virginia at the Teatro Nuovo, Naples, in 1824, the Rivista teatrale writes: "Il signor Fioravante disse maestrevolmente la sua aria".[43] Similarly another journal, Il caffè del molo, says of Adelaide Tosi in Lauro Rossi's Costanza ed Oringaldo, "Un congratulatamento con la signora Tosi, che disse ben la sua aria finale: senza gridar mai",[44] incidentally showing us once more that fine pronunciation and shouting were regarded as being at variance with each other. Adelaide Tosi was a favourite pupil of Girolamo Crescentini and thus "educata da esperto cultore".[45] She sang at the premiere of the

---

42. L'Omnibus, Naples, 28 July 1842: "Ell'è infatti quella modificazione o carattere, o timbro vocale, chè noi pure vorremmo chiamarlo, il quale succede, allorchè il cantante vuol dare volume alla sua voce, e questo ottiene rialzando il velo palatino fino a chiudere affatto l' apertura postiere delle fosse nasali, ed accanalando la lingua, la quale è tenute tesa alla sua base dalla laringe, che in questo timbro resta sempre immobile e alquanto più bassa che non nella posizione naturale. La forma che ne ottiene la faringe è cagione di questa maggior volume e rotondezza di suono vocale. Questa modificazione non si ottiene perfetta che sulle vocali e ed o strette, e sulla vocale u. Cantando sulle altre vocali ben chiare è impossibile conservare la forma su indicata all' organo vocale ... Dall' osservazione delle quali poche parole ognuno può inferire qual novella forma dovessero prendere i concetti del poeta".
43. Rivista teatrale, 29 May 1824.
44. Il caffè del molo, number 24 (Naples, 1830), p.4.
45. Il caffè del molo, number 26 (Naples, 1830), p.3.

revised Bianca e Fernando at Genoa in 1828. The same paper describes the tenor Buonfigli as Tebaldo in Bellini's I Capuleti e i Montecchi: "Il signor Buonfigli ha detto molto bene la sua cavatina".[46] Bellini himself is very frequently found using dire when referring to the singing of a specific aria, whereas the verb cantare would be used to refer to singing in general. Thus his assessment of Amalia Schütz, in the role of Giulietta in I Capuleti e i Montecchi in 1831, is couched in the following terms: "Madame Schütz canta molto bene: ha una bella voce e possiede un metodo di gusto ... la sua scena e romanza la dice come meglio non si potrebbe".[47]

Similarly he writes of Rubini in rehearsal of the finale to I puritani "Il sudd.^{tto} pezzo mi è venuto magnifico, e qui Rubini lo dice come un Dio".[48]

The naturalness of pronunciation seems always to have been held as very important and Tosi puts great emphasis on it like all the other theorists. In this context he also refers to the volume of an unaffected and natural mouth position which seems to have meant that the singer was always smiling. Tosi maintains that the singer should compose his mouth "in the manner (if allowed by the sense of the words) that tends towards the sweetness of a smile, rather than to too much solemnity".[49] In very similar terms, Mancini advises that "every singer should position his mouth, as he would normally do so, when smiling naturally; that is to say, so that the upper teeth are directly

---

46. Il caffè del molo, number 43 (Naples, 1830), p.4.
47. Vincenzo Bellini, Epistolario, edited by Luisa Cambi (Verona, 1943), p.265 (3 January 1831). Further references to this collection will be indicated by the name of the editor, Cambi, as in the following note.
48. Cambi, p.497 (5 January 1835).
49. Tosi, p.16: "in guisa (se il senso delle parole lo permette) che inclini più alla dolcezza d' un sorriso, che ad una gravità severa".

above and moderately apart from the lower ones".[50]

Such seems to be the strictness of this tradition that one suspects a direct reference to Mancini, when reading in Perrino's Osservazioni of 1810 the instruction: "let the mouth be open so that the upper range of teeth comes directly above the lower; and without the slightest discomfort and in a manner rather like that of a sweet smile, let it assume a natural and graceful expression in this position".[51]

The tradition of the gracefully smiling singer can be traced throughout the eighteenth century; and many will recall Mozart's reference to his first encounter in 1777 with Anton Raaff (1714-1797) the tenor for whom he wrote the role of Idomeneo: "In the opera he had to die, and while dying sing a very very very long aria in slow time; well he died with a grin on his face".[52]

The secret of this lies in the all-encompassing nature of the singer's place in the spettacolo as a whole. As the exponent of the dramma, as well as giving an unforced enunciation of the words, for which purpose this gentle smiling was supposed to be some sort of assistance, he also had to display the essential grace and dignity of the general concept. Milizia's idea of "Questi due effetti, Piacere ed Utile"[53] is echoed in 1849 by Giuseppe Mastriani's phrase urging writers to "adoperare il dolce per produrre quell' Utile".[54] To this end he points out that "personal beauty is also a quality required in an

---

50. Mancini, p.111: "ogni Cantante deve situar la sua bocca, come suol situarla, quando naturalmente sorride, cioè in modo che i denti di sopra siano perpendicolarmente, e mediocremente distaccati da quelli di sotto".
51. Perrino, p.18: "la bocca sia aperta in guisa che il registro della dentatura superiore venga ad essere perpendicolare all' inferiore, e che senza il menomo dissesto, in atto presso a poco di dolce sorriso serbi nell' indicata posizione una naturale aggiustatezza e grazia".
52. Emily Anderson, The Letters of Mozart and his Family, 3 vols (London, 1938), II, 550 (14-16 November 1777).
53. Milizia, p.9. See note 25.
54. Mastriani, p.10. See also Chapter 2, note 35.

artist, in as much as an ugly appearance would be ill-suited to the representation of beautiful things".(55)

The singer's very appearance was a very important part of his complete performance. P. A. Duey points out that Burney, for example, always mentions the appearance of a singer he discusses.(56) This is not in fact absolutely the case, but it is particularly likely when he discusses a singer on stage. At a rehearsal of Jommelli's *Demofoonte* at the Teatro San Carlo, for example, he says of Aprile, the castrato, "Aprile has rather a weak and uneven voice, but is constantly steady as to intonation. He has a good person, a good shake, and much taste and expression".(57)

More specifically, reference was usually made to the facial expression and general good looks of the singer. The following review of Adelaide Tosi in Pacini's *Alessandro nell' Indie* makes the connexions between physiognomy and acting clear. It seems that she was justly applauded "as much for her singing as for her expression". The journal continues: "We owe her our thanks. The expression of her physiognomy is most graceful and spontaneous. Hooray! A fine actress should not be limited just to matters of singing".(58)

It would seem that the most graceful and spontaneous expression would in its inherent dignity be taken to be that of a gentle smile. This possibly involved some limitation on the volume of sound attainable, since references to the idea tend to disappear towards the middle of

---

55. Mastriani, pp.26-27: "La bellezza della persona è pure qualità richiesta nell' Artista però che uno brutto aspetto mal converrebbe alla rappresentazione del bello".
56. Duey, p.71.
57. Charles Burney, *The Present State of Music in France and Italy* (London, 1771), p.318.
58. *Rivista teatrale*, 13 October 1824: "tanto per la parte del canto che per quella dell' espressione. Noi le dobbiamo un ringraziamento. L' espressione della sua fisonomia è più dolce e disinvolta. Evviva. Una brava attrice non dee limitarsi al solo canto".

the nineteenth century, when a more openly dramatic style was aimed at. Certainly Léon Escudier would appear to disapprove of it on these very grounds; that is to say, that smiling on the part of a singer resulted in an insupportable thinness of tone.(59)

Of the three means that singers have of expressing their ideas and emotions, the words and the tone of the voice were very closely integrated in the <u>bel canto</u> concept of singing. Milizia's third resource "consiste ne' movimenti esteriori e nelle attitudine del corpo".(60) With this idea we have to consider their oratorical manner of acting, although of course this is also closely allied to the desire for clear enunciation and the consequent importance attached to the mouth position and general physiognomy.

The general reader would probably be surprised by the extent to which contemporaries stressed the value of good acting, in some cases even above that of a fine voice. Mancini refers to the career of the great castrato Nicolini in this respect:

> "Let Niccola Grimaldi, known as 'il <u>Cavalier Niccolino</u>' be evidence of this; this artist could play the comic to such perfection that solely through this, even though deficient of other talent, and not endowed with a good voice, he nevertheless won for himself a singular fame in the profession". (61)

Crescentini also states in his singing manual that the singer who pronounces and accentuates words correctly will, even if not blessed with "il più bell' organo", produce a better effect than a singer with a fine voice but a "mancanza di ragionamento".(62)

The key to understanding what contemporaries seem to have been

---

59. Escudier, p.15.
60. Milizia, p.59. See note 26 above.
61. Mancini, pp.232-233: "Siane testimonio Niccola Grimaldi detto il Cavalier Niccolino; possedè questo artista con tanta perfezione la Comica, che con questa sola, ancorchè povero d' altro talento, e non fornita di bella voce nelle professione si acquistò nulladimeno un merito sì singolare".
62. Crescentini, section 10.

looking for in the singer/actor can be found in the importance attached to the edifying nature of their theatre. Thus, for example, the official gazette of the time in Naples, Monitore delle due Sicilie, commends a singer in Cimarosa's Gli Orazi e i Curiazi as sung at the San Carlo in 1815 for her "nobilità di azione".[63] In a similar style, the Rivista teatrale praises the tenor Curioni, who later created Orombello in Beatrice di Tenda: "It would be impossible to look more handsome; and looking at him one understands and excuses poor Desdemona's love for him. Signor Curioni moreover has a perfect nobility of gesture".[64]

Another report concerns a prima donna who frequently appeared in Naples, Boccabadati, in Rossini's Matilde di Shabran. This urges the assumption of some dignity by the leading lady: "one would again like to implore her to be rather more dignified in her movements and her gestures".[65]

A type of reference to "la maniere di stare in iscena"[66] that is to be found quite often neatly suggests the immobile nature of this type of singing. This, however, may not be wholly representative; particularly when considering the acting of tenors, when perhaps matters were already beginning to change. The following is a recommendation made to Rossini's protegé Ivanoff singing Elvino in La Sonnambula: "We would still like him to be more animated during his silent passages,

---

63. Monitore delle due Sicilie, Naples, 24 November 1815: "La Signora Dardanelli piace per nobilità di azione, per metodo di cantare e per impegno che mostra per il felice successo dello spettacolo".
64. Rivista teatrale, 17 November 1824: "E impossibile di avere un più bel personale; e vedendolo si comprede, si scusa la passione della povera Desdemona. Il Signor Curioni ha d' altronde una perfetta nobilità nel gestire". The report is of a performance of Rossini's Otello in Paris.
65. L'Indifferente, Giornale di teatri, mode e varietà (Naples, 1830), fascicolo II, p.202: "le si vorrebbe raccomandare ancora di essere un poco più nobile nel suo andamento e ne' suoi gesti".
66. L'Omnibus, 9 July 1840.

and to follow the situation on the stage with gestures and facial expressions".[67]

Bellini himself seems usually to have expected something upon these sort of lines, and makes references to the stage presence of singers, especially tenors. The following concerns the singing of Domenico Reina (who had earlier created the role of Arturo in **La straniera**) as Pollione in **Norma**: "Reina, who is not like Donzelli, put much effort into imitating his voice and appearance. Clear pronunciation and he acted with energy".[68] The trouble that he went to in persuading Rubini to act convincingly in **Il pirata** which has often been referred to, suggests much the same.[69]

Bellini's other great inspiration, the soprano Giuditta Pasta (1798-1865) seems always to have been praised for her impressive stage presence, however, The Neapolitan **Rivista teatrale** writes "where can one find an actress to match Madame Pasta?".[70] Another report describes her in terms that suggest that she comprised most of the qualities held most dear by the **bel canto** tradition. This review is from the Milanese journal, **I teatri**: "Nature, who made her for the tragic stage, endowed her with a dignified presence and a noble face, an expressive glance and fine pronunciation";[71] and elsewhere comments on her "broad and smooth **bel canto**, perfectly suited to declamation".[72]

---

67. L'Omnibus, 15 June 1833: "Ma perchè nulla è a disidararsi per soavità di voce ed anche per espressione nel suo canto, vorremmo ancora che nelle scene mute fosse più animato, e seguisse più coi moti della fisonomia e del gesto la situazione della scena".
68. Cambi, p.320 (24 August 1832): "Reina che non è Donzelli, vi mette tanto fuoco da duplicare la sua voce e la sua persona. Pronunzia chiara e si muove con energia".
69. Friedrich Lippmann, Vincenzo Bellini und die italienische Opera seria seiner Zeit, Analecta Musicologica VI (Cologne and Vienna, 1969), p.224.
70. Rivista teatrale, 30 March 1825: "ove trovare un' attrice come Madame Pasta?".
71. I teatri, Milan, 19 March 1829; quoted after Cambi, p.148: "La natura che la formò alla scena tragica, le concedette dignitosa presenza, nobile fisonomia, occhio parlante e bella pronuncia".
72. I teatri, 10 December 1828; quoted after Cambi, p.148: "bel canto spianato, perfettamente adatto alla declamazione".

This matching of the ideals of fine declamation and the broadly arched phrasing of the <u>bel canto</u> tradition is significant in a singer such as Pasta, who created some of Bellini's major <u>prima donna</u> parts; Amina in <u>La sonnambula</u>, Norma, and Beatrice. Bellini regarded her as embodying all these traditional virtues as well calling her his "Angiolo Enciclopedico".[73]

It is worth quoting one of Pasta's most ardent supporters, not so much to describe Pasta herself, as to stress in what terms contemporaries considered acting on the operatic stage. Stendhal writes of her as "an actress who is young and beautiful; who is both intelligent and sensitive; whose gestures never deteriorate from the plainest and most natural modes of simplicity, and yet manage to keep faith with the purest ideals of formal beauty".[74] He refers in a similar fashion to the great tenor Nozzari who created the Otello of Rossini, drawing attention to "the pure beauty of his gestures"[75] in this part. Indeed it is to Stendhal that we must look for the most readily accessible and most comprehensive appraisal of acting on the Italian operatic stage and, incidentally, a good measure of its aesthetic concepts in general. This is how he describes Isabella Colbran, Rossini's sometime wife and <u>prima donna</u>, as Elisabetta at the Naples premiere in 1815 of <u>Elisabetta, regina d'Inghilterra</u>:

> "the moment she stepped onto the boards, her brow encircled with a royal diadem, she inspired involuntary respect, even amongst those who, a minute or two earlier had been chatting intimately with her in the foyer of The Theatre ... she allowed herself no gestures ... her eyes alone betrayed ... her mind ... [She] used no gestures, did nothing melodramatic, never descended to what are vulgarly called <u>tragedy-queen poses</u>". (76)

---

73. Cambi, p.313 (28 April 1832).
74. Stendhal, <u>Life of Rossini</u>, new and revised edition translated and annotated by Richard N. Coe (London, 1970), p.371.
75. Stendhal, <u>Life of Rossini</u>, p.221.
76. Stendhal, <u>Life of Rossini</u>, pp.157-164.

One should certainly be warned not to take this literally as a true assessment of the quality of the singers. Stendhal was very inclined to become over-enthusiastic about certain of them. Our concern is to discern what were the values that were looked for in artists, not whether or not they actually had them. This is just as well since, despite his extensive description, only part of which has been given here, Stendhal never actually saw this performance of <u>Elisabetta</u>; and the report is almost certainly from a contemporary, or else describes a later performance. Stendhal was in fact in Milan on 4 October 1815 during the Neapolitan premiere of <u>Elisabetta</u>. According to Ottavio Matteini, he made similarly false claims to have seen the premieres of <u>La gazza ladra</u>, <u>La donna del lago</u> and other operas.[77] As it happens, Stendhal's report is supported by that of Louis Spohr, who also saw Colbran as Elisabetta two years later. He reports that she (like Bellini) was a pupil of Crescentini and that "She is far behind Catalani in voice and every mechanical point of excellence, but she sings with feeling and plays with considerable passion".[78]

Stendhal himself is a very acute observer of the Italian opera, and not blind to some of its faults; though inclined to emphasize its virtues compared with French music, as was Rousseau. He will be referred to a number of times because he sums up contemporary attitudes to singing and opera in general so well. This case is typical of Stendhal in that the literal truth of his writing is not reliable, but the views contained in it are completely representative. He explains it thus: "not <u>my</u> impressions, but the impressions which were abroad in Naples, or in Florence, or in Brescia, or wherever I happened to see

---

77. Ottavio Matteini, <u>Stendhal e la musica</u> (1981), p.173, note 101.
78. Louis Spohr, <u>Autobiography</u>, 2 vols (London, 1865), II, 29.

this particular opera; for no one has a deeper mistrust than I of
<u>personal</u> impressions ... I implore the reader to believe me, when I
state that throughout this book the personal pronoun I is simply a
conventional device, which might at any time be replaced by a different
phrase, such as: <u>It used to be said in Naples among those who frequented the Marchese Berio</u> ...;".(79) He refers to his deriving his
reports from Neapolitan opinion as "setting down one or two of the
ideas which were discussed in those Neapolitan conversations in which
I occasionally participated, and which I found so enthralling".(80)

Comparing Stendhal's views with such Italian views as reached
print, confirms his claims to being representative of the attitudes and
opinions of his contemporaries. Stendhal is valuable because he is a
more eloquent advocate of what we might call the <u>bel canto</u> approach to
opera, but his views can often be supported by reference to others.
Thus we can see echoes of Stendhal's approach in Giuseppe Mastriani's
instructions for actors and singers:

> "The actor, transformed into the character he represents,
> must be aware of what deportment, what general demeanour,
> what voice, what gestures and what facial expressions are
> most appropriate to the full depiction of the feelings and
> emotions welling up inside the spirit of a man of that
> temperament and character". (81)

---

79. Stendhal, <u>Life of Rossini</u>, p.67.
80. Stendhal, <u>Life of Rossini</u>, p.329n.
81. Mastriani, p.36: "Trasformatosi l'attore nel personaggio rappresentato, deve conoscere qual portamento, qual aria generale della persona, qual voce, quai gesti, qual espressione di fisonomia sieno più acconci a ben esprimere le passioni ed i sentimenti svilluppantisi nell' animo di un uomo di quella indole e natura".

In this respect it should be noted that Mastriani equates singers and other dramatic actors by referring to "Artista drammatico o cantante".[82] Later he remarks that "with actors I include singers, because nowadays one can be an actor without being a singer, but not a singer without being an actor".[83]

On the whole, however, precise descriptions of the acting of singers such as Stendhal's are not particularly common; and one has to bear in mind instead the general principles aimed at, and the aesthetic concepts that cause them. There are of course many paintings of singers but, apart from the fact that they are static in nature in any case, it is always difficult to be sure how stylized or accurate they are.

What is important is instead to understand how this type of oratorical gesture fits into their general conception of the declamatory singer; and how it is the practical extension, that is the realization of the poet himself. The aesthetician Ferro, referred to in the previous chapter, writes that "The art of declamation, of gesture and of modulating the voice, are the skills of the Orator, and of the Poet".[84] In this respect we might remember that, historically speaking, Italians tended to regard the singer as stemming from the practice of the dramatic poet declaiming his own verses on stage. Like Milizia, he calls on the ancient model of Demosthenes, to explain the basis for the oratorical style of acting: "Asked what was the first most important skill of an Orator, Demosthenes replied 'Acting'. What was the second? Acting. And what was the third? Acting, and so forth

---

82. Mastriani, p.33.
83. Mastriani, p.42: "e nell' attore inchiudo il cantante, chè oggi uno può essere attore senza essere cantante, e non cantante senza essere attore".
84. Ferro, II, 10-11: "L'arte di declamare, di gestire, di modulare la voce, sono le azioni dell' Oratore, e del Poeta".

until they ceased to ask him further".[85] Like so many of his contemporaries, Ferro goes on to refer to the need for simplicity and naturalness in these oratorical gestures.

In the manner of conclusion it might be remarked that the true understanding of opera of this period requires the appreciation of the role of the singer as a representative of its poetic element. The singer represented the spirit of the ancient dramatist to the theorists of the fine arts such as Milizia and Ferro. We can see him as the immediate representative of the librettist and composer. It is perhaps more usual to study opera by starting with consideration of the nature of the libretto. This is fine if one is intent on analysis of the text of an opera. If the study is to centre on the aesthetic impulse that generates this opera, one first has to look at opera as a composer might. Thus Bellini himself would not determine immediately on the subject of a libretto when considering writing an opera, but would begin by considering the company of singers for whom he might write. This was formalized in a system where the composer would be contracted to write for a theatre and would then look for the subject of the opera. Thus when considering the possibility of writing for the opening of the Carlo Felice theatre at Genoa in 1828, he writes to Florimo explaining his priorities:

> "The day before yesterday, Signor Merelli, a theatrical correspondent, came to see me at home and brought me the legal offer of a contract from the Impresarios at Genoa for the coming Carnival season: but because the company of singers is not yet complete, I did not yet want to commit myself, and so replied that if they finished contracting the singers, and provided that I liked them,

---

85. Ferro, II, 18: "Interrogato perciò Dimostene, qual si fosse la prima qualità dell' Oratore? ripose: L'azione. Qual la seconda? L'azione. Qual la terza? L'azione: e così sempre finchè sî cessò d'interrogarlo". Compare note 27.

I would accept their offer at once". (86)

Finally he did accept to write for the singers, which included Crescentini's pupil Adelaide Tosi, and the renowned tenor Giovanni Davide (1790-1851), who had created the roles of Rodrigo in Rossini's Otello and Norfolk in Elisabetta. But the sequence of priorities is clear. Bellini wanted to be assured of the singers; if he was then he would accept, as eventually he did. Afterwards he decided to adapt Bianca e Gernando (1826) for them, partly because they had been involved in the preparations for the original production in Naples which had been delayed.

This manner of approaching the decision to compose an opera was quite normal with Bellini. His letters are littered with evidence of the weighing up of prospects on the basis of the singers to be involved, rejecting some such as the prospect for Turin later that year "because that company of singers is too weak to pin one's hopes on".(87) Other possible companies he considers in the letter include Milan, Venice and Naples. At no time is the subject of the libretto mentioned. A week later he writes again to Florimo, telling him of his decision: "This morning I signed a contract with Barbaja for an opera during the Carnival at the Teatro della Scala. The singers will be Lalande, Lablache or Tamburrini, and perhaps Winter or someone else".(88)

---

86. Cambi, p.41 (16 January 1828): "L'altro ieri è venuto in mia casa il signor Merelli, corrispondente teatrale, e mi ha recato una offerta di scrittura legalmente degli impresarii di Genova pel Carnevale venturo; ma non essendo completata la compagnia, io non mi ho voluto compromettere ancora, e la mia risposta e stata, che finissero di scritturare gli attori, e che essendo di mio piacere, avrei subito accettato la loro offerta".
87. Cambi, p.104 (9 June 1828): "perchè quella compagnia è troppo debole per sperare".
88. Cambi, p.115 (16 June 1828): "Questa mattina ho firmato la scrittura con Barbaja per un opera al Carnevale in questo Teatro della Scala. I cantanti saranno Lalande, Lablache o Tamburrini, e forse Winter od altro".

"An opera" turned out to be La straniera but no sign of this is to be seen in Bellini's correspondence. Eventually Bellini got down to looking into some possibilities that Romani, who was also signed up for Milan, might couch in his incomparable poetry. Three weeks later, Bellini tells Florimo that he is in the process of looking at "many plots in order to find one suitable, and amongst them I want to read d'A[r]lincourt's Solitario which Tottola adapted, I think for Pavesi, but if I find the novel interesting, I will get Romani to make a fine version for Tamburrini and Lalande".[89]

Not only had Bellini not decided on a subject, but it seems that he had not even considered the problem. Sometimes the subject seems to have been more the concern of Romani than Bellini; but at any rate, what is clear is that the consideration of the singer had priority over consideration of the libretto. The aesthetics behind this idea are summed up by the Rector of San Sebastiano, Marcello Perrino, who points out that the singer is the "immediate instrument of the Poet and the Composer of the Music" and that therefore the singer represented the poetic element in the drama. For this reason "it is important for him to adapt not only the voice through singing to the sentiment of the words, but also the deportment, and the gestures to sustain the character represented".[90]

---

89. Cambi, pp.134-135 (7 July 1828): "Stò svolgendo molti soggetti per trovarne uno, e fra l'altri voglio leggere il Solitario d'Alincourt che trattò Tottola, credo per Pavesi, ma se trovo il Romanzo interessante lo farò trattare da Romani bene per Tamburrini e Lalande".
90. Perrino, p.55: "è l'organo immediato del Poeta, e del Musico Compositore ... gli conviene saper conformare non meno la voce col canto al sentimento delle parole, che'l portamento, ed il gesto per ben sostenere il carattere che rappresenta".

CHAPTER 4

POETRY AND DRAMA IN THE LIBRETTO

When we come to consider the place of the libretto in early nineteenth century Italian opera, it would be as well to consider first our own received opinions as to what we understand by the term. We should then be able to see how much our preconceptions as to what constitutes a good libretto lead us to expect certain virtues not looked for by Bellini and his contemporaries. It is hoped that these considerations will be seen in the light of our understanding of the aesthetic roots of this opera and of its singers, to which some attention has been devoted in the preceding chapters.

It is certainly fair to say that almost all writers on opera today consider operas in terms of their effectiveness as dramas. In particular, it is accepted that librettos, if they are judged at all, are judged according to what extent they provide a cogent dramatic basis for the composer.

To support this short adumbration of the modern approach to the subject, reference can be made to the content, not to say the success, of Joseph Kerman's Opera as Drama; which, with its consciously Wagnerian title, goes as far as making unequivocal demands that operas should exist in the form of dramatic action. For Kerman, the best operas are those that generate this dramatic action in the music, through the means of musical continuity. In this regard Kerman talks of symphonic drama "at its most articulate, in the sonata form" since this is the most closely dramatic form of all.[1]

As far as this concerns the music it is not surprising that this

---

1. Joseph Kerman, Opera as Drama (London, 1957), p.77.

energy should be seen as requiring the power of the orchestra; and it is no coincidence that, almost exclusively, it is those composers that make effective use of the orchestra such as Mozart and Verdi, that for Kerman are the supreme masters of opera. In as much as this view of opera is perfectly coherent, no adverse judgement of Kerman's views is really involved in the following consideration of opera and drama; however, it is worth pointing out that operas that do not follow this type of approach do not seem to merit much consideration in Kerman's eyes. Earlier operas, or perhaps one should say operas conceived at a time before the advent of this orchestrally-generated dramatic style of music, or which do without the related matter of the dramatic classical style, which is also emphasized by Charles Rosen,[2] are inevitably seen by Kerman as being part of what he calls 'the Dark Ages'. In his eyes Bellini would almost certainly be consigned to these 'Dark Ages'. To simplify for a moment, the drama we call for in opera results from the presence of the orchestra, whilst operatic poetry is delivered by singers. The orchestra of Bellini's time, not seen as a protagonist of the opera itself, had the duty merely of assisting in this delivery of the words.

The actual position of the orchestra in these operas must await another chapter because, as we have already seen, the early nineteenth century _melodramma_ was generated in musical terms not by the orchestra but by the singer. Some writers might say that in the absence of a sophisticated and dramatic musical texture, this was by necessity the case; but this would be to make a judgement, and usually it is a value judgement, with the handicap of hindsight. The real reason why the singer was so central to opera was that it was he that comprised and

---

2. Charles Rosen, The Classical Style (London, 1971), p.289.

exercised the various arts of poetry, music and gesture that were united in the creation of the opera of that time.

It would seem to follow quite naturally from this that what was important to opera in the period leading up to and including Bellini, was not in the first place so much drama, as poetry. 'In the first place' because the singer was regarded at the time as declaiming poetry in musical form; though this does not mean that this could never achieve effects that we might recognise as genuinely dramatic. For this reason, a researcher looking for dramatic action from operas of this period might very well be disappointed; and, if a libretto is to be studied at all, then some reference to it as poetry would have to be made. In practice, of course, there is a severe limitation to the extent to which this can be profitably pursued. The reason for this is perfectly simple. The whole point about this poetic drama is that it is transcended by its musical realization and so we, unlike Bellini's contemporaries, no longer regard it as poetry. Even these Italian writers, beyond vague admonitions as to the value of certain pieces as poetry, do not discuss their poetic nature in any detail as they would other aspects of the opera. Beyond the vague notion that the librettos were supposed to have poetic value, there is a limited amount that we should try to say about this. Stendhal, perceptive as always, pointed out the worthlessness of this at the time. In his second 'Letter on Metastasio',[3] he says that, to begin with, the poetry is never to be heard without the music so that it never in practice existed in its original form. Moreover, poetry so transformed is much less open to study since its effect is due to the music. For Stendhal, as for Eximeno before him, there was a particularly happy marriage in the

---

3. Stendhal, Lives of Haydn, Mozart and Metastasio, translated by Richard N. Coe (London, 1972), p.212.

talents of Metastasio and Pergolesi; but for later opera, Stendhal found little of the poetic value that Italians claimed for librettos, so that its success was all the more dependent on music such as Rossini's, as he was later to explain.

> "To start with, the excruciating doggerel which forms the verbal skeleton of the average Italian aria is hardly ever recognizable as verse of any description, owing to the multiplicity of repeats; the language which greets the listener's patient ear is pure prose ... and so language <u>as such</u> can never be anything more than a <u>bare canvas</u>; the task of decorating this canvas with all the glint and glitter of a thousand tints and colours lies with the <u>music</u>". (4)

It is significant that Stendhal was roundly condemned for treating librettos with such disrespect; and for allowing Rossini to do so as well. In Naples critics pointed out that the composer should respect the poetic element, and complained that Stendhal did not care whether the libretto was insipid or not.[5] In any case, it was not quite true to say that the poetry did not exist without the music, since it was present at the opera in the "slim little volume with its gilt-paper binding",[6] which was sold at performances and which contained the poetry of the opera in question. This is in fact the contemporary meaning of the word 'libretto', and it is to this that Stendhal always refers when discussing an opera, as he at one point admits.[7] It is only his contempt for actual Italian aria-texts and his great enthusiasm for Rossini that leads him to put the artistic emphasis on the music, whose initial role was decorative. There is no awareness of any capability in music to generate the drama itself, with the libretto retiring to

---

4. Stendhal, <u>Life of Rossini</u>, p.368.
5. <u>Rivista teatrale</u>, 25 August 1824. Stendhal's great work was received with scant enthusiasm elsewhere in Italy, partly because of his frequent plagiarisms in previous works, and partly because of his preference for <u>Don Giovanni</u> over Rossini's <u>Il barbiere di Siviglia</u>; see Stendhal, <u>Life of Rossini</u>, 'Translator's Foreward', p.xvi. Particularly severe on Stendhal's "storiche inesattezze" is Lichtenthal, III, 280.
6. Stendhal, <u>Life of Rossini</u>, p.74.
7. Stendhal, <u>Life of Rossini</u>, p.194.

the role of 'subject matter'. The libretto is always present in "its gilt-paper binding".

As Pierluigi Petrobelli has already shown, the poetry was more important to Bellini than the dramatic subject; and for this reason, the establishment of the fact that Felice Romani (1788-1865), a dramatic poet of considerable stature, should be the librettist had priority over the choice of subject matter.[8] Bellini's own comment on the relationship between drama and poetry in fact sums up much of contemporary thought on the subject. In a letter to Florimo of September 1828 on the possibility of using another poet to write the libretto for La straniera because Romani was ill, he writes:

> "however good a libretto Rossi might be able to provide me with, this doesn't take away from the fact that he could never ever be a poet like Romani, especially to me, for whom good verses are very important; as you can see with Il Pirata where it was the poetry and not the dramatic situations that filled me with inspiration, particularly in Come un angelo celeste, and so for me therefore, Romani is a necessity". (9)

Since we have already discussed the fact that Bellini was generally intent on securing a good company of singers before deciding on a subject matter, it should hardly come as a surprise that it was the choice of poet that had priority over the requirements of a "buon libro". That the poetry was more important than the dramatic situation, is of interest since, where Bellini has been criticized in the past, it has been on the grounds of dramatic weakness. Thus for example, Lotte Medicus says that Bellini's talent was principally a lyrical one and that his operas suffer from a lack of dramatic tension.[10]

---

8. Pierluigi Petrobelli, 'Note sulla poetica di Bellini a proposito di I puritani', in Muzikološki Zbornik VIII (1972), pp.70-85.
9. Cambi, p.158 (September 1828): "per quanto Rossi potrebbe farmi un buon libro, pur non di meno mai mai potrebb' essere un verseggiatore come Romani, e specialmente per me che sono molto attaccato alle buone parole; chè vedi dal Pirata come i versi e non le situazioni mi hanno ispirato del genio, in particolare: Come un angelo celeste, e quindi per me Romani è necessario".
10. Lotte Medicus, Die Koloratur in der italienische Oper des 19 Jahrhunderts (Zurich, 1939), p.53.

Similarly we find comments such as "Doubtless there are in his operas weak moments which justify, to some extent adverse criticism, especially as regards lack of dramatic force",[11] and, on Italian opera of the period in general, "the dramatic side comes secondary to the musical".[12]

More recent study of Bellini has reacted against this by stressing the considerable advances made by him in dramatic awareness. However, it should be understood that even these musicological works, in their determined effort to see Bellini as a worthy precursor of Verdi, accept the very preconceptions about librettos that Bellini and his contemporaries could never have shared. As a brief caveat it should be added that this study is not designed to suggest that works that are undramatic are necessarily better or even as good as the later masterpieces of Verdi, but that, as hinted in the introductory chapter, to understand what happens in Italian opera before Verdi it is worthwhile finding out the values inherent in their own approach. This, however, never happens.

Rodolfo Celletti[13] points to an equal balance of virtuosic and dramatic elements in Norma, which has always been accepted as an oasis in the arid wastes of the Italian melodramma. The foremost writer on Bellini, Friedrich Lippmann, considers him an advance on Rossini but falling short of Verdi in the development of a thoroughgoing musico-dramatic integration. Lippmann considers that one can compare the efforts of Rossini and Bellini in the substantial correspondence of particular

---

11. Grove's Dictionary of Music and Musicians, fifth edition, edited by Eric Blom, 9 vols (London, 1954), I, 609.
12. Percy Scholes, The Oxford Companion to Music, tenth edition, edited by John Owen Ward (London, 1970), p.706.
13. Rodolfo Celletti, 'Il vocalismo italiano da Rossini a Donizetti', in Analecta Musicologica V (Cologne and Vienna, 1968), pp.267-294; VII (1969), pp.214-247 (VII, 217).

musical sections with the dramatic situations and recognize the praise lavished on the *filosofia* of the composer of *Norma*. "But Bellini is on the other hand still not so thorough as Verdi in the working out of the above characteristics. Even in his masterpieces there are a few meaningless cabalettas purely for the sake of convention".[14]

As to the standard of dramatic involvement in Bellini's music, little of this seems to be inaccurate, even if, as Lippmann points out, much the same is true of Donizetti and early Verdi.[15] Lippmann's thesis that Bellini stands as a mid-way point between Rossini and Verdi in terms of cogent musical dramaturgy seems substantially correct. As a general approach to opera it is fairly conventional. The extent to which its ubiquitousness in musicological thought is limiting to the mind is shown, however, when it leads scholars to falsely interpret the plainest evidence even if it requires them to alter Bellini's own words; as in Mario Rinaldi's assertion that Bellini's promise "Give me good verses and I will give you good music" should be better understood

---

14. Lippmann, *Vincenzo Bellini* (1969), p.361: "Man vegleiche die von Rossini und Bellini zu im wesentlichen übereinstimmenden dramatischen Situazionen erfundenen musikalischen Abschnitte, und man versteht die Rede der Zeitgenossen von der 'filosofia' des *Norma*-Komponisten. Aber Bellini ist anderseits noch nicht so radikal wie Verdi in der Herausarbeitung des Charakteristischen vorgegangen. Auch in seinem Meisterwerken stehen, nur der Konvention zuliebe, einige nichtssagende Cabaletten". In a revised edition of the study, Lippman recognizes Petrobelli's contribution to the understanding of the problem, but only with respect to the latter's affirmation "che il singolo momento drammatico-psicologico è costitutivo per l' opera belliniana e che quest' ultima è costituita dal susseguirsi di tali situazioni momentanee, gustate ad una ad una" (F. Lippmann, 'Vincenzo Bellini e l' opera seria del suo tempo', nuova edizione, in Maria Rosaria Adamo and F. Lippmann, *Vincenzo Bellini* (Turin, 1981), pp.313-555 (p.513).). Since the study is essentially analytical rather than aesthetical, considerations of the priority of poetry over drama are not considered relevant. The two editions of this important work will in the present study be identified as *Vincenzo Bellini* (1969) and 'Vincenzo Bellini' (1981). Reference will be made usually to the former as the more complete.
15. Lippmann, 'Vincenzo Bellini' (1981), p.514.

as: "Give me a good drama and I will give you good music".[16] Finally, Lippmann considers that Italian opera generally had had no interest in the drama and that characterization is completely absent. He therefore sees Bellini's role as being that of preparing the essential groundwork in characterizing scenes, for Verdi's later developments. In this Bellini is shown as an advance on Rossini and his predecessors since the idea of "thoroughgoing characterization is quite foreign to Italian opera between Monteverdi's Incoronazione di Poppea and Verdi's masterpieces. However, Verdi might not have been able to introduce it into his works so soon, had not Bellini, in particular, prepared the way for him in the musical characterization of scenes".[17]

However, Rossini's indifference to the niceties of verbal expression hardly represented Italian ideals. The previous chapters show that, in theory at least, the Italians thought quite deeply about their operas and considered that the text of the opera was of prime importance. That this is not always so in practice may well be a sign that we should not be looking for the characterization and dramatic action that we expect in post-Wagnerian opera. Rossini is not necessarily representative either, and contemporaries are sometimes heard to complain at his cavalier treatment of the words. Not only was his orchestration sometimes over-exuberant, but also his word stressing was often faulty, as Lippmann has pointed out. But contemporaries saw this as a decline particular to him so that "in

---

16. Mario Rinaldi, 'Rapporti fra Bellini e Felice Romani', in Convegno di studi sull' opera 'Bianca e Fernando' di Vincenzo Bellini 1978 (Genoa, 1980), pp.156-160 (p.160): "Ubbidì però all' aspirazione del compositore: 'Datemi buoni versi e vi darò buona musica' anche se doveva capire ancor meglio che sotto quelle parole v' era un altro desiderio: datemi un buon dramma e vi darò una buona musica".
17. Lippmann, Vincenzo Bellini (1969), p.282: "Der italienischen Oper ist durchgriefende Personencharakteristik zwischen Monteverdis Incoronazione di Poppea und Verdis Meisteropern fremd. Verdi aber hätte sie viellicht seinen Werken nicht so bald einpflanzen können, hätte ihn nicht besonders Bellini in der musikalischen Charakterisierung der Szene vorgearbeitet".

choruses and in ensembles, the words are of no importance to Rossini".[18] Italians felt that the great masterpieces of the Neapolitan tradition were much more conscientious on this point, even if the musicological evidence of this is not beyond debate. This is why they criticized Stendhal for ignóring the words. It is also why Bellini seemed so much to fulfil all their traditional ideals. Their commenting on his *filosofia* is not evidence that they were welcoming him as a musical revolutionary striking out a new path in preparation for Verdi, as Dr. Lippmann supposes;[19] but that they saw him as a throwback to the older values they fondly imagined had been realized by Pergolesi and his contemporaries. The *filosofo*, it will be remembered, held these arts of poetry and music properly balanced together.

The interest in individual scenes rather than dramatic impetus is reflected in the manner in which contemporaries discuss the dramatic element in an opera. Newspaper reviews invariably refer in the first place to the poetry rather than the libretto's dramatic logic. The review of the first Neapolitan performance of *La sonnambula* in the journal *L'Omnibus* reads:

"Teatro del Fondo - *musica* di BELLINI, *poesia* di Romani" (20)

and this type of headline to an article was almost universal at the time.

A similar approach is to be found in printed librettos. It is well known that the original dramatic basis of the opera was regarded as at least nominally important until late on in the century, so that the librettist's name would be placed above that of the composer. As

---

18. *Rivista teatrale*, 25 August 1824: "ne' cori e ne' pezzi d' insieme, oh allora sí che le parole per Rossini sono un vero nulla".
19. See F. Lippmann's consideration of the Milanese reception of *La straniera*, with its reference to "quella filosofia, costante in Bellini nel seguir sempre con la sua musica le frasi poetiche e le situazioni", in Lippmann, *Vincenzo Bellini* (1969), pp.250-251.
20. *L'Omnibus*, 15 June 1833.

an example, the first libretto for Norma, reproduced here, describes the opera as a tragedia lirica by Felice Romani, and mentions Bellini at the bottom of the cast list:

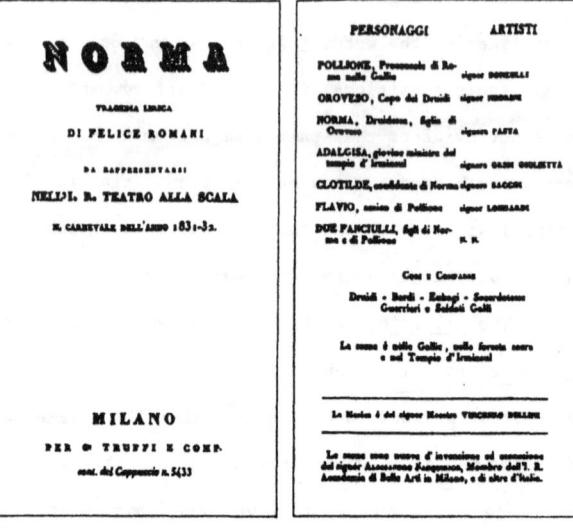

A similar description can sometimes be seen in scores as in this frontispiece for I Capuleti e i Montecchi:

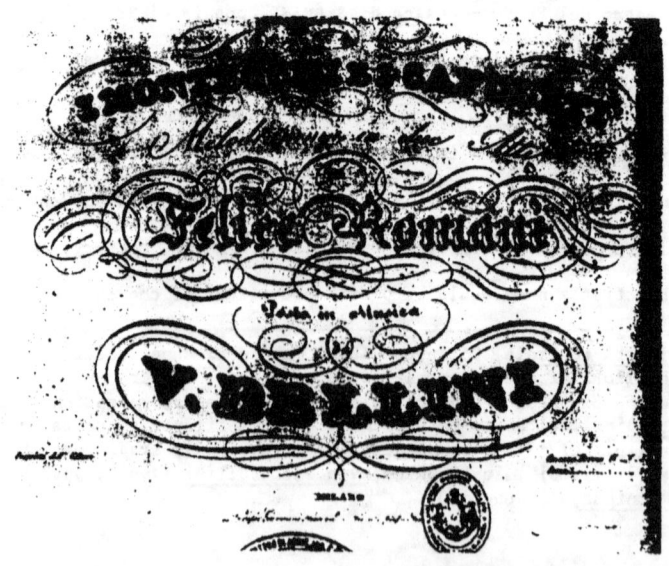

In this, we can see illustration of the extent to which Italians saw the _dramma_ as remaining intact in a musical setting. Thus the text for Rossini's _Maometto secondo_ is described by the Neapolitan paper _L'Indipendente_ as being "embellished with the graces of music",[21] no doubt with the "glint and glitter of a thousand tints and colours" as Stendhal puts it. In this important respect the views of Italians conflict directly with what is received opinion today. For us the libretto is transformed by its musical setting and no longer exists independently; to some extent, for Italians it still did.

Quite often, too, one can find a title page for a libretto that refers more directly to the poetic element, and moreover goes on to include other matters that were part of the general synthesis of the arts that was the contemporary _spettacolo_. As one example among hundreds, the libretto for Mercadante's _Elena da Feltre_, at the Teatro San Carlo, Naples in 1838, refers to: "Poesia del Sig. Cammarano / musica del Sig. Maestro Saverio Mercadante / Architetto de' Reali Teatri e Direttore delle decorazioni / sig. Cav. Antonio Niccolini ...".

There then follow the names of many of those responsible for staging and other matters, including the designers of four scene-changes, the "Appaltatore della copisteria e proprietario assoluto degli spartiti in partitura", "Direttore del macchinismo", "Capi macchinisti", "Direttore del vestiario", the designer of the "Attrezzeria", the "Pittore pe' figurini del vestiario", the "Direttore ed inventore de' fuochi chimici artificiali", and the "Direttore appaltatore dell' illuminazione". Only after this are we told the names of the singers. Quite often the names of at least the principal _professori_ of the orchestra would follow.

---

21. _L'Indipendente_, Giornale politico, letterario e commerciale, Naples, 4 December 1820: "Ad abbellir questo dramma colle grazie della musica fu destinata la penna di Rossini".

The extent to which the opera being presented to the public is described in terms of a fusion of various arts must inevitably remind one of Arteaga's description of opera as an "aggregate of poetry, of music and of decoration". What was referred to in Ferro's thesis about opera being a unification of the arts (but that only poetry should prevail, and the other arts should help it) is also relevant here.[22]

Bearing this in mind, it is only to be expected that Italians looked for poetry in librettos and judged them accordingly. That is to say, librettos are not criticized if they fail to generate dramatic excitement, but only if they are not poetic. The librettos of A. L. Tottola who provided Bellini with that for <u>Adelson e Salvini</u>, were often held to be suspect on this score. "The poetry by Signor A. L. Tottola ... say verses rather than poetry; no, more like words or chatter", was the sour comment of one Neapolitan reviewer on his <u>Imelda de' Lambertazzi</u> for Donizetti.[23] Good dramatic poetry was often remembered independently of the music, though no doubt because of it: "who does not know the poetry of <u>Otello</u>? and who does not know that of <u>Elisabetta</u>? Who has not got the verses of so many operas ringing in his ears?" as one Milanese journal put it.[24] To some extent therefore Bellini's contemporaries saw the poetic drama as a distinct feature still intact after being set to music, and to be judged as good or bad in poetic terms.

Further details as to what constitutes good poetry in a libretto tend to be lacking, however. Even individual librettos are not discussed

---

22. See Chapter 2 notes 29 and 32.
23. <u>Il caffè del molo</u>, number 29 (1830): "Poesia del Signore A. L. Tottola ... Metti versi invece di poesia; no meglio parole, meglio chiacchiere".
24. <u>L'Eco</u>, Giornale di scienze, lettere, arti, mode e teatri, Milan, 17 July 1833: "Chi non conosce la poesia dell' <u>Otello</u>? chi non conosce quella dell' <u>Elisabetta</u>? Chi non ha pieno gli orecchi de' versi ... di tante opere melodrammatiche ...?".

in detail beyond the passing of rather casual value judgements, which might be considered curious in the light of the importance that they attached to the matter. Thus Romani's librettos for Bellini are praised but rarely in detail. That for <u>Beatrice di Tenda</u> is therefore treated respectfully, but rather superficially: "The tragedy, as treated by our <u>Romani</u>, presents interesting situations, and abounds in fine poetry, as is always the case in all his <u>Drammi</u>". [25]

The references to "situazioni" and "buona poesia" are, like that to the "posizione drammatica" in Pietro Raimondi's <u>Le nozze de' Sanniti</u>,[26] quite typical. This view of drama as consisting of dramatic situations, accepted by Lippmann for Bellini, strongly contrasts with the more modern view of dramatic action with its concern for correct pacing, which is so typical of Verdi. "The fundamental mode of presentation in drama is action", proclaims Kerman,[27] showing at once why such an approach is anachronistic to Bellini. This is not because Italians tried, but were incapable of, dramatic pacing before Verdi; but because they put the emphasis on poetic depiction of situations. Thus Bellini himself always refers to the drama in terms of situations and to the poetry provided for them by Romani. Even in his last opera he seems to have considered his projected final ensemble as being effective, in an essentially static manner. He says "I believe it will be good, the situation for all on stage being very interesting".[28]

That Bellini and his contemporaries did not say precisely what

---

25. <u>L'Eco</u>, 20 March 1833; quoted after Cambi, p.341: "la tragedia come fu trattato dal nostro <u>Romani</u> presenta delle situazioni interessanti, ed abbonda di buona poesia, come avviene sempre in tutti i suoi <u>Drammi</u>".
26. <u>Rivista teatrale</u>, 13 August 1824.
27. Kerman, p.74.
28. Cambi, p.486 (30 November 1834): "credo che andrà bene, essendo la situazio[ne] per tutti i soggetti in scena interessantissima". The section being considered by Bellini is a projected <u>cabaletta finale</u>, similar to the end of Act I of <u>La sonnambula</u> (preceded by a <u>largo concertato</u> for "i due bassi, tenore, donna e cori") to end the whole opera.

they required to create good poetry in a libretto might be explained by the fact that there was always a model which to point to instead. For some time that model had been Metastasio. Eximeno regarded him in the 1770s as the height of perfection: "Now that music has achieved complete perfection, so has lyric poetry been brought to an equal level by the great Metastasio".[29]

As indicated in Chapter 2, at that time there was no nostalgic harking back to an earlier golden age, unless it be to settings of the same Metastasio by Pergolesi. Later writers had less confidence and requested poets to follow Metastasio as a model. Thus Bellini's poet for Bianca e Gernando, Domenico Gilardoni, is advised that "Metastasio ... has left us infinite models for this type of duet; and we invite both Signor Gilardoni and Signor Bellini to study them at length".[30]

Composition to Metastasian librettos had of course largely died out, even though some operas continued to be written to adaptations of them during the early nineteenth century.[31] The survival of the Metastasian libretto was therefore largely an academic chimera. The texts underwent great transformations, particularly in subject matter. Since these have been dealt with extensively by Friedrich Lippmann,[32] it is hardly necessary to discuss them in detail here. One matter that remained, however, was its essentially poetic nature. The precise dramatic construction according to three pairs of lovers had

---

29. Eximeno, p.334: "Oggi però che la Musica è giunta alla somma perfezione, à portato ad egual grado il gran Metastasio la poesia lirica".
30. Giornale delle due Sicilie, 13 June 1826: "Il Metastasio ... ci ha lasciato di questa specie di duetti infiniti modelli; e noi invitiamo tanto il Sig. Gilardoni che il Sig. Bellini a più posatamente consultarli".
31. Examples include: G. S. Mayr, Demetrio (1823); Donizetti, Olimpiade (unfinished; written in 1817); Giovanni Pacini, Temistocle (1823) and Alessandro nell' Indie (1824); Mercadante, Didone abbandonata (1823). An even older model is found in an adaptation of Zeno's Lucio Vero in Zingarelli, Berenice (1811).
32. Lippmann, Vincenzo Bellini, pp.1-52.

changed into a dependence on an eternal triangle, and the choice of subject matter was influenced by newer Romantic tastes; but its existence as a poetic form had only been changed in certain aspects of its style of language and not in its constitution. The most notable manifestations of this are the separation of recitative and aria texts, and the survival of the traditional double quatrain form for the arias themselves. The separation of texts into <u>versi sciolti</u> and rhymed quatrains for arias is quite obvious in contemporary librettos and maintained by Bellini's settings. The trend through the first half of the nineteenth century was towards integration of the two, spurred by the underpinning of both by the orchestra. Lippmann points to Bellini's aria-like passages to recitative texts, but these are never as formal as arias. There remain extremely long sections of Bellini's operas that are predominantly recitative, particularly when compared to the early works of Verdi. These are for Werner Oehlmann[33] the most obsolescent features of Bellini's operas and they represent Bellini's continuing commitment to the idea of music serving the words, not the underlying dramatic action as with Verdi. Pacini and Mercadante, in the years immediately following Bellini's death, were inclined to shorten the recitative drastically.[34] Verdi tended to do the same so that his early works are often a good deal shorter than those of Bellini and his contemporaries. He tended to compose over transitions orchestrally, avoiding the slackening of dramatic tension brought about by recitative more barely composed like that of Bellini.[35] Bellini's

---

33. Werner Oehlmann, <u>Vincenzo Bellini</u> (Zurich and Freiburg, 1974), p.20.
34. An example of a very short introductory recitative is afforded by that to Viscardo's <u>sortita</u> 'Bell' adorata incognita' in Act I of Mercadante's <u>Il giuramento</u> (1837). Its dramatic position and proportions are already more prophetic of 'Celeste Aida' than reminiscent of a <u>sortita</u> such as that of Pollione in <u>Norma</u>.
35. Further on this difference between Verdi's operas and those of Bellini's style; Julian Budden, <u>The Operas of Verdi</u>, 3 vols (London, 1973-81), I (1973), p.32.

recitatives on the other hand are so important, as at the beginning of Act II of <u>Norma</u>, as to be worthy of a separate study.

The extent of the inheritance from Metastasian opera can be seen when we turn to look in more detail at Romani's texts for Bellini. To put a famous aria text such as 'Casta Diva' in its proper context, it is best shown along with some of its preceding recitative text, and compared with an example of a <u>preghiera</u> from a libretto by Metastasio. This example from his <u>Zenobia</u>, first set by Luca Predieri in 1740, closes the second act. The situation is not quite the same as in <u>Norma</u>, in that Zenobia's is a personal prayer for justice (she is suspected by her husband Radamisto of continuing her attachment to her former lover Tiridate who, however, has attracted the love of Zenobia's sister, Egle), whereas Norma's is a prayer for peace on behalf of all the Druids. Leaving aside matters of dramatic situation, however, it is most striking how similar the two texts are in construction. This is obvious immediately in the manner in which the aria texts are set off from those of the recitatives.

Metastasio, <u>Zenobia</u>,II, 8[36]
Zenobia:
>Salvar lo sposo
>Eran le parti mie: le vostre or sono
>Protegger l'innocenza. Han dritto in Cielo
>Le suppliche dolenti
>D'un'anima fedel; né col mio pianto
>Rea d'alcun fallo innanzi a voi son io:
>Vien da limpida fonte il pianto mio.
>
>>Voi leggete in ogni core;
>>Voi sapete, o giusti dèi,
>>Se son puri i voti miei,
>>Se innocente è la pietà.
>>
>>So che priva d'ogni errore,
>>Ma crudel non mi volete;
>>So che in Ciel non confondete
>>La barbarie e l'onestà.

---

36. Tutte le opere di Pietro Metastasio, edited by Bruno Brunelli, 5 vols (Milan, 1943-1954), I, 953-954.

Romani, *Norma*, I, 4 (36a)

Norma:

Io nei volumi arcani
Leggo del cielo: in pagine di morte
Della superba Roma è scritto il nome ...
Ella un giorno morrà; ma non per voi.
Morrà pei vizi suoi,
Qual consunta morrà. L'ora aspettate,
L'ora fatal che compia il gran decreto.
Pace v'intimo ... e il sacro vischio io mieto.

    Casta Diva, che inargenti
    Queste sacre antiche piante,
    A noi volgi il bel sembiante
    Senza nube e senza vel.

    Tempra tu de' cori ardenti
    Tempra ancor lo zelo audace,
    Spargi in terra quella pace
    Che regnar tu fai nel ciel.

In both these cases, the recitative text is written in <u>versi sciolti</u> (unrhymed endecasyllables), with an occasional seven syllable verse (<u>verso settenario</u>) and a closing rhyming couplet. The aria texts, however, are bound to a strict rhyme scheme and cast in the classical format of double quatrains, using eight syllable lines (<u>versi ottonari</u>). The stress in such verse falls normally, as here, on the third and seventh syllables. During the eighteenth century, the most usual way to set such a text was in the form of a <u>da capo</u> aria, with the second stanza providing the words for the middle section. This naturally entailed returning to the first stanza for the repeat. In the libretto for Luca Predieri's <u>Zenobia</u>, for example, this return is actually indicated in the text, thus: "Voi, &c.".[37]

Turning to explore further details of these two aria texts, we can see that the final lines of the stanzas are rhyming <u>ottonari tronchi</u>. As it happens, in both cases the initial lines also rhyme giving an overall scheme of ABBC ADDC. Such a strict pattern as this is by no means universal, and other schemes are also common; but it is

---

36a. *Norma*, Libretto di Felice Romani (Milan, n.d.: reprinted 1974), pp.12-13. The ellipses form part of the text. Stage directions have been omitted.

37. *Zenobia*, dramma per musica (Vienna, 1740), p.41.

usual to find a rhyme between the <u>versi tronchi</u>. The important point, however, is that such texts, set off from recitative texts, are in a consistent metre with a formal rhyme scheme and are planned as poetry rather than merely as a bare canvas for music. Although Romani's verse may sometimes differ from the above plan in details, as indeed does Metastasio's own, the essential poetic intention remains.

With regard to the type of actual language used, we can certainly find greater differences, as one might expect from the poetic styles of different centuries. Friedrich Lippmann sees Romani's verse as being informed with a Romantic sensibility that marks it off from those of earlier periods. Following Scherillo, he compares the manner in which Mandane in Metastasio's <u>Artaserse</u> complains that she cannot forget her beloved Arbace despite his unworthiness, with the Romantic style of Elvino's complaint in <u>La sonnambula</u>.[38]

Metastasio, <u>Artaserse</u>, I, 14	Romani, <u>La sonnambula</u>, II, 4
Mandane:	Elvino:
Dimmi che un empio sei, Ch'hai di macigno il core, Perfido traditore! E allor ti crederò.	Ah! perchè non posso odiarti, Infedel, com'io vorrei! Ah! del tutto ancor non sei Cancellata dal mio cor.
(Vorrei di lui scordarmi, Odiarlo, oh Dio! vorrei; Ma sento che sdegnarmi Quanto dovrei non so.)	Possa un altro, ah! possa amarti Qual t'amò quest' infelice! Altro voto, o traditrice, Non temer dal mio dolor.
Dimmi che un empio sei, E allor ti crederò. (Odiarlo, oh Dio! vorrei; Ma odiarlo, oh Dio! non so.)	

Lippmann maintains that Elvino's text is more direct in expression and that it flows more naturally, in accordance with the natural style of Bellini's age.[39] He fails to remind the reader, however, that what is being compared is not like with like, but an <u>opera seria</u> with an <u>opera semiseria</u>. It is also relevant that the verse lengths

---

38. Michele Scherillo, <u>Vincenzo Bellini. Note aneddotiche e critiche</u> (Ancona, 1882), pp.56-57.
39. Lippmann, <u>Vincenzo Bellini</u> (1969), p.41.

are different, as we shall see. Lippmann also omits to point out that
Artaserse was first produced in 1730, set to music by Leonardo Vinci.
This is a very early date from which to expect to find identical sentiments to those of 1830. A general survey of Artaserse settings has
not been attempted, but already by 1743 we find that Karl Heinrich
Graun's setting omits this text, there only being ten scenes in the
first act.[40]

Bearing all this in mind, the two texts seem more striking for
their similarities rather than for their differences. Romani's text
is very similar in construction to those already examined, being again
in versi ottonari with rhyming versi tronchi. In this example,
Romani's rhyme scheme is even more consistent than Metastasio's,
being once more ABBC ADDC. Metastasio's versi settenari differ a
little from this, in that we now have three stanzas, although the third
is mostly an amalgam of lines from the preceding two. The rhyme scheme
of the first two stanzas, ABBC DADC, actually diverts only marginally
from the scheme we have seen so far. The effect of using lines in
versi settenari in the text from Artaserse, which Romani also uses in
many arias, is more fundamental. Whereas Romani's versi ottonari have
a very strict stress on the third and seventh syllables, as in 'Casta
Diva', Metastasio's versi settenari may put the stress on any of the
first four syllables, as well as on the penultimate. This is a
standard feature of such verse, and its effect can be seen in Mandane's
aria. Due to these technical differences, Romani's text has a more
even stress pattern, and this may well have much to do with the more
natural flow that Lippmann finds in it.

We must conclude therefore that the overall poetic intention of
Romani's verse for Bellini is still in the mainstream of the Metastasian

---

40. The libretto of 1743 is reproduced in: Italian Opera Librettos 1640-1770, vol.III (New York and London, 1978).

tradition, at least with regard to details of construction. Were Bellini's settings of the texts to completely ignore the rigours of this poetic construction, it might be reasonable to reply that such details are no longer relevant; but such is certainly not the case. The present study deals with the ideas and priorities that conditioned Bellinian opera rather than analyses of the scores themselves, but it might be pertinent to point out that the essential poetic structure is reflected in the resulting arias. In the case of Elvino's aria, the strict poetic metre gives rise to an equally strict musical metre, with the third and seventh syllables serving for the first beat of each bar. The second stanza introduces a contrasting phrase (in the relative minor), a regular feature with Bellini. With the earlier example, 'Casta Diva', the second poetical stanza is accorded a second musical one, but here again the lines are set in their original sequence. The poetic metre determines the rhythmical pattern of the music, especially interesting in this case as this pattern becomes increasingly complex towards the end of each stanza. Lippmann declares that Romani's verse strikes the heart more strongly but this is a curious value judgement, since what was so much valued in Metastasio was not his formal aspect but his natural and unforced poetic sensibility, which spoke directly to the heart in uncomplicated language; exactly the claim Lippmann makes for Romani in the face of Metastasio. It will hardly be surprising, therefore, to find that Romani was compared with Metastasio by contemporaries. While drawing attention to the similarities between <u>Anna Bolena</u>, <u>Beatrice di Tenda</u> and <u>Parisina</u>, an article in the <u>Giornale di Commercio</u> agreed that Romani "revived the <u>dramma per musica</u> in Italy that had declined from the level to which Metastasio had raised it".[41] The review continues to show

---

41. <u>Giornale di commercio, arti, industrie, manufatture e varietà</u>, Naples, 30 July 1834: "egli rilevò in Italia il dramma per musica decaduta dalla dignità alla quale aveало innalzato il Metastasio".

the links between Metastasio and Bellini himself:

"It was well said by whoever likened Bellini to Metastasio ... certainly Metastasio is the poet that better than any other, finds his way to the heart, he is the poet of noble and tender emotions, but no one could deny that he produced a style that was gentle and graceful that often sacrificed the truth and energy of grand and powerful passions. Thus, turning to Bellini again, we must admit that our composer ... even if he is successful in dealing with delicate, graceful, pathetic and gentle emotions, in powerful and tragic situations he is often weak". (42)

Thus Bellini is already seen as a composer limited to tender emotions, a point which Lippmann strongly disputes the validity of.(43) Later writers tended to consider him rather elegaic compared with the more dramatic opera of their own time; but here he is already being judged so in comparison with Rossini. He seems to have been attracted to Romani's verse for poetic rather than dramatic reasons, and that for Norma was judged in comparable terms: "everyone applauded the philosophical music, the varying emotions, and the tender words of this lyric tragedy. This work of Signor Romani is beautiful, theatrical and poetic".(44)

It can easily be seen that it was precisely these tender words that attracted Bellini to Romani as well as being the style universally held in favour in Italy. Hence the high esteem in which Bellini and Romani were held. In the passage just quoted the cities besides Naples that are listed as applauding Norma are "Milano, ... Venezia, Bergamo,

42. Giornale di commercio, 30 July 1834: "Ben disse chi paragonò il Bellini al Metastasio ... certamente Metastasio è il poeta che meglio d' ogni altro ricerca le vie del cuore, è il poeta de' nobili e gentili affetti; ma niuno potrà scovenire ch' egli aveasi formato un linguaggio tenero e pietoso al quale sacrificava sovente la verità e l'energia di grandi e forti passioni, Così ancora dicendo del Bellini, ci è d'uopo confessare che questo nostro scrittore di musica ... se piace negli affetti delicati, dolci, patetici, soavi, nelle forti e tragiche situazioni sovente riesce snervato".
43. Lippmann, Vincenzo Bellini (1969), pp.352-355.
44. L'Omnibus, 13 July 1833: "àn tutte applaudito alla filosofica musica, a' contrastati affetti, e alle tenere parole di questa tragedia lirica. E, bello, teatrale, poetico è questo lavoro del Signor Romani".

Genova, Ancona e ultimamente Londra".[45] This can be more easily understood by accepting that Bellini and Romani were seen as realizing long held ideals, rather than as Romantic revolutionaries paving the way for Verdi.

If we compare Metastasio and Romani's texts directly we can sometimes find examples of a similarity in style. Dr. Lippmann's assertion that Bellini is not limited to tender affections would be as valid for Metastasio. Consider how similar is Serse's denunciation of his confidante Sebaste in Temistocle to Norma's denunciation of her erstwhile lover Pollione. Norma's text is introduced by

"Oh non tremare, o perfido,
No, non tremare per lei ..."

as she denounces Pollione on finding that he has seduced Adalgisa. Sebaste's treachery has been political rather than romantic, but one can see that the texts differ little, even with regard to vocabulary.

Metastasio, Temistocle, III, 7[46]
Serse:

Non tremar, vassallo indegno;
È già tardo il tuo timore:
Quando ordisti il reo disegno,
Era il tempo di tremar.

Ma giustissimo consiglio
È del Ciel che un traditore
Mai non vegga il suo periglio,
Che vicino a naufragar.
[Parte

Romani, Norma, I, 9[47]
Norma:

Vanne, sì, mi lascia, indegno;
Figli, oblia, promesse, onore ...
Maladetta dal mio sdegno
Non godrai d'un empio amore.

Te sull' onde e te sui venti
Seguiran mie furie ardenti:
Mia vendetta e notte e giorno
Ruggirà d'intorno a te.

Again we see double quatrains of versi ottonari, bound to formal rhyme schemes; Metastasio's being a variant of what we have seen already: ABAC DBDC. The main difference lies in the fact that whilst Serse's is an exit aria, Norma's text introduces a trio. Consequently

---

45. L'Omnibus, 13 July 1833. This enthusiasm for Norma increased in the following years. In April 1836 Norma was to be found playing in three Neapolitan opera houses at the same time, as reported in an article 'NORMAMANIA', in I curiosi, Naples, 30 April 1836: "Tutto è Norma".
46. Metastasio, I, 913-914.
47. Norma, Libretto, p.25. The ellipsis forms part of the text.

there are further stanzas for Pollione and Adalgisa which rhyme with Norma's, accounting for the fact that the final lines of Norma's two quatrains do not rhyme with each other as do Serse's. Instead, the rhyme is with the equivalent lines in the subsequent stanzas, giving rise to the complex scheme: ABAB CCDE FBFB CCDE GBGB CCDE. What is perhaps more striking is the similarity in style and choice of language used in each case to deride the 'indegno' and to tell him 'non tremare'. The element of curse marks Norma's text as more obviously belonging to the nineteenth century; but, significantly, curses are by no means common in Bellini's operas, unlike many of his contemporaries' works.

For contemporaries both Romani's and Metastasio's verse shared the qualities of poetic sentiment, expressed neatly and concisely within this classic double quatrain structure. To us it may seem an excessively formal scheme, particularly if we still see opera as something more approaching Kerman's ideal, where such polite sensibilities are sacrificed on the altar of musical drama. Compared with what Verdi was looking for, words are treated here as poetry rather than mere texts for musical expression. The prime features of this style would seem to be the sentimental affection of the language and the formal conciseness of the poetic structure. Milizia points out that since poetry is an edifying and delightful imitation of Nature,

> "the lyric style ought to be simple and fluent, without verbosity, without studied eloquence, precise, sparing of words, strong, natural, limpid and graceful ... But what need of further rules? Metastasio's drammi provide the true rules for lyric style". (48)

This can be compared with Bellini's injunctions to Pepoli over studied poetical conceits, in this famous passage concerning the latter's text for I puritani:

> "Musical contrivances murder the effects of the dramatic situations, all the more so poetic ones in a libretto; to be effective, poetry and music require naturalness and nothing more: anyone that turns away from this is lost, and will have produced in the end a ridiculous and

---

48. Milizia, p.44: "lo stile Lirico deve essere semplice e rapido, senza verbosità, senza eloquenza ricercata, preciso, avaro di parole, forte, naturale, facile, grazioso ... Ma che più regole? Le vere regole dello stilo Lirico sono i Drammi del Metastasio".

tedious work, which will please only pedants but will never touch the heart". (49)

In short, Bellini is here giving Pepoli a lesson in contemporary aesthetic thought. All that is lacking is a direct reference to Metastasio as <u>auctoritas</u>. But the end result should, as with Metastasio, touch the heart. For this Bellini required poetry that "depicts the emotions in the most realistic way";(50) that is, in a way that is most natural and true to life, although naturalness in a medium as patently artificial as opera might seem to us a curious concept.(51)

The precise style of language that was deemed worthy of a libretto is a subject properly left to a native speaker. Luigi Dallapiccola has done this in a famous essay 'Words and Music in Italian Nineteenth Century Opera',(52) which points out characteristics that accord with the idea that Italians wanted an edifying spectacle; although in actual fact the libretto, from a literary point of view, was usually without merit: its style had nothing in common with spoken language and, confined to librettos, was brought to life only by the music with which it was associated. Dallapiccola sees this largely in terms of "carelessness of imagination and of misplaced affection". In this respect he

---

49. Cambi, p.400 (May 1834): "Gli artifizi musicali ammazzano l'effetto delle situazioni, peggio gli artifizi poetici in un dramma per musica; poesia e musica, per fare effetto, richiedono naturalezza e niente più: chi sorte di questa è perduto, ed alla fine avrà dato alla luce un' opera pesante e stupida che solo piacerà alla sfera dei pedanti mai al cuore".
50. Cambi, p.422 (4 August 1834): "che dipingono le passioni al più vivo".
51. A comparatively extensive account of how, in the opinion of a contemporary, the 'natural' element in Metastasio was seen to work is provided by Stendhal, <u>Lives of Haydn, Mozart and Metastasio</u>, pp. 214-220. He considers the entire scene leading to the famous aria 'Se cerca, se dice', as set by Pergolesi in <u>Olimpiade</u> (1735). Stendhal still sees this as a model of "<u>truth to nature</u>".
52. Luigi Dallapiccola, 'Words and Music in Italian Nineteenth Century Opera', in <u>The Verdi Companion</u>, edited by William Weaver and Martin Chusid (London, 1980), pp.193-215. The essay had been printed previously, as <u>Words and Music in Italian Nineteenth Century Opera</u> (Dublin, 1964); and as 'Parole e musica nel melodramma' in <u>Quaderni della Rassegna Musicale</u> II (1965), pp.117-139.

points out the conventionalized use of antiquated formal and dignified terms in the place of perfectly normal Italian language. He points to the use of **accenti** rather than **parole**, **sacri bronzi** rather than **campane**, **tempio** rather than **chiesa**, **appressarsi** rather than **avvicinarsi**, **destra** rather than **mano**, **bellezza**, **beltade** and **beltà** rather than **donna**.

This dependence on the use of grandiloquent and antiquated word-forms, which Dallapiccola refers to as an "absurd language", really has to be seen in terms of the supposedly edifying nature of contemporary Italian opera, that "**non plus ultra** del diletto e dell' utile".[53] We have seen how this consideration directed much of the thought concerning the actions of the singer on the stage, and how it stems from their classical derivation of opera. It was, moreover, not just a consideration of abstract theoreticians but permeated all writings on the subject. The following extract comes from the Neapolitan paper *Il galiani*: "The well directed theatre ... would be able to exert the greatest influence on the moral character of nations".[54] This elevated view of the purpose of the Italian theatre is reflected in their expectations of its dramatic side. "Tragedy is written as the imitation of the life of Heroes", claims Milizia,[55] and so therefore its language was to be suitably elevated to match this. For this reason **tempio** meaning **temple**, was much more suitable than **chiesa**, Dallapiccola's alternative.

There may well have been also the desire on the part of librettists to follow in the great traditions of Italian literature. Many of the most common and notable antiquated words that make up Italian libretti, including such words as Dallapiccola's mentioned **beltà**, and

---

53. Milizia, p.39.
54. *Il galiani*, 10 December 1823: "Il teatro ben diretto ... potrebbe avere la più grande influenza sul carattere morale delle nazioni".
55. Milizia, p.15: "La *Tragedia* è l'imitazione della vita degli Eroi".

words such as _cangiare_ (rather than _cambiare_), _periglio_ (rather than _pericolo_), _palagio_ (rather than _palazzo_), are to be found easily enough in the vocabularies for the works of Dante and Petrarch.

The choice of poet as we have seen took priority over the choice of subject, for Bellini as for his contemporaries. Nevertheless, Italians also had clear ideas as to what constituted suitable material, determined by its duty to elevate the soul and delight the senses. "Its purpose is to elevate the soul and edify our sensibilities, to humanize us, to render us prudent and honest. The means conducive to so great an end are terror and compassion",[56] maintains Milizia, giving as concrete examples of suitable dramas "Achille in Sciro, Didone abbandonata, Alessandro nell'Indie by the illustrious Metastasio".[57] Subjects suitable are those that incite awe in the audience, but not, as we shall point out, horror. In his list of Metastasian dramas it is notable that he commends them particularly for their exotic subject matter; that is for what Milizia calls "meraviglie" in exotic locations.

Since what was important was the static situations that were made to affect the emotions, the emphasis remained on individual scenes rather than dramatic ebb and flow. This accords with Bellini's manner of composition, which was to set the text piecemeal as Romani sent him parts of the libretto for individual scenes; though this was sometimes a matter of necessity in any case. It was therefore not expected, or even always possible, that these scenes should be drawn together into a logical dramatic process, let alone an exciting one such as was later

---

56. Milizia, p.16: "Il suo fine è di elevare l'anima, di formare il cuore, di umanizzarci alla pietà, di renderci prudenti e probi. I mezzi conducenti a sì gran fine sono il terrore e la compassione". This idea stems ultimately from Aristotle, Poetics, chapter 14
57. Milizia, p.42: "L'Achille in Sciro, la Didone Abbandonata, l'Alessandro nell' Indie del chiarissimo Metastasio, sono soggetti proprj d'un' Opera in Musica".

to interest Verdi. On the subject of Bellini's early outline of the overall structure of I puritani, Charlotte Joyce Greenspan has pointed out, in a recent thesis, that "Bellini does not explain how all the touching situations of the plot were to be resolved, the plot summary does not contain an end for the story".[58] It might also be added that logical causes for such situations were similarly unimportant, so that they remain discrete from any logical dramatic process within any plot itself. For this reason Bellini explains the situation where the innocents suffer by saying merely that "it is brought about by fate".[59] This approach to the drama accounts for the episodic nature of so many of the operas of Bellini's contemporaries, even more perhaps than those of Bellini himself. The unimportance of logical causes for dramatic scenes can be seen as late as Cammarano's famous libretto for Il trovatore (1853). It is only to a later age that these seem logically under-prepared, or under-motivated.

The sentimental style involved in singing over the suffering innocents, and the 'tenere parole' of Romani's verse, are elements that connect Bellini with general considerations of what was to be aimed at in contemporary melodramma and with its roots in Metastasian style.

The dignified view of Italian opera permitted the treatment of such sentimental subject matter along with the more heroic style that we can see in Romani's text for Norma, perhaps because it was sanctioned by Metastasian precedent, but also since it was inclined to lift the spirit and instil it with pity through the means of "il terrore e la compassione".

On this point, however, we should say that whilst terrore (which

---

58. Charlotte Joyce Greenspan, 'The Operas of Vincenzo Bellini' (unpublished Ph.D. dissertation, University of California, Berkeley, 1977), pp.330-331.
59. Cambi, p.395 (11 April 1834): "il destino ne è creatore".

might be translated as 'awe' or 'dread') and compassion were sanctioned in the interest of edification, this seems not to have included <u>orrore</u>. A firm line seems to have been drawn between the two which Milizia explains under the title "<u>Terrore e compassione</u>": "One offers Tragedy to arouse awe and pity, but not, of course, horror; spectacles of a gory nature are frightful and barbaric, and offend human sensibilities. They are offensive to moral standards too, and coarsen finer feelings, as happens with butchers and surgeons".[60] For the first part of the nineteenth century this standard was maintained and the 'gothick' inspired operas found in France and Germany are rare in Italy. Giuseppe Mastriani in 1847 still holds the same values as Milizia and maintains that so also should those on stage: "sensing to this very day the dignity of art ... let them show that theatre is not nowadays fashioned to arouse immoral passions, but to use artistic beauty to give useful edification".[61]

Consequently operas that dealt with sordid subjects or protagonists rather than with "<u>Amore pudico</u>", as Milizia puts it,[62] risked running a gauntlet of criticism. Donizetti's <u>farsa</u>, <u>L'ajo nell' imbarazzo</u> (1824) was such an opera, as was his later <u>Francesca di Foix</u> (1831).[63] The judgement of <u>La farfalla</u> was that "The plot of the libretto did not strike us as worthy either of the

---

60. Milizia, pp.18-19: "la Tragedia si propone d'ispirare terrore e pietà, ma non già orrore; e gli spettacoli sanguinosi sono orrendi e barbari, e offendono l' umanità. Offendono anche il costume, e induriscono il cuore, come accade ai Macellai ed ai Chirurghi".
61. Mastriani, p.29: "sentendo oggimai la dignità dell' arte ... facciano vedere che il Teatro non è oggi fatto per eccitare colpevoli passioni, ma si per servirsi del bello artistico a dare utili insegnamenti".
62. Milizia, p.18.
63. In <u>Francesca di Foix</u>, an <u>opera semiseria</u>, courtiers intrigue to seduce the pretty young wife of a Count who has locked her away, pretending that she is ugly. Finally the courtiers mock his attempts to avoid being cuckolded. It antedates <u>Rigoletto</u> by twenty years but significantly lacks the later opera's 'Gothick' flavour.

theatre, or of recounting here".(64) The opera proved to be most unsuccessful, only running a few nights.

Other operas that offended contemporary taste were spared the strictures of newspaper critics only by being banned from the stage altogether. Theatrical censorship is a subject on its own, embracing influences on the opera beyond the aesthetic sensibilities of contemporary theatre-goers; but we can see that too much has been made in the past of purely political, not to say Austrian imperialist, motives for censorship, and not enough of moral and 'educational' ones. Theatrical censorship could threaten an opera on three grounds: for political, religious or moral offences. The city where the opera was to take place affected which offence was most likely to be penalized. Moral and religious matters were particularly sensitive in Rome; political matters much more so in Naples. Torresani, the prefect of police in Milan, elegantly summed up the philosophical justifications for theatrical censorship and in doing so shed light on how they fit in quite logically with the traditional view of the spettacolo in terms of edification.

> "Theatres are designed to correct morals, and must therefore never present anything but moral themes, or, if they present vice and wickedness, it must be done in such a way that virtue appears glorious and beautiful as a result". (65)

Milizia summed up this view of the moral side of theatrical education in the phrase "Hatred of vice, love of virtue".(66)

In making a distinction between terrore and orrore, it might be added that when exception was taken by contemporary audiences and critics to the subject matter, this was inextricably bound up with how

---

64. La farfalla, 4 June 1831: "L'Argomento del libretto non ci è sembrato degno nè del teatro, nè della ricorrenza".
65. David R. B. Kimbell, Verdi in the Age of Italian Romanticism (Cambridge, 1981), p.24.
66. Milizia, p.19: "Odio al vizio, amore alla virtù".

this appeared on stage. In this connexion, the dignity required of the singer representing the character on stage, discussed in Chapter 3, is naturally also relevant here. However, it should be said that what was permissible in this respect was already beginning to change.

An early mad-scene in an opera such as Paër's <u>Agnese di Fitzhenry</u> (1809) offended taste as it introduced vulgar elements of the comic theatre into opera-seria, producing an effect that one newspaper described as "comico-lamentevole", and rejected as an "insufferable medley of the lugubrious and the ludicrous".[67] Invidious comparisons were made with Paisiello's <u>Nina pazza per amore</u> (1789) in which was depicted the "gentle alienation of Nina's mind".[68]

This purely sentimental approach was much more acceptable to Italians generally than that of Paër. In fact Paër's opera seems tame indeed compared with later operatic mad scenes, but there is no doubt that Bellini's mad scenes in <u>La sonnambula</u> and <u>I puritani</u> stem more from the Neapolitan tradition of Paisiello with its "dolce alienazione della mente" than the more Romantic type mixing comic and lugubrious elements. As Pierluigi Petrobelli has pointed out, Bellini made his reference to Paisiello quite explicit[69] and in his early plan for the second act 'mad scene' of <u>I puritani</u> he describes it as "terzetto for two basses and la Grisi; this is like the quartet in Nina, where the ensemble is all her so that it will seem more like a <u>scena</u> for her alone".[70] Later he describes the whole role of Elvira, as

---

67. <u>Monitore delle due Sicilie</u>, 16 January 1813: "quale insoffribile mescolanza di lugubre e di scempiato".
68. <u>Monitore delle due Sicilie</u>, 16 January 1813: "la dolce alienazione della mente di Nina".
69. Pierluigi Petrobelli, 'Bellini e Paisiello. Altri documenti sulla nascita dei <u>Puritani</u>', <u>Il melodramma italiana dell'Ottocento, Studi e ricerche per Massimo Mila</u> (Turin, 1977), pp.351-363.
70. Cambi, p.439 (21 September 1834): "terzetto di due bassi e la Grisi questo è come il quartetto della Nina, ove questa ha tutto quindi sembrerà una scena per lei piuttosto".

adapted for Malibran, as "very interesting because it is of a style like Nina pazza; and has heart-rending situations".(71) Petrobelli considers that the scene in Nina acts as an archetype for Bellini's thoughts on this subject; which, bearing in mind his Neapolitan upbringing, discussed in Chapter 1, is most probable.

Bellini's contemporaries were much more progressive, however, and not at all limited to the Neapolitan tradition of mad scenes. By the 1830s blood-stained scenes such as that of Edgardo's suicide in Lucia di Lammermoor (1835) are not uncommon. These would no doubt be classed under Milizia's 'spectacles of a gory nature', where terrore had become orrore. At such a time reviewers were quite happy to look back with relative fondness to the much maligned Agnese of Paër. Thus the Milanese Eco describes Donizetti's Il furioso all'isola di S. Domingo in 1833:

> "It is certainly by no means a beautiful spectacle seeing a madman floundering about the stage with torn clothing, an ashen face, with a dazed expression, with dishevelled hair, going from one excess of fury to another; nor, indeed, is having to be a witness to such misery. The interest and the compassion that a similar misfortune might excite, is changed to horror by the repulsiveness of the long and over-realistic representation of it; and the audience is left with just a succession of disgusting impressions instead of the pleasure it has a right to expect in the theatre ... In Paër's Agnese it is a father abandoned by his daughter that loses his mind; this motive is much more likely to arouse interest than the mad ravings of Il furioso". (72)

---

71. Cambi, p.455 (13 October 1834): "La parte delle Malibran sarà interessantissima perché è d'un genere come la Nina pazza; ed ha delle situazioni laceranti".
72. L'Eco, 4 October 1833: "Non è certamente il più bello spettacolo il vedere agitarsi sulla scena un pazzo cogli abiti laceri, con volto pallido, cogli occhi incantati, coi capelli irsuti e trascorrere da eccesso in eccesso di furore, nè bello è l'essere testimoni di tal miserie. L'interesse, la compassione che una simile sventura eccita, dal ributtante della lunga e troppo naturale rappresentazione di essa, è cangiato in orrore; e gli spettatori, in vece del diletto che hanno il diritto di trovare in teatro, non ne provano che un seguito di disgustose impressioni ... Nell'Agnese di Paër egli è un padre che perde il senno perché sua figlia lo ha abbandonato; questo motivo è più atto a destare interesse, che non lo è la pazzia del Furioso".

The review concludes by noting that "the audience reacted with the good sense it should: it laughed instead of feeling awe".[73] In other words, the complaint is substantially that compassion and awe (terrore) had been replaced by horror (orrore). The result was an unedifying spectacle that offended aesthetic theory, and the memory of the more gentle earlier models followed by Bellini. Despite the shock registered by the press, however, Il furioso was one of Donizetti's most popular and widely performed works; showing perhaps that audiences were beginning to accept a more obviously theatrical representation of madness than Bellini offered.[74] Certainly one does not find a work such as this often prohibited by moral censorship. Lucrecia Borgia, however, was an opera that often suffered at the hands of censors; and, for different reasons, Maria Stuarda was killed off at birth. Censorship was to become much more of a problem to composers, and much more politically orientated after the revolutions of 1848. This is why Verdi suffered so much.

Bellini himself seems to have escaped much restriction from censorship, which perhaps gives some clue as to the unexceptionable nature of his subject matter. His almost complete lack of interest in politics and his general lack of concern for this side of opera prevented him from attempting anything that would smack of the Risorgimento, which is never mentioned in his letters. He was later to accept the Legion d'Honneur from Louis Philippe in Paris, and dedicated the score of I puritani to his Bourbon Queen; and then expressed wounded puzzlement that he should receive criticism from Florimo and other friends in Naples.[75] Perhaps he, like one English traveller's Italian teacher, accepted that

---

73. L'Eco, 4 October 1833: "il Pubblico giudicò col buon senso che gli è proprio: esso rise invece di provare terrore".
74. Herbert Weinstock, Donizetti and the World of Opera in Italy, Paris and Vienna in the First Half of the Nineteenth Century (New York, 1963), p.333.
75. Cambi, p.529 (27 February 1835).

"Universally the men of talent are enemies to the political change".[76] Certainly there is very little, outside the Druids' chorus in Norma, of that nationalistic style that is so noticeable in Rossini's L'Italiana in Algeri ('Pensa alla patria'), and more seriously in L'Assedio di Corinto ('Questo nome che suona vittoria') and Guillaume Tell.

Many of the considerations governing the nature of operatic librettos, both in respect of its topic and of its poetic form, stem from contemporary appreciation of its traditionally noble nature. This explains its often elevated subject matter and grandiloquent language, and why Metastasio, as "il poeta de' nobili e gentili affetti", was held as a model of its poetic element just as Pergolesi was of its musical side. Bellini's concern for this aspect of the libretto and its dignity is quite consistent with traditions. Where there was anything that might arouse disgusting impressions, he actually admits to trying to eradicate it, or at least that his music would make the opera as a whole transcend it. He saw this possibility arising with the evil character of Filippo in Beatrice di Tenda: "I admit that the subject matter is horrible; but I sought by colouring it with my music, sometimes with awe, sometimes with pathos, to correct and neutralize the disgust aroused by Filippo's character".[77] The forbidden element of orrore here could be the victorious perfidy of Filippo or else the entry of the tortured Orombello. At any rate, Bellini's concern is for theatrical good taste.

Therefore wildly Romantic subject matter is rare in Bellini's

---

76. John Scott, Sketches of Manners, Scenery &c. in the French Provinces, Switzerland and Italy, second edition (London, 1831), p.244.
77. Cambi, p.395 (11 April 1834): "Confesso che il soggetto è orribile; ma io, con la musica, colorandolo ora tremendamente ed ora mestamente, cercai di correggere e far scomparire il disgustante che eccita il carattere di Filippo".

works, restricted mostly to Il pirata and, more particularly, La straniera; which perhaps significantly never gained a secure hold on the repertory. None provides such a 'grotesque' end as Edgardo's suicide on stage at the end of Lucia di Lammermoor, however, which is too much even for Joseph Kerman.[78] More in keeping with the dignity of the Art would be where such an unhappy ending was transformed by its inherent virtue and nobility. The touchstone and model for this is provided again by Metastasio, this time in his Attilio Regolo, the story of the Roman general captured by Carthaginians and sent to Rome to persuade them to sign a treaty with Carthage to their disadvantage. Regolo nobly urges Rome against such folly and returns to Carthage to accept his cruel fate. Metastasio's ending provides a text for a chorus but no final aria, and Regolo takes his farewell in recitative. It is in the light of such an example that we should see the striking end to Romani's Norma, rather than seeing it as a sort of proto-Wagnerian music drama.

Indeed, when we finally come to consider Bellini's choice of plots, Norma is an interesting case in point. Its essential nature lies in the traditional conflict between love and duty, which is brought to a crisis when Norma hears of the approach of Pollione, an enemy of the Druids but whom she still loves. The opera is in fact described as a tragedia lirica (not a music drama), and fulfils many of the edifying ideals of theorists. Nor is its subject matter new. There are obvious echoes of the fallen vestal virgin Giulia in the Italian version of Spontini's La vestale, first produced at Naples on 8 September

---

78. Kerman, p.145.

1811[79] and, as mentioned in the opening chapter, a regular standard at Naples. It is not to be doubted that Bellini knew the opera well and he owned a copy of the score which he left with Florimo along with scores of La donna del lago, Mosè in Egitto and others.[80] Other examples of operas on similar material include: Mayr, Medea in Corinto (Naples, 1813), with a libretto by Romani; V. Fioravanti, La foresta di Hermanstad (Naples, 1812), with a text by Tottola; and Pacini's La sacerdotessa d'Irminsul (Trieste, 1820) also with a libretto by Romani. The score of the opera Norma Bellini dedicated to his mentor at Naples, Zingarelli.

Other operas of Bellini also use subjects that were not particularly modern. Notable of course is that of Zaira, which is taken from Voltaire. Perhaps more characteristic is his I Capuleti e i Montecchi, which subject had been treated by Zingarelli's Giulietta e Romeo in 1796. Famous singers of the role of Zingarelli's Romeo included Crescentini and Giuditta Pasta.

More obviously progressive and Romantic plots occur in Il pirata and La straniera; but this leads us to an important observation about Bellini. At the end of the preceding chapter it was pointed out that choice of subject matter was something that was only finally settled after securing a worthwhile company of singers. In this Bellini fits into the system then prevalent in the first half of the nineteenth century, as did Verdi. However, it will come as no surprise to find that

---

79. Monitore delle due Sicilie, 9 September 1811: it was referred to as a "dramma serio spettacoloso" but was not immediately successful, most of the report concerning itself with the arrival of "LL. MM. il Re e la Regina con tutta la Real Famiglia". Later performances established the opera, however, and next month it was reported: "Il Teatro di S. Carlo prosiegue le rappresentazioni della Vestale con piu fortuna che non si sperava ne' primi giorni" (Monitore delle due Sicilie, 4 October 1811). Its ensuing "series of brilliantly successful performances" was still remembered by Berlioz twenty-five years later (The Memoirs of Berlioz, translated and edited by David Cairns (London, 1969), p.209).
80. Francesco Pastura, Bellini secondo la storia (Parma, 1959), p.103.

often this choice was not so much Bellini's province as that of his librettist. Romani, born in 1788, was already a mature craftsman with his own opinions, an admirer of Metastasio and detractor of Manzoni. His relationship with the young Bellini was therefore very different from that between Verdi and, for example, Piave. It is a striking feature of Verdi's approach that he tended to have an enthusiasm for a particular dramatic subject, and would then try to make some poor librettist adapt it to his demands, as even with early works such as Ernani and Attila. This type of approach was quite as foreign to Bellini as it was to his contemporaries; and it is much more common to find that his subjects came not from his own reading, but from his librettist's.

Thus we find Romani claiming responsibility for the suggestion of Il pirata as a subject for Bellini in a 'Necrologia' issued after Bellini's death.[81] In other words, this most romantic of subjects was not Bellini's choice at all, whose considerations as to suitable librettos tended to revolve round Romani's poetry and old-fashioned sentimental situations such as those in Nina or I puritani. In other places too, Bellini seems to have been happy to defer to Romani's ideas. Thus the decision on La straniera, which as we have seen was left until after the singers were assured, also seems to have been left in doubt for some time. Thus in August 1828 we find Bellini writing that he is expecting Romani to arrive and that, as he puts it, "I hope that Romani will have some good ideas about other plots, which I will need particularly if Rubini can't come".[82] Later, when Romani was with Bellini to work on the opera, he started sorting through possibilities. Bellini

---

81. Weinstock, Vincenzo Bellini, pp.210-211.
82. Cambi, p.150 (6 August 1828): "spero che Romani avrà in testa altri buoni soggetti, che mi saranno necessari specialmente se non potrà venire Rubini".

reports "among those he has re-read to date, he finds la Straniera good, but would take it from the novel and not from the play".[83]

Another highly romantic plot that was later to crop up as a possibility was Ernani. This may well have been Romani's suggestion too, since the reason that it was finally dropped was that when censors demanded changes, Romani did not wish to compromise his artistic integrity. Bellini seems rather detached in his cursory account of the matter, evidently lacking Verdi's later enthusiasm for the subject: "You will know that I am not writing Ernani any more, as the plot would have had to be altered to get through the police, and so Romani, not wanting to be compromised, is now writing la Sonnambula or I due fidanzati svizzeri".[84]

In conclusion it should be pointed out that what is shown here is not that Bellini did not care about his librettos, which he certainly did. What was important to him, however, was not its mere subject matter, but the poetry in which it was couched. It can be seen that, in this respect, he was very much in line with contemporary and traditional thought about operas. Modern writers would tend to be shocked by his non-committal approach to drama, however; and rather gloss over this aspect of his operas, lest it make him seem as frivolous as Rossini was seen to be. It is much easier to understand the dramatic side to Bellini's operas if we see it in the context of operatic aesthetics as a whole. Then we can see that there is a certain logic in

---

83. Luisa Cambi, 'Un pacchetto di autografi', in Scritti in onore di Luigi Ronga, edited by Riccardo Ricciardi (Milan and Naples, 1973), pp.51-90 (p.61 (16 August 1828)): "Egli sin'ora fra quei che ha riletto trova bono la Straniera, ma tirarlo dal Romanzo, e non dalla commedia". Reference to the name "Cambi" will otherwise concern her Vincenzo Bellini, Epistolario (Verona, 1943), as in the following note.
84. Cambi, p.265 (3 January 1831): "Sapete che non scrivo più l'Ernani poiché il soggetto doveva soffrire qualche modificazione per via della polizia, e quindi Romani per non compromettersi l'ha abbandonato, ed ora scrive la Sonnambula ossia I due fidanzati svizzeri".

the Italian approach to the poetic drama, both with regard to its imagined ancestry and bearing in mind Italian attitudes to the power of music to help drama.

The role of the instrumental music, to be explained in the next chapter, was to support the singer and not to emphasize more overtly dramatic articulation in the manner demanded by Joseph Kerman. The idea of drama created in the music is one that only came later in opera. For this reason, other aspects were salient in the libretto. Today the precise words are no longer what is vital in operatic drama, rather it is orchestrally motivated drama. If we understand how the opera of Bellini's time works, however, it is possible that we might be able to see other virtues in his operas rather than merely mourning, or having to ignore, the absence of those we expected to find. In the meantime we are in a similar state to the French audiences Bellini encountered: "in Paris they want music before anything else - they don't understand the language, and they don't care whether the words are beautiful or ugly".[85]

---

85. Luisa Cambi, 'Un pacchetto di autografi', p.81: "a Parigi ci vuole musica avanti tutto - non conoscono la lingua, e non si curano delle belle o delle brutte parole".

CHAPTER 5

THE CONSTITUTION OF THE ORCHESTRA AND
ITS PLACE IN THE MELODRAMMA

The purpose of this chapter is to show in what ways attitudes to opera and music in early nineteenth-century Italy conditioned the constitution and role of the orchestra. This is a very important part of our understanding of opera at this time, because of the emphasis that is now put on its value in any consideration of opera composers. Dramatic articulation through orchestral contributions is a concept that has little place in either the Italian idea of the power of music, discussed in Chapter 2, or in their conception of drama in the libretto, discussed in the last chapter. Therefore it is important to realize that for Italians the orchestra was not something that existed in its own right, but only as part of a greater whole. In this respect it should be remembered that orchestral music was much less developed in Italy than elsewhere, particularly in the south, and that generally speaking "what we call a symphony [meant] nothing to them".[1] Italian opera orchestras developed out of traditional accompaniments to singers and were therefore conceived of from the bass line upwards. As we shall see, this maintained an emphasis on the top and bottom lines of the operatic texture that was briefly referred to at the end of Chapter 2.

That Italians looked askance at instrumental music has already been explained in reference to their understanding of music as being inextricably linked with words. They considered instrumental music to

---

1. The Memoirs of Hector Berlioz, p.186. That orchestral music did develop for a brief time further north is shown by archival evidence from Emilia-Romagna, collected in Marcello Conati and Marcello Pavarani, eds., Orchestre in Emilia-Romagna nell' Ottocento e Novecento (Parma, 1982).

be inferior because bereft of its poetic element. The French and Germans were supposed to have resorted to it because they were not naturally musically gifted and had therefore never learnt to sing properly. This meant that instrumental sections in Italian operas were less important than further north. Ballets, for example, were regarded as extraneous to the poetic element in opera and were never integrated into it as they were in French operas. Consequently ballet music that had to be provided for Italian <u>spettacoli</u>, by different composers, was placed between the two acts but not incorporated into them. Italians continued to prefer their opera without <u>ballabili</u> and large ballets. Thus, in Verdi's <u>Les vêpres siciliènnes</u>, the half-hour ballet proved to be the only unsuccessful part of the opera when transferred to Italy, as it was unacceptable as part of a <u>melodramma</u>.[2] At Bellini's time any music that seemed dance-like risked the ultimate accusation that it tickled the ears instead of touching the heart because it was instrumental in character. "The pleasure aroused by dance-like sections is merely a sensual one that does not affect the heart ... And it seems to us that dance-like sections are really nothing more than instrumental music".[3]

Here we can see how "instrumental music" has become a pejorative term. That is to say, that music that was instrumental in character was criticized as being unpoetic, and vocal music that displayed these characteristics was particularly undesirable. The <u>cabaletta</u> that Rossini had invested with his rhythmic élan was particularly prone to criticism on these lines. As we have seen, this sort of music was

---

2. Budden, II (London, 1978), p.239. The ballet, 'Les quatre saisons', was eventually discarded in Italian productions.
3. <u>Rivista teatrale</u>, 22 January 1825: "Il piacere che destano i <u>ballabili</u> è piacere mero de' sensi che non affetta il cuore ... E mi pare veramente che i <u>ballabili</u> altro non sieno che musica instrumentale e nulla di più".

regarded as a pleasure of the senses; but to become truly acceptable to Italians, music had to revive the *filosofia* of the ancients by working some poetic effect on the heart. This involves accepting that music itself was incapable of expression without words. Therefore cabalettas that seemed to develop a purely musical character of their own were regarded as slightly suspect.

Bellini, on the other hand, was immediately seen as harking back to some golden age by his strong attachment to the words, even at the expense of some purely musical interest. They saw that through his *filosofia*, Bellini tended to shy away from the rhythmic continuity that gave such a dance-like quality to Rossinian arias. This was praised as it suggested a more serious concern for the words, as in this review of La straniera:

> "He is not seduced by the charms of some musical motif that he has invented, and to whatever extent he might consider it capable of great effectiveness, if he sees that the words change, he will then abandon it, and seek out another one that suits the new sentiment. Such is his philosophical approach, that often his phrases remain incomplete, but is this a defect? It is for those people that have become used to *cabalettas* more like country dances, yawning in the audience when they can't hear them, and mechanically clapping momentary effects; they are quite content to just gratify their ears without any sensation ever being felt by the heart". (4)

This is quite an instructive passage as it shows the gravity with which Italians approached the subject of opera, rather than the frivolousness that they are usually credited with. Here again we see how the instrumental character of any piece of operatic music was looked

---

4. L'Indifferente Anno I (Naples, 1830), fascicolo II, p.154: "Il brillante di un imaginato *motivo* non lo seduce e benchè possa egli reputarlo di qual si voglia ottima effetto, se vede che il sentimento dalle parole cangia, ei lo abbandona, ed altro ne va rintracciando che al nuovo sentimento si addica. Una tanta filosofia fa che le sue frasi le spesse volte non sieno finite: ma è questa una colpa? Lo è per coloro, che avezzi alla *cabalette* che sanno di contraddanze, sbadigliano nel teatro qualora non ne ascoltano, e freddi applaudenti di un effetto momentaneo son paghi di solleticar solo il loro orecchio, senza mai che alcuna sensazione ricevono al cuore".

upon with disdain because of its association with mere dance music. Bellini himself seems to have been of a similar opinion since he talks of his ambitions in terms of his joint effort with the singers rather than his ability to create effective instrumental music: "Don't doubt that I will once more have the happy occasion to gain true glory with the singers and my music, without the battle scenes, volcanoes, ballets and other spectacles, that attract great crowds to theatres".(5) His mention of "Vesuvi" probably refers to Pacini's Gli ultimi giorni di Pompei produced at the San Carlo, Naples in 1825. Such spectacular effects were, like ballets, parts of operas that relied on orchestras rather than singers, and as such looked down on by Bellini, who regarded his opera as being a combined presentation by singers and composer. Orchestras in Italy were designed for this purpose rather than Pacini's, as this chapter will show.

To show how different this traditional attitude to the power of music was compared with the growing instrumental culture developing in northern Europe, it is fascinating to compare the utterances by Stendhal and E. T. A. Hoffman on the subject. Stendhal still saw instrumental music as essentially artificial as in the views of Eximeno, Milizia and Lichtenthal referred to in Chapter 3.

> "A hunting horn, echoing over the hills of the Scottish highlands, can be heard at a considerably greater distance than the human voice. In this respect, but in this respect only, art has out-distanced nature: art has succeeded in increasing the volume of sound produced. But in respect of something infinitely more important, namely inflexion and ornamentation, the human voice still maintains its superiority over any instrument yet invented, and it might even be claimed that no instrument is satisfactory except in so far as it approximates to the sound of the human voice". (6)

---

5. Cambi, pp.104-105 (9 June 1828): "non dubitare che avrò ancor io il felice momento di farmi vero onore con i cantanti e la musica, senza Combattimenti, Vesuvi, Ballabili ed altri spettacoli, che l'insieme attira il gran mondo al teatro".
6. Stendhal, Life of Rossini, p.367.

One can best see the heart of the difference between this outlook and that of the German school by comparing it with E. T. A. Hoffman's review of Beethoven's instrumental music:

> "When we speak of music as an independent art, should we not always restrict our meaning to instrumental music, which, scorning every aid, every admixture of another art (the art of poetry), gives pure expression to music's specific nature, recognizable in this form alone?" (7)

Hoffman's enthusiastic view dates from considerably earlier than Stendhal's and shows the contrast that had developed between the views of committed professional musicians and traditional literary approaches to music. The German school is the one that grew in influence in the nineteenth century so that Berlioz, who had great contempt for Stendhal's views on music,(8) was able to develop the expressive powers of orchestral music and centred his approach to the subject of Romeo and Juliet on a purely instrumental love scene. Such a view of the powers of music was something that came to Italy only much later. Italians continued to consider the orchestra as an extension of the bass line that accompanied singers, as we shall see. This means for us that we have to completely adjust our view of the role and constitution of it if we are to see it in the same light. Since the time of Wagner and Mahler, we have become accustomed to opera as being under the general control of a conductor, standing as it were outside the orchestra and treating it as a self-sufficient entity. In the opera-house, he usually also holds the role of the director of music. In considering opera at this time, we have to be aware both that such a position did not exist in Bellini's day, and also that the very terms

---

7. Strunk, *Source Readings*, p.775. This dates from 1813, but an earlier version devoted to Beethoven's Fifth Symphony appeared in AMZ in 1810 and, translated, can be found in Ludwig van Beethoven, *Symphony No. 5 in C Minor*, edited by Elliot Forbes, a Norton Critical Score (London, 1971), pp.150-163.
8. See Matteini, pp.293-299.

used had different meanings at the time.

Because, for musical reasons, the post of conductor was non-existent, and because the music, as we shall see, was, for historical reasons, more under the control of the maestro al cembalo, the term direttore delle opere should not be taken to mean conductor but overall 'musical director'. Financial control was under the impresario or appaltatore. This meant, for most of the period at La Scala and at Naples, Domenico Barbaja. Mention of musical directors was in any case rare at this time. Newspaper reviews, which are generally speaking sporadic in Naples until about 1830, only refer to musical directors directly in the case of the appearance of the composer in the orchestra during particular performances. Such a position was not standard at other times. Thus the list of the appalto for the Carnival season 1823-24 at Naples does not mention the orchestra at all, despite listing in detail "the leading artists who have appeared in these productions",[9] including all the main and secondary singers and ballerini, as well as the composers; no mention is given at all of anyone who directed proceedings, either on or off stage.

In overall charge of musical, as opposed to financial, matters when Bellini arrived at Naples in 1819, was Rossini; who is described as "charged with the direction of operas at the Royal Theatres" in a subscription prospectus of 1820 in the State Archives.[10]

This post of overall supervision of musical matters existed in the absence of a conductor. It was later held by Carlo Coccia (1782-1873) and Donizetti. As conductors in a more modern sense rose from

---

9. Rivista teatrale, 21 February 1824: "gli artisti primari che hanno agito in questi spettacoli".
10. Naples, Archivo di Stato (henceforth A/S), Sezione Amministrativa, Fondo Teatri (henceforth F.T.), fascio 133 (Imprese diverse), 'Prospetto d'abbonamento': "e incaricato da Direzione delle Opere de' Reali Teatri".

the ranks of the orchestra, this role became more an honorary title. Thus Mercadante is described as "direttore onorario delle musiche de' Reali Teatri"[11] in 1851, when he was past the most important part of his composing career and had, in 1840, become director of the Conservatory of Music. Effective musical control changed with the gradual rise of musical <u>direttori</u> from the orchestra or from the <u>maestro al cembalo</u>. From which of the two the post of the conductor, and thus the real musical director, came is a matter of dispute and probably varied from theatre to theatre. The problem will be considered later in the chapter.

An idea of the hierarchy at the San Carlo at Naples can be gleaned from the listings in a contemporary handbook, the <u>Almanacco de' Reali Teatri</u> for 1834.[12] In this the mention of the orchestra and its leadership comes very far down the list on page 13. The <u>Primo violino e direttore dell' orchestra</u> is the name of the post, but does not signify control of the opera as a whole; which is important to the nature of the opera itself. The top of the hierarchy is accorded to the main officers of the <u>impresa</u>, the "Società Commerciale in anonimo d'Industria e Belle Arti". This is followed by the directors of stage machinery, decoration and scene-painting: it will be remembered that Arteaga listed the three most important ingredients of opera as <u>poesia</u>, <u>musica</u> and <u>decorazione</u>. Next but still far above the orchestra comes a list of the main posts under the title "Poesia e Musica".[13] These are:

"D. Giovanni Schmidt, poeta
D. Andrea Passaro, poeta e concertatore
D. Salvatore Cammarano, poeta e concertatore
D. Giuseppe Doglia, concertatore al cembalo

---

11. A/S, F.T., fascio 127 (Orchestre personale).
12. <u>Almanacco de' Reali Teatri S. Carlo e Fondo dell' annata teatrale 1834</u> (Naples, 1835), pp.3-29.
13. <u>Almanacco de' Reali Teatri</u>, pp.6-7.

D. Giuseppe Trimarchi, concertatore de' cori
D. Giuseppe Latilla, concertatore de' cori"

In this particular list, no mention is made of an overall direttore delle opere such as Rossini or Mercadante. However, in the listing of the appalto for that year, Carlo Coccia is named as "Maestro Idrettore della Musica" by a Neapolitan newspaper.[14]

In agreement with the importance given to the poetry, the librettists' names come first. The names of composers appear much later in the Almanacco, partly because they were not regarded as staff of the impresa but instead were scritturati. The titles of the poets or librettists make clear the fact that they were responsible for direction on stage during rehearsal.[15] Their duties as concertatori would therefore make them more akin to what today would be called opera producers.

The Almanacco also mentions D. Domenico Cartosia as Direttore del palcoscenico.[16]

Perhaps most important of all for the understanding of opera at this time, however, is the position of D. Giuseppe Doglia as Concertatore al cembalo. His inclusion in this list of important offices for Poesia e Musica shows that the office of maestro al cembalo still had more respect than anything in the orchestra. The idea of a conductor which, in the case of Habeneck in contemporary Paris, developed out of the orchestral leader, had so far made little impact on Italian opera. Today the office of the maestro al cembalo, except where occupied by the composer himself, would seem more akin to the répétiteur than anything else. But at this time, the office stood in place of the composer in the orchestral pit. In fact it would probably be fair to say

---

14. L'Omnibus, 31 May 1834, 'Teatri, Prospetto di appalto pel Real Teatro di S. Carlo dal 30 maggio 1834 a tutto il carnevale 1835'.
15. See Kimbell, p.54.
16. Almanacco de' Reali Teatri, p.5.

that much of the orchestral texture that had developed in Italian opera by Bellini's time was an extension of that of the basso continuo. For this reason the constitution of the orchestral accompaniment will be considered first from the point of view of the maestro al cembalo. Afterwards the growth of new methods of operatic direction will be considered.

We shall therefore try to see the orchestra in terms of a development of the practice, described by Mancini, of providing an instrumental standard of pitch for singers. This was obviously, in the first place, a practical aid and not an end in itself so that we should hardly be surprised that unnecessary sophistications are not encouraged. "In fact to anyone who understands music, the ancient rules for accompanying singing class are well known, the fingers should be used on the keyboard with discretion, it is not necessary to introduce decorations in a fanciful manner, instead a very firm and simple accompaniment is required, so that the singer is in no way incommoded".[17] This manner of using the accompaniment primarily as a means of ensuring good intonation is also advocated by Marcello Perrino.[18]

In all these cases the instrumental part is almost disregarded from the artistic point of view, and is no more than the means by which the pitch could be maintained. Rather like the setting of a jewel, it is a necessity rather than the contributor to an artistic whole. The idea that these discrete elements should be integrated was one that came later. In many ways the characteristics demanded by Mancini of the accompaniments are expressed negatively and limit the encroachment

---

17. Mancini, pp.73-74: "Infatti, a chiunque conosce la Musica, son note le vecchie vecchissime regole, che per accompagnare un Professore di canto, devonsi adoperare sul Cembalo poche dita, non vi vogliono grazie aggiunte a capriccio, ma richiedesi il più sodo, e semplice accompagnamento, acciò [che] il cantante in verun modo non sia disturbato".
18. Perrino, p.22.

of instrumental music on vocal music. It was supposed to be a simple accompaniment that in no way disturbed the singing. For this purpose he recommends the use of "poche dita".

Mancini is here referring to solfeggios, which are important as showing the strong link that existed between composer and performer. Eximeno writes that "before the student begins to tackle the study of counterpoint, he should get practice in song ... with the sole aim of acquiring good taste".[19] Composers began to study through solfeggios in much the same way that singers did as is pointed out by Andrea della Corte, noting that later these would be used by composers to accustom singers to their particular style.[20]

What this means is that solfeggios served the purpose of developing a composer's style so that it would be genuinely vocal, and also of familiarizing singers with a composer's particular technical demands. Such a close link between singer and composition is radically different today; but certainly existed up until the time of Bellini, some of whose solfeggios still exist. Our precise knowledge of the solfeggios is limited by the fact that there were no Italian publications of them. Any good singing teacher was supposed to be able to write solfeggios himself, and only, as Tosi puts it, "if the teacher is unable to compose let him provide himself with good solfeggios of varying styles which develop imperceptibly from the easy to the difficult, according to the progress that he notices the student making from them".[21] He thus composed them in much the same way as composers wrote them as exercises. Interest in Italian *bel canto* grew in France and it was with this development that solfeggios began to be published. The first

---

19. Eximeno, p.312, note ii: "prima che lo Scolare intraprenda lo studio del contrappunto si eserciterà nel canto ... solo per formare il gusto".
20. Andrea della Corte, Canto e bel canto (Turin, 1933), p.233.
21. Tosi, p.13: "Se'l Maestro non sa comporre si provegga di buoni solfeggi di stile diverso, che insensibilmente passino dal facile al difficile a misura del profitto, che scorge nello Scolaro".

examples were in a vast collection, Solfèges d'Italie (Paris, 1772), which contained examples by Neapolitan composers such as Leo, Durante and A. Scarlatti and went through many editions. Mancini also emphasizes solfeggios and advises students to move on from elementary examples to well written pieces by Leo, Porpora and Hasse.[22]

An example (No.1) will show how such compositions displayed the archetypal baroque texture of a sustained vocal line and a single bass line designed to support it:

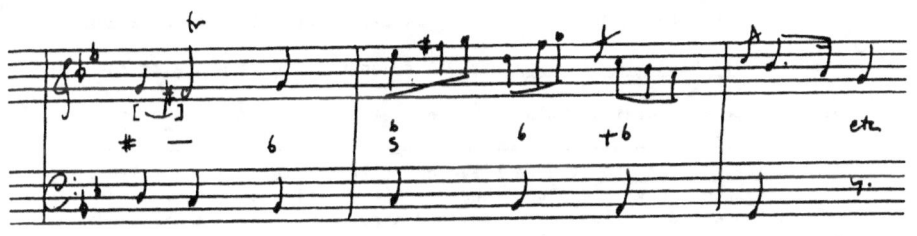

Example 1: Solfèges d'Italie avec la basse chiffrée, no. 88 (Paris, 1798)

In the preface to the collection, the editors make it plain that even the chordal figures were not supplied in the original manuscripts: "The majority were not figured because it is usual in Italy to

---

22. Mancini, p.244.

accompany without this help".[23] Thus the two-part texture is further emphasized in the originals. Crescentini's solfeggios in his Raccolta di essercizi of 1811 are quite similar, but Rossini's Gorgeggi e solfeggi of 1827 are more modern in that they are supplied with piano accompaniments as are most nineteenth century collections.

This two-part texture was important, but so also was the fact that the composer learnt his craft primarily from the point of view of the singer's accompanist. In the performance of his works this became formalized in the role of maestro al cembalo, as one part of an age-old system of dual command; controlling proceedings in harness with the orchestral leader, whose responsibilities were more purely tied to the instrumental contribution.

It was, as Stendhal writes, the general rule that "the maestro who wrote the opera [is] required to conduct the performance of his own music from the piano during the first three performances".[24] This practice was established by contract, as can be seen in Rossini's contract for Il barbiere di Siviglia,[25] to ensure his presence at the performances to receive applause[26] as well as to direct the first

---

23. Solfèges d'Italie avec la basse chiffrée (Paris, n.d. (c. 1798)), 'Preface', p.v: "La plus grande partie n'était pas chiffrée parce qu'on est dans l'usage en Italie d'accompagner sans ce secours".
24. Stendhal, Life of Rossini, p.445. The original also refers to the use of the piano; Stendhal, Vie de Rossini, edited by Henri Martineau, 2 vols (Paris, 1929), II, 272: "Il est de règle que le maestro qui a écrit l'opera dirige l'execution de son musique au piano, durant les trois premières représentations".
25. This is printed in Giuseppe Radiciotti, Gioacchino Rossini. Vita documentata. Opere ed influenza su l'arte, 3 vols (Tivoli, 1927-1929), I, 178-180. Dated 15 December 1815, it tells us: "Il maestro Rossini sarà inoltre obbligato a dirigere la sua opera secondo l'uso e d'assistere personalmente a tutte le prove ... anche di assistere alle prime rappresentazioni che saranno date consecutivamente e di dirigere l'esecuzione al cembalo ecc.". Rossini would then be paid, "terminate le tre prime rappresentazioni che dovrà dirigere al cembalo".
26. It would seem that in Bellini's time, the composer was actually received on stage as reported by I teatri of Milan in 1830 (see Cambi, p.241), whereas this "onore che venne accordato al maestro ... non confortò mai il maestro Rossini" (Il caffè del molo, number 3 (Naples, 1829), p.4).

three nights. Stendhal's references are to Rossini at the piano rather than the harpsichord[27] and it may indeed seem surprising that harpsichords could have been available in nineteenth-century Italy. Burney had already pointed out that they were all "more wood than wire" in Italy in 1770,[28] so they were unlikely to have been much cultivated. Some positive references to harpsichords do exist, however: thus Stefano Pavesi (1779-1850) is identified as taking charge of his Il trionfo dell' amore at the "gravicembalo" in 1811;[29] and, turning to a reference in English, Byron reports the premiere of Edoardo e Cristina at Venice in 1819 by saying that "there has been a splendid Opera lately at San Benedetto - by Rossini - who came in person to play the Harpsichord".[30]

Bellini, too, had to make such appearances. His first important biographer, Filippo Cicconetti, refers to it as standard practice of earlier times when writing of the premiere of Zaira at Parma in 1829: "At that time the unpleasant and cruel custom still obtained, that the composers, already shaken by severe anxiety, had to appear at the keyboard".[31] Other references are to Bellini at the premiere of Beatrice di Tenda in 1833 being applauded "at his first appearance at the keyboard",[32], "there between the cello and violone".[33] In

---

27. Stendhal, Vie de Rossini, I, 156: "Nous avons laissé Rossini faisant répéter son opera a un mauvais piano"; I, 160: "Rossini se lève de sa place au piano ... il fait trois saluts, est couvert d'applaudissements", etc.
28. Charles Burney, Music, Men and Manners in France and Italy 1770, edited by H. Edmund Poole (London, 1974), p.69.
29. Monitore delle due Sicilie, 6 June 1811: "Il sig. Pavesi, che stava assiso al gravicembalo in capo all'orchestra, riceve i segni lusingieri della generale approvazione".
30. Byron's Letters and Journals, edited by Leslie A. Marchand, 12 vols (London, 1976), VI, 132.
31. Filippo Cicconetti, Vita di Vincenzo Bellini (Prato, 1859), p.46: "In quel tempo durava tuttavia il costume non civile e tormentatore, che i maestri di musica già da penosa ansietà internamente agitati dovessero assistere al cembalo".
32. L'Eco, 20 March 1833; quoted after Cambi, p.341: "Al suo primo comparire al cembalo fu salutato".
33. Gazzetta privilegiata di Venezia, 18 March 1833; quoted after Cambi, p.339: "lì fra il violoncello e il violone".

fact the practice seems to have lasted some time, perhaps partly based on the idea that the composer turned the pages for the principal cello and double-bass, a practice that Pacini claimed to have stopped at Naples in 1839.[34] However, the role is properly understood as a continuation of that of the <u>maestro al cembalo</u>. This is explained clearly by Lichtenthal in his <u>Dizionario</u> of 1826 as a natural progression from the early rehearsals by composer or répétiteur to the full presentation:

> "The rehearsals of an Opera begin usually just with the singers at the **keyboard**, attended by the composer himself, or else by the maestro who is to sit at the **keyboard** in the theatre; after which come the so-called <u>provette</u>, or string rehearsals, that is with Violins, Viola and Bass; then follow the <u>full orchestral rehearsals</u>, then finally the two <u>dress rehearsals</u>". (35)

Just as the instrumental part of a solfeggio was still confined to a bass line, so was the main weight of the instrumental part of an opera. This can be seen both in the composition of opera scores and in their orchestral performance. The aesthetic reasons for this were historically well established by this time and easy to find. J. J. Rousseau praised Italians in his <u>Lettre sur la musique française</u> (1753) for their avoidance of counterpoints which would conflict with vocal lines and for their concentration on the bass line:

> "I well understood how the bass, being the foundation of all harmony, should always prevail over the rest, and that when the other parts stifle it or cover it up, this causes a confusion which makes the harmony less distinct; and I saw in this the reason why the Italians, so economical with the right hand in accompanying, ordinarily play the octave of the bass with the left; why they have so many double-basses in their orchestras; and why they so often make their violas proceed with the bass, instead of giving them a separate part as the French never fail to do". (36)

---

34. See Kimbell, p.44. He is described by Mendelssohn, <u>Reisebriefe aus den Jahren 1830 bis 1832</u>, ed. P. Mendelssohn-Bartholdy (Leipzig, 1865), p.110 (17 January 1831): "Nun erschien Pacini am Clavier und wurde empfangen".
35. Lichtenthal, II, 139: "Le prove d'un' Opera principiano ordinariamente co' soli cantanti al Cembalo, assistiti dallo stesso Compositore della musica, oppure dal maestro che è destinato di stare al Cembalo del teatro; dopo di ciò si fanno le così dette <u>provette</u>, o prove di quartetto, cioè: co' Violini, Viola e Basso; poscia seguono le <u>prove a grand' orchestra</u>, indi l'<u>antiprova generale</u>, e finalmente la <u>prova generale</u>.
36. Strunk, p.646.

Algarotti also makes a plea for the reinforcement of the bass line, and avoidance of "a multitude of fiddles etc., that ... in general produce no better an effect than to astonish the faculty of hearing and to drown the voice of a singer. Why is there not more use made of the basses, and why not increase the number of bass viols, which are the shades of music".[37] The reader will remember that Ferro is still saying the same in 1807.[38]

All available accounts of Italian opera orchestras seem to suggest that the old Italian custom of employing more double-basses than cellos prevailed during the first half of the nineteenth century:[39] Spohr describes the orchestra at Florence for L'Italiana in Algeri in 1816 as using six or eight double-basses to one rather weak cello. He particularly lamented the lack of any individual cello writing in the tenor range in the German manner.[40] Indications of orchestral constitutions tend to confirm Spohr's lament that Italians were not interested in writing for middle voices and conforms to the idea adumbrated by Rousseau that counterpoints should be avoided. Thus the cellos are relegated to doubling the basses at the octave, rather than being melodic instruments sometimes doubled themselves at the lower octave by the double-basses. This holds good for the accompanimental textures that occur throughout Bellini's works and this is their origin. In the following example (No.2), taken from I Capuleti e i Montecchi, the bottom line is marked "Bassi" in the autograph manuscript, and the cello line is left blank, but to be understood as following the bass. No other instruments are used, and the harmonic infilling is thus left to the violins, which manage not to interfere with the voice by avoiding

---

37. Strunk, p.668.
38. See Chapter 2, note 42.
39. See Adam Carse, The Orchestra from Beethoven to Berlioz (Cambridge, 1948), p.27.
40. Spohr, I, 286-288.

the important beats, and to the violas. The violas are divided despite their paltry numbers, and this practice is reflected in orchestral layouts, as we shall see. Consequently the texture is essentially two-part reflecting its ancestry in the two-part texture of solfeggios:

Example 2: Bellini *I Capuleti e i Montecchi*, aut. MS p.130 (Catania, Museo Belliniano).

The general character of this texture reflects the long history of Italian opera from the Baroque era onwards, despite the obvious changes in the style of composition. With regard to Baroque orchestration, Bukofzer has described the heavy reinforcement of the outer lines which left the less essential middle parts to the improvised realizations of the continuo.[41] Naturally this implies no poverty in the actual harmonizations, but only reflects the initial Baroque conception of the music. Consequently the inner parts of an eighteenth-century aria were not generally fully worked out. With the greatly increased size of Italian orchestras, numbering as many as seventy players in the largest eighteenth-century theatres, such harpsichord accompaniments began to be inadequate as harmonic support for the whole orchestral texture. Newer styles of composition required more sustained accompaniments. These harmonies were assigned to the string parts instead, needing no addition from harpsichords. It was rare, however, for such inner parts to be elaborated further so as to become sources of musical interest in their own right. The only articulation to such a texture in the Bellini example is the discreet see-sawing of the violins, more to sustain the harmony than to offer competing part writing to the voice.

With regard to the bass line, Adam Carse has shown comprehensively that it was only towards the end of the eighteenth century that the bass part in the full score ceased to be a bass part in general, and began to be split into separate parts, each designed for specific instruments.[42] In the German symphonic tradition this had changed considerably by the early nineteenth century, but Italians lacked such a tradition and were not surprisingly more conservative. This explains

---

41. Manfred Bukofzer, Music in the Baroque Era, p.382.
42. Adam Carse, The Orchestra in the Eighteenth Century (Cambridge, 1940; reprinted New York, 1969), p.146.

Spohr's complaints about the lack of individual cello writing in the tenor register. It is an indication of the influence still exerted by the long history of generalized continuo basses.

Carse devotes considerable space to describing the variability of performance of such generalized basses, including the question of the various instrumentations used, whatever the actual indications in the scores.[42a] The growing rigour of German symphonic orchestrations naturally began to rule out such licence, but it seems reasonable to expect its effect to have been still felt in Italian opera of Bellini's time. The comments of Ferdinand Simon Gassner (1798-1851) in his Dirigent und Ripienist (1844) suggest fairly explicitly that cello players were still expected to be competent to fill out a figured bass by providing the correct chords, whilst the Double Bass maintained the written bass.[43] This was still particularly useful in the performance of recitatives. The extent that such skills were actually called upon would presumably have depended on the density of the textures already present in the scores.

In this respect it has to be admitted that it is not particularly easy to determine precise details of performance practice in Italy during the early nineteenth century. That many of these old-fashioned practices were still held to is suggested by the following passage from Lichtenthal's dictionary of 1826. There are strong echoes in this of the traditions of continuo-harmony. Lichtenthal is explaining various practices generally employed to compensate for the weaknesses of three-stringed Italian Double-Basses through the addition of what he calls 'strumenti di Rinforzo'.

> "In full orchestral music one often reinforces the Double-basses. The instruments that help in this capacity are:
> 1) The violas, which (not using them for true four-part

42a. Carse, The Orchestra in the Eighteenth Century, pp.122-126.
43. Robert Haas, Auffuhrungspraxis (Potsdam, 1934), p.264.

writing), as a four-foot register linked to the eight-foot register of the Violoncellos, are placed against the sixteen-foot Violone".

To the violas, Lichtenthal adds

"the second violins, which produce a good effect in various ways, reinforcing patterned basses".

He concludes that

"Someone has proposed using the violas or other higher pitched instruments in perfect fifths with the Bass, thereby imitating the 'quint' of the full organ, but as yet no one has hazarded an attempt at this proposal".

Other instruments advocated by Lichtenthal in this regard include bassoons, trombones, horns, trumpets, clarinets, oboes, flutes in their upper octaves, and piccolos.[44]

To a modern reader this seems rather excessive, and no doubt the list represents all the different instruments so employed at various times. It seems less strange when the long history of Italian continuo technique is borne in mind, and the great importance accorded to bass lines by writers such as Algarotti, Rousseau and Ferro. Quite apart from the question of actual orchestral practices, there is little doubt as to the certainty of his views and the traditions they embody. Lichtenthal was more cosmopolitan than many of his Italian contemporaries, being Austrian by birth, and "an ardent supporter of Mozart's chamber works".[45] His dictionary and bibliography suggest he was generally well acquainted with contemporary practices and writings on music. Yet, compared

---

44. Lichtenthal, II, 155-156: "Nelle musiche a grand' orchestra si usa sovente a rinforzare i Contrabbassi. Gli strumenti che a tal uopo servono sono:
1) Le Viole, le quali (non trattandosi di scrivere un vero a quattro), come Registro di 4 piedi unito al Registro di 8 piedi dei Violoncelli, tengono il contrapposto al Violone di 16 piedi. 2) I Fagotti ... 3) Il Trombone ... 4) I Violini secondi, i quali in varj casi producono un grand' effetto, rinforzando in Basso figurato. [It is not impossible but less likely that this refers instead to "figured bass" in the English sense.] ...
5) Il Corno e la Tromba, 6) Il Clarinetto ne' suoi gravi suoni, 7) L'Oboè pure ne' suoni profondi, 8) Il Flauto nelle sue più acute Ottave, e finalmente 9) l'Ottavino.
Taluno ha proposto di far andare le Viole od altri strumenti più acuti in Quinte perfette col Basso, imitando così il Registro di ripieno di Quinta nell' Organo; ma nessuno ha ancora azzardato d'approfittare di tale proposizione".
45. Alfred Loewenberg and Bruce Carr, 'Lichtenthal', in The New Grove, 20 vols (London, 1980), X, 825.

with what was already happening with French and German composers, the attitude here is old-fashioned in its unscored use of bassoons to double the bass line. By this tradition the Italian orchestra would sound not so much like 'a big guitar'[46] as like a full organ.

Naturally enough French and German musicians were no longer in sympathy with this type of <u>basso-continuo</u> orchestra, and often referred to it contemptuously. The tradition of <u>strumenti di Rinforzo</u> was ridiculed by Weber thus: "Oboi col Flauti, Clarinetti col Oboi, Flauti col Violini, Fagotti col Basso, Viol 2do col Primo, Viola col Basso, Voce ad libitum, Violino colla parte".[47]

The difference of point of view is quite clear, of course; but in fact Weber makes a technical error here. Whereas the point of his ridicule is that the whole orchestra is <u>colla parte</u>, in fact he would have done better to dismiss the orchestra as <u>col basso</u> in apposition to the vocal line. What was lacking was the existence or even interest in contrapuntal filling in, which is the source of Berlioz's disgusted comment that "even in the kind of music that Italian orchestras normally play" the habitual use of more double-basses than cellos was unjustified.[48]

Before northern musicians had worked up such disdain for Italian traditions, however, some correspondents reported the effect favourably as in this report of 1802 in the Leipzig <u>Allgemeine Musikalische Zeitung</u>: "At any rate, I have noticed that the Italians lay out their orchestra with a stronger bass than is usual amongst us, and I always found the resulting effect very good; and also the other voices were

---

46. Compare differing reactions to this 'big guitar' idea in Dyleney Hussey, <u>Verdi</u> (London, 1940), p.28; and Leslie Orrey, <u>Bellini</u> (London, 1969), p.133.
47. From Max von Weber, <u>C. M. von Weber, ein Liebesbild</u>, 3 vols (Leipzig, 1864); quoted after Carse, <u>The Orchestra from Beethoven to Berlioz</u>, p.268.
48. <u>The Memoirs of Hector Berlioz</u>, p.196.

thus brought out more clearly rather than being covered up".[49] In other words, the effect, at least in theory, was that emphasis of the bass line brought out better the other voices. In the case of the Italians this could hardly refer to anything but the vocal line.

Lists of early orchestras in Naples and elsewhere in Italy are rare. Such eighteenth century ones as exist show the orchestras to have been very large in the main theatres.[50] That at the San Carlo in Naples numbered seventy in 1740 with two cellos, four double-basses and two harpsichords, with a similar number at La Scala in 1778 including thirteen "bassi da arco". The Enciclopedia dello spettacolo[51] conjectures this as being divided into eight cellos and five double-basses, but does not explain on what basis, except presumably that of modern practice; and indeed the reverse seems more in line with contemporary usage. Ulisse Prota-Giurleo provides lists for the San Carlo in Naples as reorganized by Paisiello in c.1796 which note fifty-one players including twenty-five violins, four violas, two cellos and six double-basses, and two harpsichords; and also for the smaller Teatro Nuovo and Teatro Fiorentino.[52]

A slightly larger orchestra can be found at the San Carlo in 1808 listed in a petition for payment preserved in the State Archives.[53]

---

49. AMZ IV, col. 784n. (23 August 1802): "Wenigstens habe ich bemerkt, dass die Italiener ihre Orchester mit Bässen stärker besetzen, als bey uns gemeiniglich geschiehet, und die Würkung davon fand ich immer sehr gut; auch wurden die andern Stimmen dadurch mehr gehoben, als verdeckt".
50. See Adam Carse, The Orchestra in the Eighteen Century, p.24; see also the article 'Orchestra' in Enciclopedia dello spettacolo, 11 vols (Rome, 1954-1966), VII, col. 1392; Ulisse Prota-Giurleo, La grande orchestra del R. Teatro San Carlo nel Settecento (Naples, 1927).
51. The author of this part of the article is not specified.
52. Robinson, p.161. See Prota-Giurleo, p.53.
53. A/S, F.T., fascio 125 ('Personale degli artisti di canto'), Petition dated 13 December 1808 and signed "Francesco Mercier primo violino per tutti". The list indicates that Mercier is the leader of the orchestra; by 1810 Giuseppe Maria Festa (1771-1839) is referred to in this post; see below note 79.

The list, which includes the players' names, shows it constituted thus:

14	Violins I	2	Flutes
10	Violins II	2	Oboes
6	Violas	2	Clarinets
6	Cellos	2	Trumpets
10	Double-basses	2	Corni di Caccia
1	"Cembalista"	2	Bassoons
		1	Tympanist

Also referred to are two "Pmo violino di Ballo".

Another list, in the Allgemeine Musikalische Zeitung, shows the orchestra similarly constituted, given the estimate of twenty-four violins, in 1818.[54] This report shows the layout of the orchestra, which divides the strings into two halves:

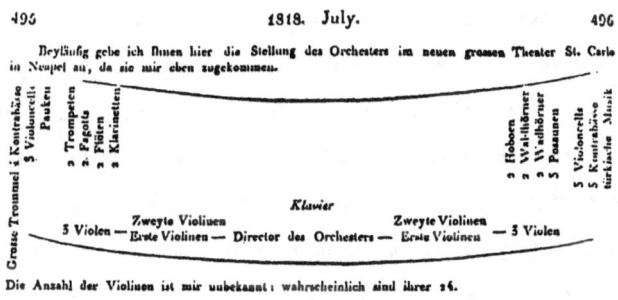

This can be compared with a similar list for the Milan orchestra at La Scala in 1825:[55]

---

54. AMZ, XX, cols. 495-496 (8 July 1818); see also Carse, The Orchestra from Beethoven to Berlioz, p.475.
55. AMZ XXVII, cols. 131-132 (23 February 1825); see also Carse, The Orchestra from Beethoven to Berlioz, p.474, where, however, the list is taken from The Harmonicon and mistranslates "Primo violino de' secondi": it should be understood as referring to the leader of the second violins.

```
                                                                    I Serpentono
     Banda.                II Corni                                 III Tromboni
 (türkische Musik)  II Corni  (abwechselnd)  II Fagotti  II Clarinetti  II Oboe  II Flauti  II Trombe             Timpani
```

```
                    VI Violini secondi    Primo Violino    VI Violini secondi.  II Viole.
                                          de' Secondi
```

```
 IV Contrabassi.
 II Violoncelli.                                                           III Contrabassi.
 I Violoncello Cembalo I Contrabasso                                       III Violoncelli.
     VI Violini primi.    Capo d'orchestra.    VI Violini primi.    IV Viole.
```

The divisions of the lower strings on the plans are into equal groups, and the position of the violas as <u>strumenti di Rinforzo</u> rather than as individual voice parts in their own right is shown by their similar fragmentation despite their paltry numbers. This division into two groups of three violas may well have been responsible for their habitual use <u>divisi</u> in the works of Bellini and his contemporaries as harmonic infilling, as in Example No.2. Any idea of greater interest being accorded middle voices, such as viola parts, would seem to have been summed up by Donizetti's (possibly apocryphal) couplet:

"Quattro rose fanno un mazzo
Ma quattro viole non fanno un c ..." (56)

The stability in numbers of the San Carlo orchestra may well have bred complacency, but it is hard to assess the actual standard at Naples because contemporary reports depend on the sympathies of the writer to Italian practices. Thus Stendhal is wildly enthusiastic, comparing it of course favourably to French orchestras, and even to

---

56. Gino Monaldi, 'Orchestre e direttore del secolo XIX', in <u>Rivista Musicale Italiana</u> XVI (1909), pp.123-142, 531-549 (p.138).

that of La Scala, where the orchestra "cringes before the singers".[57]
In 1817, Spohr also reported that the orchestra under Giuseppe Maria
Festa (1779-1839) was "precise but lacking in nuances of piano and
forte".[58] Even Berlioz was not dismissive, saying "I went to the
San Carlo and there, for the first time since coming to Italy, heard
music. The orchestra, compared with those I had encountered till then,
struck me as excellent. One could safely listen to the wind instruments. The violins were competent, and the cellos played with a good
singing tone, though there were too few of them".[59]

Nor should we assume, because the role of the orchestra was very
strictly confined in contemporary aesthetic thought, that its actual
quality was totally ignored by Italians themselves. It had to know its
place; but it also had to be good. Thus at a performance of Rossini's
Zelmira in 1824 the Rivista teatrale complained that "all the tempi
were wrong, so that often one tempo was immediately changed as many as
three times, some bars were reduced to hardly a half or an eighth of
their length, and another was increased accordingly, not of course to
follow the singer's greater or lesser animated delivery, but in opposition to it".[60] Italians were not uncritical of orchestras but saw
their role as being that of the follower of the singer: already the lack
of a conductor was causing noticeable problems.

Domenico Barbaja, the impresario at Naples, very soon found that
standards were not as high as he hoped, because of absenteeism.[61]
Later he proposed changes to the authorities because of the age of

---

57. Stendhal, Life of Rossini, pp.449-450.
58. Spohr, II, 13.
59. The Memoirs of Hector Berlioz, p.196.
60. Rivista teatrale, 14 July 1824: "tutti i tempi sono stati falsi, che spesso uno stesso tempo ha subito sino a tre variazioni, che qualche battuta è giunta appena ad un quarto e un ottava, ed alcune altra è cresciuta d'altrettanto, ma non già per seguire l'espressione più o meno animata del cantante, ma in opposizione di quello".
61. A/S, F.T., fascio 127, letter of 15 May 1813.

many of the professori of the orchestra which resulted in "all the deficiencies which have so far given rise to justified grounds for continuous remonstrations from the public in general and particularly from connoisseurs following the frequently imperfect playing in the operas and always most imperfect playing in the ballets".[62]

The orchestra seems to have been reformed in 1833 when Barbaja lost his control of the Reali Teatri temporarily to the Compagnia d'Industria e Belle Arti under the control of Alessandro Lañari, with whom Bellini had much fruitless correspondence. A list of the new players including all their names appears in a 'Notamento' of March 1833 supervised by Bellini's friend, Florimo.[63] This list is again larger than earlier ones, listing seventy-eight names; but the precise number in the orchestra cannot easily be determined, although it must have been a large one, as another list appeared published in the Almanacco de' Reali Teatri for 1834 which augments it even further.[64] Evidently the potential forces were large but had to serve the Teatro del Fondo, the smaller Real Teatro, as well. Of the two lists, the 'Notamento' seems the more probable. What is immediately obvious compared with the lists of 1808 and 1818 is that there is no mention of a

---

62. A/S, F.T., fascio 127, letter of 10 March 1825 to the Duca di Noja, Presidente delle Real Deputazione de' Teatri e Spettacoli in Napoli: "tutti gl' inconvenienti che han dato finora giusti motivi di continue rimostranze al Pubblico in generale e maggiormente a' Conoscitori in seguito della esecuzione spesso non perfetta nelle Opere, e sempre imperfettissima ne' Balli". There are also further letters from Barbaja on the same subject, noting professori retired on grounds of old age; letter of 17 December 1832, "A. S. E. Il Ppe di Ruffano, soprintend^e de Teatri e Spettacoli".
63. A/S, F.T., fascio 127, 'Notamento degli Individui scelti dalla Commissione di esame per far parte dell' Orchestra e del corpo de' Cori pel servizio de' Reali Teatri nel nuovo anno teatrale 1833 al 1834'; this is signed "Il Presidente delle Commissione, Giulio Sarmiento: per copia conforme Fr. Florimo Leg^e". There is also another, apparently preliminary list, 'Notamento del Professori di Violino esaminati' of 19 March 1833 addressed to Giuseppe Festa, "primo violino direttore dell' Orchestra del Real Teatro S. Carlo", on which the names of the final 'Notamento' are based.
64. Almanacco de' Reali Teatri, pp.13-16.

'cembalista' or of a 'klavier'.

	'Notamento' A/S	Almanacco
Violins I	15	) 29
Violins II	11	)
Violas	6	7
Cellos	7 or 8	10
Double-basses	9	12
Piccolo	1	2
Flutes	2	4
Oboes	2	3
Clarinets	2	4
Bassoons	2	2
Horns	4	4
Trumpets	2	3
"Tromba a Chiave"	1	
Trombones	3	3
Cimbasso in A	1	1
Serpent	1	
Cor anglais	1	
Timpani	1	
Bass drum	1	
Triangle	1	1
Cymbals	1	1
Tamburro	1	1
Harp	1	1
Armonico [Glass harmonica?]	1	1
Total	78	89

It has to be admitted that it is hard to pin down exactly the size of the orchestra at, say, the San Carlo. Against this it has to be pointed out that earlier lists make it plain that the orchestra at the San Carlo was already large by this time, and the Almanacco makes the comment that for this re-organization "The orchestral and choral bodies were enlarged".[65] A comparison of the two lists suggests that the 'Notamento' gives us an approximation of the orchestral forces of the San Carlo and that the Almanacco expands this to show those players used at the Fondo to supplement those of the San Carlo principals not also required to serve at the Fondo. The 'Notamento' makes no mention, for example, of the leaders of the Fondo orchestra in the opera (viz., Gaetano Coccia) and the ballets (viz., Antonio Vaccaj). The Fondo would also appear to have had its own particular wind players.

---

65. Almanacco de' Reali Teatri, p.125: "Fu aumentato il corpo d' orchestra e de' cori".

The standard printed contract for other players, however, obliged the <u>professori</u> to "play the said instrument in each and every production, performance, <u>feste di ballo</u>, that is given in the Theatres under the control of Sig. Barbaja, and where required to play also on the stage".[66] This meant both the royal theatres of San Carlo and the Fondo. Moreover, in the 'Notamento' of 1833, it establishes that "all the <u>professori</u> with the exception of the leader, the leader of the seconds, the principal cello and principal double-bass will be required to play in both the operas and the Ballets".[67] Even this honour evades the leader of the violas; if indeed there was one.

As a result of this it would seem that the orchestra was expected to be very large. It is clear that the type of work being performed was not a vital factor in determining the size of an orchestra, which is not surprising if we bear in mind the relatively restricted repertory offered by opera houses. Instead, according to traditional custom, "the number of players in a musical performance generally should be in proportion to the grandeur of the location", says Lichtenthal.[68] The San Carlo Theatre would, on this basis, as "il più vasto e magnifico teatro ch'esiste",[69] have to have one of the largest orchestras. This is confirmed by a review of the Royal Italian Opera at Her Majesty's Theatre in London in the late 1830s, which is described as "the largest theatrical orchestra in existence, as far as the stringed

---

66. A/S, F.T., fascio 63 ('Artisti di canto e ballo'), dated 27 February 1819; it is made out to Clemente Zanetti of Bergamo, "professore di Arpa": "per suonare il detto istromento in ogni e qualunque spettacolo, rappresentazione, Festi di Ballo, che si eseguirà ne' Teatri condotti del Sig. Barbaja, ed occorredo suonare anche sul palcoscenico".
67. A/S, F.T., fascio 127, 'Notamento', note 9: "tutti i Professori ad eccezione del concertino, del Primo Violini dei secondi, del primo Violoncello, e del primo Contrabasso saranno obbligati di suonare tanto nelle Opere, che nei Balli".
68. Lichtenthal, II, 71: "Il numero degli artisti per un' esecuzione musicale in grande debb' essere proporzionato alla grandezza del locale".
69. <u>Almanacco de' Reali Teatri</u>, p.29.

instruments are concerned, with the solitary exception of that of San Carlo in Naples".[70] The figures it gives for the London orchestra are not comprehensive but list twenty-six violins and seven double-basses for 1838, and twenty-nine violins and eight double-basses for 1839. The importance given to the violin and double-bass figures would therefore seem not to be restricted to Italy.

Later lists of orchestras at the royal theatres give eighty-six names in 1838 (with thirty-four violins, nine cellos and twelve double-basses),[71] and eighty-nine names in 1840 (including thirty-one violins, six violas, ten cellos and twelve double-basses).[72] A separate list for the smaller Fondo theatre dates only from 1849 but is still quite large with sixty players (including sixteen violins, four violas, four cellos and six double-basses).[73]

It seems certain, then, that the orchestra at the San Carlo was very large and increasing in size. Eventually it would be capable of orchestral effects as ends in themselves. Already in the _Almanacco_ for 1834 there is mention of the Glass harmonica which Donizetti presumably used in the mad scene in _Lucia di Lammermoor_. During Bellini's era, however, the emphasis was strictly devoted to the sonorous bass line.

One might imagine that the vast size of the orchestra would give a particularly smooth character to the sound at the San Carlo, particularly in pianissimo. No doubt a simple and non-contrapuntal style ensured that the singer was not lost against an orchestra of this size,

---

70. The Italian Opera in 1839: its Latest Improvements and Existing Defects Impartially Considered (London, 1840), p.2.
71. A/S, F.T., fascio 125, 'Stato degl' Impegnati e Scritturati dell' Impresa de' Reali Teatri dal giorno 8 Aprile 1838 a' 23 Marzo 1839', dated 27 June 1838. Giuseppe Festa is still named as 'Direttore', but he died the following year.
72. A/S, F.T., fascio 125, 'Notamento degli Scritturati Salariati dell' Impresa suddetta per l'annata 1839-1840'.
73. A/S, F.T., fascio 127, letter of 23 April 1849 to "Sua Eccelenza il Soprintendente de' Teatri e Spettacoli".

whether at La Scala or San Carlo, as determined by the size of the theatres themselves:

> "they have often heard a very numerous orchestra exert all its powers, without in the least covering the voice, or disguising the sense: and the reason is simply this, that what is called the 'fortissimo' or extreme force of the orchestra, is not continued uniformly throughout the accompanyment ... - but that this extreme exertion is instantaneously called forth either in those particular notes which are peculiarly significant of the rhythm, such as the first of the bar &c. or on some note or notes where the sense itself requires it". (74)

The type of simple accompaniment that was required was one that strengthened the bass line (in the manner of Algarotti's "shades of music") with all the emphasis of the <u>strumenti di Rinforzo</u>, in apposition to the vocal line, and restricted the harmonic infilling to a few divided violas; a texture commonly seen in scores up to and including those of Bellini. It was never something that would disturb the old traditional poetic conception of opera. As soon as orchestras began to develop a life of their own, however, and devote more interest to enlivening the middle and upper parts, as already Rossini sometimes did, then there grew demand for some more sophisticated means of control, apart from merely adhering to the principle of following the singer. To this extent the development of orchestral direction can be seen as a 'barometer' of the change from poetic opera into orchestral drama, which in Italy was a slow process.

Thus it is probably a measure of the extent to which the Italian opera orchestra of Bellini's time continued to be essentially an extension of the idea of <u>continuo</u> accompaniment, orchestrated principally for strings, that the old methods of orchestral direction from the bass line lasted for so long. The honour of being the first regular Italian opera conductor is usually accorded to Angelo Mariani (1821-1873) as

---

74. John Brown, <u>Letters</u>, pp.83-84.

"maestro concertatore e direttore delle musiche" at the Teatro Comunale in Bologna in 1860.(75) Since Mariani had originally been a violinist-director at Messina in 1844, this suggests that the Italian opera conductor rose from that of violinist conductors, as happened in the case of Spohr and Habeneck further north. Carse places the development at about the same time, but points to its origins in the maestro al cembalo. At La Scala, the maestro al cembalo had become Maestro concertatore by 1859 and Maestro concertatore e direttore delle opere by 1869; whereas the capo d'orchestra "subsided into the position of a mere primo violino".(76)

Lichtenthal, in 1826, naturally enough does not mention conductors as such; under 'Direttore di musica' he writes "V. Capo d'orchestra".(77) Elsewhere he remarks on the relationship this position has with the bass line:

> "The first violin and (in many regions) the Maestro di Cappella or director must place themselves in a prominent position, from where they can be seen by all the players ... The positioning of the double-basses is very advantageous, if they are arranged above a hollow floor and turned round with their sound holes facing the audience; in this manner their tone will be a third as full and strong again as normally". (78)

In other words, the arrangement of the orchestra revolved around the commanding position of the leader and the equally important arrangement

---

75. Nino Pirrotta and Giorgio Graziosi, 'Direzione e Concertazione', in Enciclopedia dello Spettacolo, IV, col. 741. See also Piero Mioli, 'Il Teatro Comunale', in M. Conati and M. Pavarani, eds., Orchestre in Emilia-Romagna, pp.325-342 (p.336), where Mariani is described as "Direttore delle Opere" in 1861, and "Direttore e maestro concertatore delle opere" in 1864. In 1870 he conducted Lohengrin there.
76. Carse, The Orchestra from Beethoven to Berlioz, p.316.
77. Lichtenthal, I, 228.
78. Lichtenthal, II, 131: "Il Primo Violino ed (in molti paesi) il maestro di Capella o direttore debbono occupare un posto eminente, onde essere veduti da tutti i suonatori ... La posizione de' Contrabassi è assai vantaggiosa, se sono collocati sopra un fondo cavo, e voltati coi loro ff verso gli uditori; il loro suono in allora sarà di un terza parte più pieno e robusto del solito".

of the double-basses. It is noticeable again how every effort is made
to boost the bass line, again presumably with the maestro al cembalo
sharing control. The first orchestral list that does not mention the
cembalo, it will be remembered, dates from 1833, after Bellini had
left Naples.

Descriptions of the manner of direction of the primo violino e
direttore dell'orchestra are rare, but evidently tended to arouse suspicion that the orchestral part was beginning to rise above its
appointed station. The following description of Festa[79] in charge
of a performance of Spontini's La vestale in 1813 illustrates how music
of some orchestral complexity was beginning to make its effects felt:

> "If anyone asked Signor Festa, the eminent director of
> the orchestra of this Royal Theatre, situated in a
> prominent position, why he beat time with his bow,
> like a maestro di cappella in a Church choir, something
> quite unknown and unheard of in the days of Paisiello,
> Piccini, Guglielmi, etc., he would no doubt reply that
> in those happy days the instrumental music served with
> gentle and graceful accompaniments the vocal music, and
> was subordinate and submissive to it, but that nowadays
> ... accompaniments have become true Haydn symphonies". (80)

The reviewer makes reference to Festa doing what we can only
interpret as conducting, at what must, for Italy, be regarded as an
early date. He also makes reference to the only such form of direction
customary up to that time, choral conducting. Burney in 1770 makes

---

79. Carse, The Orchestra from Beethoven to Berlioz, p.271, following Spohr's account (see note 58 above), points to Festa as director from 1817; but he is referred to as "pmo violino" as early as 1810 (A/S, F.T., fascio 125, letter of 6 May 1810 from the Prefettura di Polizia).
80. Monitore delle due Sicilie, 3 November 1813: "Se alcuno domandasse al Signor Festa, egregio direttore dell' orchestra di questo Real Teatro, perchè situato in luogo eminente, egli batta col suo archetto il tempo, come un maestro di cappella in una cantoria di Chiesa, cosa affatta in usitata e sconosciuta ai tempi dei Paisiello, dei Piccini, dei Guglielmi ecc; egli risponderebbe senza dubbio che a quei tempi felici la musica strumentale serviva con dolci e graziosi accompagnamenti la vocale, ed a quella era subordinata e sommessa, ma che adesso ... gli accompagnmenti sono quasi divenuti vere sinfonie Haidiane".

several such references to Latilla and Galuppi conducting with rolled-up manuscript paper, but only with regard to choral music.[81]

At La Scala, a similar role to Festa's was taken by Alessandro Rolla (1757-1841) from 1803,[82] and would have taken charge of the orchestral parts in Bellini's operas produced there, as in La straniera where he is reported as "taking up again the baton"[83] after a period of illness.

Despite the reports of Festa conducting from a "luogo eminente" in 1813 it seems unlikely that he actually discarded violin playing as Habeneck was later to do. The idea of a maestro standing in front of an opera orchestra, and directing it, as it were from outside, caused considerable amazement to Italians as is shown in the report made of a rehearsal for "una sinfonia di Bethoven" made in 1824 when there was nothing new worth reporting on stage:

> "As soon as the symphony was finished, up jumped a vigorous maestro waving around a piece of cardboard in his hand who seemed to want to put in doubt the ability of the players and continually criticized them for mistakes and laxness". (84)

This report is obviously unusual, not least for its curious mention of Beethoven, and raises the possibility that the use of the "batter la solfa" as it was called might have been used in rehearsals whilst not regarded as seemly for a finished performance on the grounds

---

81. Burney, ed. Poole, pp.70, 80, 114, 160.
82. Paganini was one of his pupils in Parma in 1795.
83. I teatri, 16 February 1829; quoted after Cambi, p.194: "Rolla risanato ha ripreso il bastone della nostra sceltissima orchestra". See also the report of his direction in 1816 given in Spohr, I, 258.
84. Rivista teatrale, 17 November 1824: "Finita quella sinfonia, eccoti un vigoroso maestro con un pezzo di cartone in mano che qua e là contorcendosi par che volesse far dubitare dell'abilità di que' professori, e lor facesse continue rimprovero d'inesattezza e d'insufficenza". The report opens with the characteristic explanation: "Non avendo notivà sul scena; discendiamo un poco in orchestra".

that it was "a crutch, an aid, an imperfection that should be concealed and not made a song and dance of".[85]

Barbaja voiced concern for effective methods of leadership in his letter of 1825 to the Duca di Noja, complaining of very imperfect playing in the ballets. Indeed it was the purely instrumental ballets that led the way to stricter orchestral control. Barbaja goes on to complain that he was having to sign up a new leader, Gaetano Coccia (father of the better known Carlo Coccia (1782-1873)), previous leaders "not having had enough exact control to sustain a sufficiently interesting leadership". He says that "Signor Coccia has been given a contract ... he is particularly charged with playing and directing the ballet music for the Real Teatro S. Carlo".[86]

The implication is that it was the purely instrumental music that was encouraging Barbaja to look for orchestral organization. This attitude is by no means uncommon and was one source of the disdain with which *ballabili* were treated by Bellini's contemporaries, on the grounds that it was mere instrumental music. In an art form of the dignity of opera, however, it would not be expected that there would be any failings on the part of the *professori*; and that therefore there would hardly be the need "for a director of an opera house of the first rank

---

85. *Rivista teatrale*, 17 November 1824: "il batter della solfa è un puntello, un aiuto, una imperfezione che bisogna nascondere e non farne pompa". Elsewhere the review, which takes the form of a lengthy discussion, comments that the practice of waving around "quel sudicio cartone" is "uno di que' regali che ci vengono da paesi pe' quali la musica non è dono di natura ma forza d'arte e di studio"; a revealing glimpse of the characteristic chauvinism that kept Neapolitan traditions pure of foreign influences during Bellini's period there.

86. See above, note 62. A/S, F.T., fascio 127: "non potendo aver la rigoria necessaria à sostenere una tanta intèressante direzione ... Si è scritturato il Signor Coccia ... è particolarmenta incaricato di suonare e dirigere le musiche di Ballo nel Real Teatro S. Carlo". Gaetano Coccia also held the post of "primo violino e direttore del orchestra del Real Teatro di Fondo per le opere" mentioned by Barbaja and in *Almanacco de' Reali Teatri*, p.13.

to conduct the orchestra".[87]

A very productive source of information on the hierarchy within orchestras is furnished by librettos, which often give a summary of the orchestra used, noting the most important members of it. For example, the libretto for the premiere of <u>Zaira</u> (Parma, 1829) gives a 'Nota de' Signori professori d'orchestra' which starts characteristically with <u>Maestro al cembalo</u>, followed by <u>Primo violino e Direttore d'Orchestra</u>. Amongst the seventeen principals mentioned is the <u>Primo Contrabasso al Cembalo</u>. After this mention is made of "altri quaranta Professori della Città".

For the orchestra at La Scala a similar position can be seen in the librettos for <u>Il pirata</u> (Milan, 1827) and for <u>La straniera</u> (Milan, 1829). The list of orchestral principals is almost identical and that for <u>La straniera</u> is interesting as a version of it appears in the <u>Harmonicon</u>,[88] with English versions of the Italian titles. In this, the <u>Maestro al Cembalo</u>, Sig. Vincenzo Lavigna, is translated as 'Conductor' in the <u>Harmonicon</u> indicating a position of some importance; whereas <u>Primo Violino Capo d'Orchestra</u> Sig. Alessandro Rolla is translated as 'Leader'. Amongst the many other principals mentioned are, as at Parma, <u>Primo Contrabasso al Cembalo</u> and <u>Primo Violoncello al Cembalo</u>, indicating again their close co-operation with the cembalist as a continuo group.

A slightly different situation can be seen developing at the Teatro della Pergola in Florence. A relatively early libretto such as that for Rossini's <u>Tancredi</u> in 1822 lists the <u>Primo violino e Direttore dell'Orchestra</u> and the <u>Maestro al primo cembalo</u>. In this case there is

---

87. <u>L'Omnibus</u>, 28 September 1833. The comment is part of a disdainful reply to the <u>Passatempo per le Dame</u> of Palermo, which "voleva che un Direttore d'un primo teatro facesse il battitore in orchestra".
88. <u>The Harmonicon</u> (London, 1831), pp. 105-106.

also an <u>Altro Maestro</u>, no doubt because <u>Tancredi</u> (1813) still used the old <u>secco recitative</u>. That a second <u>cembalo</u> was required when it was actually to be used for recitative suggests that here, at least, the <u>primo cembalo</u> was not used at all. The <u>Enciclopedia dello spettacolo</u> suggests that a second cembalo was already used in the eighteenth century to exempt the maestro from having to play <u>continuo</u> during the arias.(89)

Signs of change can be found quite early at Florence, however. The libretto for <u>La straniera</u> (Florence, 1830) does not list a <u>maestro al cembalo</u>, but instead a <u>Maestro Direttore delle Opere</u>, Pasquale Sogner; but still placed below the <u>primo violino e Direttore dell' orchestra</u>. In the libretto for Bellini's <u>Zaira</u> (Florence, 1836), however, the <u>Maestro e direttore dell'Opere</u>, Andrea Nencini, appears above that of the <u>Capo e direttore dell'Orchestra</u>. He would appear to be of the <u>maestro al cembalo</u> type, described as "professore di Contrappunto nell'I. e R. Accademia di Belle Arti".

It may be suggested from this that at the Teatro della Pergola the <u>maestro al cembalo</u> was freed from his duties as an accompanist and assumed more complete responsibility for the direction of the opera as a whole at a relatively early date. If this is true, then we can see a process different from the one that occurred in France and Germany, where it was the orchestral leader who rose to direct the orchestra. It would seem, however, that such advances were not yet paralleled at Naples, where the lists in the <u>Almanacco 1834</u> and contemporary librettos do not show the same concern for general musical director of the operas as a whole.

A position is to be found at Venice quite different from that at Florence. In librettos for the Teatro La Fenice for Bellini's <u>Il</u>

---

89. Pirrotta and Graziosi, 'Direzione e concertazione', in <u>ES</u>, IV, col. 740. Prota-Giurleo's list of Paisiello's orchestra in 1796 also lists two harpsichords; Robinson, p.161.

pirata (Venice, 1830) and for the premiere of I Capuleti e i Montecchi (Venice, 1830), the orchestral lists begin with a Maestro e Direttore dell'Opera e Capo Orchestra. This is an unusual designation but no doubt indicates a violinist-conductor with perhaps more control than Festa at Naples. A long way down the list comes the Maestro al Cembalo e Direttore de' Cori, Luigi Carcano. Two years later the situation approaches more that of Naples: in the libretto for Anna Bolena (Venice, 1831) given at "Il Carnevale dell anno 1831-32" the Fenice orchestra is led by the Direttore dell'Orchestra, Gaetano Mares; and, still much lower in the listing, Luigi Carcano again appears, this time as Maestro al Cembalo Istruttore, e Direttore de' Cori di Donne e Uomini.

The same position obtains in the libretto for the premiere of Bellini's Beatrice di Tenda (Venice, 1833). During the following decade, however, the positions of Mares and Carcano at the Fenice Theatre became directly reversed, and show a process much like that at Florence; in that, contrary to practice in France and Germany, the Maestro al Cembalo eventually assumed general control. An example such as the Fenice libretto for Norma in 1844 now places the Maestro al Cembalo, Luigi Carcano, at the head of the list in large letters above the Primo Violino e Direttore dell'Orchestra, Gaetano Mares.

Still quite apart from either in the organization of the operas was, as at Naples, the position of Direttore della musica, evidently held at this time by one Pietro Romani.[90] This is presumably the same Pietro Romani (1781-1877) who supplied 'Manca un foglio' as a substitute for Bartolo's 'Un dottore di mia sorte' in Il barbiere di Siviglia. He is often cited as an early Italian conductor. Pietro was a pupil of Fenaroli at Naples and succeeded the aged Giacomo

---

90. Sandro della Libera, 'Teatro la Fenice, Cronologia degli spettacoli 1792-1866' (typescript in Venice, Archivio del Teatro La Fenice), p.188.

Tritto (1733-1824) who had taught Bellini counterpoint there.[91] He is named as <u>Maestro direttore della musica</u> at the San Carlo in 1835,[92] the same position accorded Carlo Coccia the year before.[93] He certainly went to the Teatro della Pergola in Florence[94] and information in encyclopedias suggests that he was the first Italian conductor of many important French and German operas.[95] It is very easy, however, to confuse him with his nephew and pupil Carlo Romani (1824-1875) who wrote the recitatives for <u>Der Freischütz</u>'s Italian premiere in 1843, also at Florence.[96] Important premieres there also include <u>Les Huguenots</u> in 1841 and <u>Le Prophète</u> in 1852. They would seem to have been professional directors with histories as <u>maestri di cembalo</u>, rather than as violinist leaders in the German and French manner.

Bellini would seem to have been writing just before the advent of conductors in Italy, in a tradition of control from the <u>maestro al cembalo</u>, on the one hand, and violinist director on the other. The evidence seems to suggest that the bass-orientated orchestra of Italian conceptions led to the rise of organized control from that particular post rather than from the violinist. French and German taste had developed an interest in pure instrumental music and this prompted the rise of the violinist leader to that of conductor, rather than the external <u>maestro al cembalo</u>.

The rise of Italian conductors came after those in France and Germany but in certain places rather before the time suggested by Adam

---

91. Weinstock, <u>Vincenzo Bellini</u>, p.31; <u>The New Grove</u> XVI, 127.
92. <u>L'Omnibus</u>, 18 April 1835, 'Prospetto di Appalto pel Real Teatro San Carlo dal 19 Aprile 1835 a tutto carnevale 1836'.
93. <u>L'Omnibus</u>, 31 May 1834; see above, note 14.
94. <u>Riemann-Lexicon</u>, Personenteil (1961), II, 533.
95. <u>Die Musik in Geschichte und Gegenwart</u>, XI, col. 783.
96. <u>Dizionario Ricordi della musica e dei musicisti</u> (Milan, 1959), IV, 42; G. Gatti, ed., <u>La Musica, Dizionario</u> (Turin, 1966), II, 873. See, however, F. J. Fetis, <u>Biographie Universelle des Musiciens, Supplement</u> (1880), II, 436.

Carse, though not during Bellini's time. The earliest indications are found at Florence's Teatro della Pergola by 1836, a theatre for which Bellini did not write. At Milan we have Carse's dates of 1859 and a conductor at Naples in 1860 is noted by the Enciclopedia dello spettacolo.(97) What is fairly safe to maintain is that the process in Italy comes from the rise in power of the maestro al cembalo, reinforcing the historical importance given to this role with its roots in bel canto.

Bellini himself had on occasions to fulfil that post of maestro al cembalo, and we have seen that, historically, the two roles are linked. Exactly what he did is rather a matter for conjecture; and, for later composers, increasingly so, as orchestrations became fuller and conductors more necessary. At this earlier period, however, Bellini and his contemporaries would still seem to have exerted some control in the role, in sometimes not too happy conjunction with the leader. His comments on the premiere of Bianca e Fernando at Genoa in 1828 show that he had an active role: "The orchestra in particular is horrible; with me directing, it did not go too badly: but with the first violin, who although he is a fine player is none too experienced, they are making some real balls-ups".(98)

It was always a problem to maintain a balance between the instrumental parts with the violinist-leader, and the vocal parts trained by the maestro al cembalo. In early opera this was no problem, as instrumental sections of operas were kept as discrete items in the work. Even in the eighteenth century opera seria the violinist-leader would be able to direct the string accompaniments to arias provided that he

---

97. Pirrotta and Graziosi, 'Direzione e concertazione', in ES, IV, col. 740.
98. Cambi, p.77 (10 (?) April 1828): "L'orchestra specialmente è un orrore; con me andava non tanto male: ma col p$\overline{m}$o violino, che sebbene bravo non è tanto prattico, fanno delle grandi coglionerie".

did not have to cope with a large body of wind (as opposed to wind solos) as well. When, however, many disparate elements, both orchestral and vocal, had to be brought together, such as in grand ensembles, or where the orchestration became more complex, then some means of central control became necessary. In Italy, because of the emphasis on the bass line, this was most easily devised by promoting the <u>maestro al cembalo</u>. The weight of this emphasis lasted as long as composers viewed their operas in the light of traditional <u>bel canto</u> accompaniments. The charge that Italian opera orchestras were not balanced as a whole, but were bottom-heavy, as made by Spohr and Berlioz, must be answered by replying that they did not exist as wholes, but were balanced by the vocal part. The middle parts had as little significance for Bellini and his contemporaries as they had done for his predecessors.

It was precisely when composers attended to the chordal reinforcements through brass and wind, rather than bass reinforcements through <u>strumenti di Rinforzo</u>, that the same system was adopted as elsewhere in Europe. This first happened in the late 1830s, in the scores of Mercadante, Pacini and then in the later Donizetti, and particularly in Verdi. But what is interesting here is how the orchestral constitutions and conceptions as reflected in its methods of organization, go hand in hand with the type of musical texture composed, and with the attitudes to harmony and counterpoint. Often composers took direct control of the whole performance, as in the case of the production of Mercadante's <u>Il proscritto</u> at the Teatro San Carlo in 1842.[99] The need for this can be seen as a reflection of the musical textures themselves.

Perhaps more important historically was the effect on Italian

---

99. <u>L'Omnibus</u>, 6 January 1842: "ha tutto diretto il Mercadante".

composers of having their operas performed by foreign orchestras, particularly those at Paris. Carse maintains that the orchestra of the Paris Opèra "shone as a large and bright star amongst even the most brilliant of European opera houses"[100] and was a sine qua non of the "dazzling effects" developed by operatic composers. Hand in hand with this went the control of proceedings under one man as at the premiere of Donizetti's La Favorite at the Opèra in 1840, reported by a Paris correspondent as "wonderfully directed throughout by M. Habeneck",[101] whose sole control of the Opèra orchestra from 1831 to 1846 was somewhat dictatorial. There is no doubt this had considerable importance for composers such as Rossini (Guillaume Tell (1829)), Donizetti and Verdi (Les vêpres siciliènnes (1855)), not to mention Meyerbeer and Halevy. Bellini, too, worked at Paris, of course, but at the Théâtre Italien whose orchestra was smaller "but of the same first-class quality".[102] This naturally had some influence on his approach to orchestration; particularly since, as mentioned at the end of the last chapter, he was aware that in Paris they wanted music before anything else and were not interested in the niceties of the poetry.

Effects of Parisian influence probably worked back to Italy only slowly, at least to the established opera houses; but occasional performances might have been different. The premiere of Rossini's Stabat Mater at the Liceo Musicale di Bologna was conducted by "Maestro Direttore Gaetano Donizzetti", perhaps prompted by his experience of the effects of having Habeneck conduct his own La Favorite. The constitution of the orchestra here is quite different from earlier Italian lists:[103]

---

100. Carse, The Orchestra from Beethoven to Berlioz, p.77.
101. L'Omnibus, 24 December 1840: "sempre mirabilmente diretta da M. Hanebeck".
102. Carse, The Orchestra from Beethoven to Berlioz, p.82.
103. L'Omnibus, 31 March 1840.

"Suonatori prime parti	Altri
Primo violino direttore dell Orchestra)	
Primo violino di spalla)	23
Capo dei secondi Violini)	
Primo Violoncello	6
Primo Contrabasso	5
Primo Viola	5
Primo Flauto	1
Primo Oboè	1
Primo Clarinetto	1
Primo Fagotto	1
Primi Corni (2)	2
Prima Tromba	1
Primo Trombone	2
Timpanista	"

[total 63]

This orchestra is now much more like a standard classical orchestra with double wind and a more normal balance of cellos and double-basses. There is not even any mention of a cembalo though perhaps Donizetti may have conducted from one. He is in any case the most striking feature of the performance. Bologna might well have been generally rather progressive on such matters, and of course the list is not one of an opera orchestra. It is salutary to compare the balance of strings here, twenty-six violins and six double-basses, with the still bass-heavy orchestra of the Real Teatro del Fondo seven years later, with its sixteen violins to six double-basses; or with the thirty-one violins and twelve double-basses at the Teatro San Carlo in 1839/40.[104]

Throughout this period the Italian opera orchestra shows itself very much as part of a greater whole; that is, balanced against the voice rather as a continuo bass had been, rather than complete in itself. The concern of the reader has been drawn to details of individual orchestras and their constitutions, not as an end in itself, interesting though the lists may be as the basis of comparisons with orchestras elsewhere, or of today; but to show that the nature of the

---

104. See above, notes 71-73.

beast was strongly conditioned by the role it was expected to play. Contemporary aesthetic views naturally came into consideration here as well; in particular, the conviction that the instrumental part should remain simple and act as a servant of the vocal part. In other words, the condition of the instrumental part has to be considered in the light of its position with regard to all the other parts, and therefore to its position in the aesthetics of opera as a whole. Likewise attention has been drawn, in consideration of the methods of direction, to many names, not for their intrinsic interest so much as to see what their positions and the names of those positions mean in relation to each other; and the implications they hold for the understanding of the importance accorded to the orchestra compared with the many other parts of the <u>opera</u>. This is important for us as we are used to considering, nay judging, opera, according to the interest, or lack of it, that is to be discovered in the orchestral part. This is particularly the case where comparison with Mozart, Wagner or other symphonically minded composers is perpetrated. So far as the orchestra is concerned we should, instead of seeing it from the external point of view of the conductor, see it from the point of view of his ancestor in the Italian opera, of the <u>maestro al cembalo</u>.

CHAPTER 6

THE HERITAGE OF THE BEL CANTO

This final chapter will deal with those aspects of the transmission of the vocal culture of the era of the castratos into Bellini's time that follow on from the matters dealt with in previous sections of this study. It will therefore consider how musical expression was realized in bel canto, bearing in mind Italian interests in poetic drama for which instrumental music took essentially a secondary place. Later, consideration will also be given to the types of voices that still contributed to realizing these bel canto ideals in the early nineteenth century.

Whilst mistrust of instrumental music as artificial, and a concern that harmony should not become more important than melody, were views that Italian theorists inherited from Jean-Jacques Rousseau and the other Encyclopedists, their conception of the singer's role in the opera became much more fully developed than it ever did with the French theorists. In time it also became conditioned by the evolution of particular Italian methods of voice-production and of singers' own practice. In this, national characteristics of harmony and counterpoint, which naturally differed from French styles, could not fail to make themselves felt.

We have seen how the singer was felt to be the immediate instrument of the poet and the composer,[1] and that he was the protagonist of the drama as the declaimer of its poetry. This was carried out with a minimal orchestral support that provided a firm bass, but not competing orchestral voices. The singer therefore encountered no obstacle to his expression of the text,

---

1. See above Chapter 3, note 90.

the orchestra being merely a continuo-derived pedestal upon which he had to stand to declaim the poetry. When commentators began to complain that the orchestra was beginning to take over so as to strain the voices of the singers, it was because they had not yet realized that the 'pedestal' could ever have any expressive power in its own right. Celentano therefore complains: "you no longer see the statue on the stage, and its pedestal in the orchestra, but find instead the orchestra as the leading element and the voices accessory to it".[2]

It is a mistake to see in this merely a love of singing for its own sake. Celentano is a late example of the type of commentator whose view was that, since music had no expressive power without words, it was a mistake to rely on the orchestra rather than the singer. We must see this in the light of the discussions that have been offered regarding the proud insular traditions of Neapolitan musicians, and the genuine seriousness with which they treated opera; opera, that is, to the exclusion of instrumental music from countries further north. In the introductory chapter reference was made to Mercadante's article, published the same year as Celentano's book (1867), which seemed to exclude foreign claims on the history of opera. An even more suspicious attitude was taken to instrumental music in the first third of the century.

The statue on the stage, then, had no reason to fear competition from his pedestal. If there was one simple thing that this meant for the Italian ideals of <u>bel canto</u> it was that, compared with singing today, the level of sound required from the singer was much lower. The lack of interest in vocal power shown at this time is probably the one single feature that is, at the same time, the least obviously important

---

2. Celentano, p.9: "non più vedi la statua sul palcoscenico, e il piedistallo nell'orchestra, ma trovi invece l'orchestra per principale, e le voci da accessario".

to the commentator, and the most far-reaching in its effect. It is least obviously a matter to be mentioned by a musicologist because it is so simple and does not manifest itself readily in the score, whilst it is in effect most important because it meant that the poetic conception of opera permeated all features of vocal production.

Therefore in an earlier chapter on the nature of the singer on the stage, mention was made of the fact that the principal tenets of the bel canto traditions of singing were based on the desire to deliver the words in the clearest manner possible. Singing was therefore seen not in terms of the interpretation of the words so much as their most elegant and noble enunciation, and this is the true meaning of Crescentini's dictum that "Il canto deve essere un imitazione del discorso".

It can be readily understood that what was meant by expressive singing was 'expression of the words' in a sense more literal than is understood today; it meant their clear pronunciation. A corollary of this is that it was not dependent in the same way as would be expected today on the expressive power or colouration of the voice. This idea is perhaps a delicate one but can be best understood in the light of the consideration given to early nineteenth century Italian ideas of pure abstract, instrumental music and its derivation from poetic vocal music. As was pointed out earlier, the new awareness of the expressive power of absolute music that had been awakened further north by Beethoven's instrumental music was as yet not felt in Italy, partly as a consequence of its continued isolation from such influences. Such concepts were thus quite foreign to contemporary aesthetic views of opera. For Italians music therefore had no expressive value in itself, and it was the presence of the poetic element that caused it to qualify as art. In the same way as this conditioned contemporary attitudes to the role and nature of the instrumental contribution to opera, so it did also to the vocal part. Vocal expression was perhaps more restrained than is usual today and more a matter for clear pronunciation; but this does not mean that, in their terms, *bel canto* singing was not expressive.

Henry Pleasants notes that few devices of musical terminology are employed less precisely than *bel canto* and "none whose origin is so obscure",[3] a point echoed by Owen Jander in The New Grove.[4] Charles Brauner uses the term to describe, in a loose fashion, the operatic style of Rossini, Bellini and Donizetti, where the vocal melody is of paramount importance; equivalent to the contemporary development of German Romanticism.[5] In this chapter I wish to refer to it as meaning something else: that is, as a method of singing in the first place, and as a style of composition only to the extent where one is determined by the other or inextricably linked to it. This is the "kind of singing that flourished in Italian throats in the seventeenth and eighteenth centuries".[6]

The origins of the term are obscure. Pleasants says that the "term did not exist" at the time with which it is associated.[7] According to the best modern book on the subject, it appears first in Italian writing about 1860. This seems, from the evidence available, a little too late, though it is accepted by Owen Jander.[8] Its appearance would seem to depend on the awareness of methods of singing

---

3. H. Pleasants, The Great Singers (London, 1967), p.19.
4. O. Jander, 'Bel canto', in The New Grove, II, 420.
5. Charles S. Brauner, 'Vincenzo Bellini and the Aesthetics of Opera Seria in the First Third of the Nineteenth Century' (unpublished Ph.D. dissertation, University of Yale, 1972), pp.12 and 83, note 53. Despite its title, Dr. Brauner's thesis concerns itself with formal conventions of opera rather than aesthetical ones, and on "how the total product of libretto and music creates music drama" (Brauner, p.1).
6. Pleasants, p.19.
7. Pleasants, p.19.
8. Jander, 'Bel canto', p.420. The first date recorded in the OED (Supplement, 1972) is 1894.

that were evidently not beautiful, that were seen to come in from abroad. Thus Lichtenthal does not mention *bel canto* but refers to "l'arte del Canto", and points out that little was known of the precepts underlying any traditions of singing other than the Italian one:

> "It would certainly be of the greatest use to have a book explaining not just the various methods of the old Italian singing schools ... but also the different style we can see in the great singers of the very same school". (9)

Stendhal refers to "Le *beau chant*" in 1824, considering Rossini's revolutionary departure from it in his operas, following his encounter with the castrato Giovanni Battista Velluti (1780-1861),(10) and associates it rather with the singers of the previous century. Moreover the *Rivista teatrale*, the next year, talks of the "raffinamenti dell'arte del bel canto" as something very much to be upheld.(11) Perhaps illuminating as to its precise meaning is the reference to the singing in 1828 of Bellini's favourite *prima donna*, Giuditta Pasta, as

> "bel canto spianato, perfectly suited to declamation, skilful in breath control and in bringing forth the voice, which can cover over two octaves from low G to high B ... expert in swelling and fading at will the high head notes ... singing that is one continuous melodic language of the emotions". (12)

In this early exegesis of the term, attention should be drawn to the fact that it is a *spianato*, that is to say a *legato* style, and that it is associated, in Pasta's case, with fine declamation and in the *messa*

---

9. Lichtenthal, I, 129: "Sarebbe certamente della massima utilità un libro, il quale spiegasse non solo i varj metodi delle antiche scuole di canto italiane ... ma anche il differente stile, osservato ne' gran cantanti dell'una e medesima scuola".
10. Stendhal, *Vie de Rossini*, ed. H. Martineau, II, 144. For the context, see note 18 below.
11. *Rivista teatrale*, 15 January 1825.
12. *I teatri*, 10 December 1828 (plus appendix); quoted after Cambi, p. 148 note 2: "bel canto spianato, perfettamente adatto alla declamazione, perizia nel fare uso del fiato e nel mettere la voce, voce che comprende diciotto suoni dal *sol* basso al *si* acuto ... abilissima nel crescere e smorzare a suo grado gli acuti di testa"; appendix: "un canto che è una continua lingua melodiosa del sentimento".

di voce, of which more later. It also incorporates the emphasis on vocal extension and the integration of this with the head voice. One cannot necessarily rely on it to describe Pasta's actual voice, any more than with any perhaps partisan journalism; but what we are concerned with is what constituted the values held to be paramount in the bel canto spianato. With its final reference to a "melodic language of the emotions", it can be seen as embodying most of the values that will be discussed in this chapter.

Other references antedating Duey's date of 1860, refer to bel canto as something specifically Italian, as in the full title of Vaccaj's Dodici ariette per camera in chiave di violino per insegnamento del bel canto italiano (1840). Vaccaj's pieces inhabit a later musical environment, however, and perhaps look back on something precious but recently departed, as does Carlo Ritorni, referring to "that precious inheritance of italian bel canto" and "the so called bel canto, glorious faculty of the Italian genius" in 1841.[13] This linking of bel canto with Italian genius can be taken a step further and associated particularly with Naples. This is a point made in the great pioneering study on the subject by Franz Haböck, who goes on to say that the development of singing, and particularly castrato singing, is inextricably bound up with the rise of the schools at Bologna and Naples.[14]

A somewhat bland view of what the old bel canto school meant to those looking back on it from mid-century is afforded us by Mastriani, explaining that the practice by which "without falling from being

---

13. Carlo Ritorni, Ammaestramenti alla composizione d'ogni poema e d'ogni opera appartenente alla musica (Milan, 1841), pp.64-66: "quella preziosa prerogativa del bel canto italiano"; "il cosi detto bel canto, gloriosa prerogativa delle italiche Muse".
14. Franz Haböck, Die Kastraten und ihre Gesangkunst. Eine gesangsphysiologische Kultur- und musikhistorische Studie (Stuttgart, 1927), p.119.

beautiful and pleasing, [the voice] succeeds in expressing such a rich diversity of emotions, is the most important undertaking in studying singing".(15)

But to gain some idea of the intensity with which passions could be, and were expected to be, expressed requires us to search the literature that is actually contemporary with what Stendhal referred to as "Le beau chant". This means taking into consideration the traditions of the great soprani with which the whole idea of bel canto is inextricably bound up. Castrati such as Pier Francesco Tosi, whose Opinioni of 1723 was translated into English, French and German, and Giambattista Mancini, are examples of the most influential theorists of this tradition. Their importance and the consistency of their views have been shown by Franz Haböck and Duey.

Following Haböck, Duey considers that all the precepts underlying bel canto were entirely motivated by castrati and following Garcia, dates the decline of bel canto from their departure from the stage.(16) The bond between ideas of bel canto and the reign of the castrati is also emphasized by Rodolfo Celletti.(17) Stendhal typically sums up this view:

> "The Art of bel canto was created in the year 1680 by Pistocchi, and its progress was hastened immeasurably by Pistocchi's pupil Bernacchi (c.1720). The peak of Perfection was attained in 1778, under the aegis of Pacchiarotti, but since that date, the race of male sopranos has died out, and the art has degenerated". (18)

---

15. Mastriani, p.51: "senza lasciare di essere bello e piacente, riesca ad esprimere passioni tante e sì fra loro diverse, è il più grave studio da fare intorno al canto".
16. Duey, pp.58-59.
17. Celletti, in Analecta Musicologica V (1968), p.272.
18. Stendhal, Life of Rossini, p.351. The original reads in Vie de Rossini, ed. Martineau, II, 144: "Le beau chant commença en 1680 avec Pistocchi; Bernacchi, son élève, lui fit faire d'immenses progrès (1720). Le perfection de cet art a été en 1778, sous Pacchiarotti. Depuis l'on n'a plus fait de soprani et il est tombe". Of the soprani that Stendhal mentions in his Vie de Rossini, special emphasis is put on Pacchiarotti, Marchesi (1755-1829) and Crescentini, and the transmission of their skills to Giuditta Pasta (ed. Martineau, II, 192).

The difficulty in assessing the extent of the heritage of vocal ideals bestowed on opera by the reign of the castrati is only too obvious. It is thus hard for us to glean much from Stendhal telling us that "Crescentini would suffuse his whole voice and inflexion with a broad and indefinable colouring of satisfaction".[19] That their singing was quite unlike anything that we have today is shown by such remarks as exist from contemporaries concerning the difficulty of describing the peculiar but ravishingly delicate nature of their sound.

> "I defy the skill of the most perceptive of writers to give a description to those that have not heard it, of the singing style of a Pacchierotti. The techniques of his method consisted of minute gradations of smorzare, rinforzi, gruppetti, mordenti, trilli, appoggiature, mezzetinte, sfumature, etc. such as human speech has no means of being able to express". (20)

It is important to realize that it is not vocal force but this vocal flexibility that seems to ravish the senses of listeners to castrati and their followers. It is one of the three main requirements of singing, along with the stressing of the right notes, and the colouring of the voice to suit the nature of the composition, that are demanded by Crescentini in his Raccolta di Essercizi of 1811. He refers to "that elasticity, suppleness and flexibility" needed by the voice to regulate attacks and diminuendos of intensity without strain.[21] This was a particular faculty of castrati such as Crescentini himself, and it is explained by Arteaga who notes that castration renders the ligaments of the throat "more suitable to vibrate, and consequently to

---

19. Stendhal, Life of Rossini, p.354.
20. Majer, p.170: "Sfido l'ingegno del più acuto scrittore a dare un idea a quelli che non l' hanno udito, del modo di cantare di un Pacchierotti. Consisteva l'artifizio del suo stile in alcuni minimi gradi di smorzare, rinforzi, gruppetti, mordenti, trilli, appoggiature, mezzetinte, sfumature ec. che il linguaggio umano non ha mezzi da poter spiegare". Majer, incidentally, already regards this as "la ormai quasi perduta arte del canto" (Majer, p.170).
21. Crescentini, sections 2-4: "quella Elasticità, morbidezza e ondeggiamento".

execute the infinitesimal gradations of song, it renders the opening of the glottis more supple and disposes it to produce the high notes better than others do. Such a consideration necessarily gave them priority in opera".[22]

In these analyses it is noticeable that no reference is made to vocal power. What is valued in the castrato voice is its extension of the upper register without any implication of brilliance [assumed by writers today] and the adaptability of the voice to render the finest shadings of song.

This delicacy and flexibility is what permitted the effects remarked on by Stendhal and Majer. The expressive purpose of the vocal elaborations made possible has been explained in an earlier chapter. This delicacy, and the vocal extensions remarked on by Arteaga, are well summed up in what is probably the most effective attempt at a description of the castrati and their ethereal art.

> "It is impossible to give any tolerable idea of the Excellencies of these three celebrated Eunuchs, or the Beauty of their several Voices: In short they are above Description ... This Eunuch [Pauluccio] ... was indeed the Wonder of the World. For besides, that his voice was an Octave, at least (and I speak within Compass) higher than any ones [sic] else, it had all the Warblings and Turns of a Nightingal, but only with this difference, that it was much finer, and did not a Man know the contrary, he would believe it impossible such a Tone could proceed from the Throat of any Thing that was human. Jeronimo, (or Momo) had a Voice so soft, and ravishingly mellow, that nothing can better represent it than the Flute-stops of some Organs.
>
> ... you are ravished with the high Warblings of Pauluccio, and when you think you are almost satiated with those

---

22. Arteaga, I, 351: "gli rende più atti a vibrarsi, e conseguentemente a eseguire le menome graduazioni del canto, assotiglia l'orifizio della glottide, e la dispone a formar i tuoni acuti meglio degli altri. Cotali circostanze doveano dar ad essi la preferenza in Teatro". Whatever might be the advantages so gained, such continued to be the opprobrium cast on the process that unlikely pretexts were still offered as excuse for it. The excuse in Crescentini's case would seem to be that he had fallen down the steps of his home and hurt himself so badly as to require "an operation" (Raffaele Rossi, Appunti biografici intorno a Girolamo Crescentini (Udine, 1873), p.6)!

Luxuriances of Sound, you are most agreeably charmed a new with the soft strains of Jeronimo (which I have sometimes almost imagined have been not unlike the gentle Fallings of Water I have somewhere in Italy often heard) lulling the mind into a perfect Calm and Peace". (23)

This type of description is naturally rather impressionistic but it is noticeable that the emphasis is on delicacy of sound rather than impressive volume. This is interesting since it has usually been assumed that castrati were singers of great power due to their combination of the larynx of a youth with the fully developed chest and lungs of an adult.[24] This would seem, however, to be applying our own expectations anachronistically. Not only do the castrato theorists never lay any particular value on bigness of sound as Duey himself admits,[25] but it also conflicts with the values inherent in contemporary reports of singers, and indeed in the substance of the reports themselves. The unusual resources of breath control would seem to have manifested themselves in extended passaggi and in the traditional messa di voce. More important from our point of view is the fact that writers in the nineteenth century looked back on the castrato era and mourned just this type of skill rather than the supposed power of their voices,[26] as we shall see presently.

---

23. Italian Love; or Eunuchism Display'd (London, 1758), pp.30-31. An earlier edition exists as Eunuchism Display'd (London, 1718) which originated as a much expanded version and translation of Charles d'Ancillon, Traité des Eunuques (Paris, 1707).
24. See for example Duey, p.52; Donald Jay Grout, A Short History of Opera, second edition in one volume (New York, 1965), p.198; Willi Apel, The Harvard Dictionary of Music, second edition (London, 1970), p.137.
25. Duey, p.55.
26. An echo of the report in Italian Love; or, Eunuchism Display'd can be found in the nineteenth century description of a castrato in the Sistine Chapel by Enrico Panzacchi (1840-1904) as "a voice that combines the sweetness of the flute and the animated suavity of the human larynx" (Angus Heriot, The Castrati in Opera (London, 1956), pp.36-37). The only recordings of a castrato, made of Alessandro Moreschi in 1902, are unedifying, but show the upper register to be more promising than the lower.

Then, too, such vocal flexibility was regarded as capable of great emotional power.   So much is usually made of the ridiculous arrogance of castrati and the ignorance of their idolators, by unsympathetic northern writers, that one could be forgiven for imagining that <u>bel canto</u> was beautiful and not much more.[27] Stendhal, however, reports that it was a serious matter that required committed listening, which was why Rossini had no time for it: "The older style of singing could stir a man to the innermost recesses of his soul; but it could also prove rather boring; Rossini's style titillates the <u>mind</u>, and is never boring".[28] That such singing could send contemporaries into rapture is indicated by the report of an English traveller in Rome, dating from 1790. It must be set against all the more usual disdainful views on the inattentiveness of Italian audiences. It should also be compared with the idealized accounts of the singing of the ancients as "the language of impassioned souls" which stirred the hearts of the listeners; and whose "mysterious and magic eloquence stood wholly in its ravishing melody".[29]   <u>Bel canto</u> was something that was taken seriously even if contemporary travellers did not always understand it. Thus Dr. John Moore writes of the audience at Rome:

> "I never saw such genuine marks of satisfaction displayed by any assembly, on any occasion whatever. The sensibility of some of the audience gave me an idea of the power of sounds which the dulness of my own auditory nerves could never have conveyed to my mind. At certain airs, silent enjoyment was expressed in every countenance; at others the hands were clasped together, the eyes half shut, and the breath drawn in with a prolonged sigh, as if the soul was expiring in a torrent of delight. One young woman, in the pit, called out 'O Dio dove sono; che piacer via caccia l'alma?'* ([note:] *'O God, where am I! what pleasure ravishes my soul?')". (30)

27. Pleasants, p.19.
28. Stendhal, <u>Life of Rossini</u>, p.352.
29. <u>La farfalla</u>, 7 May 1831: "Il linguaggio delle anime appassionate" (see chapter 2, note 13) has obvious echoes of <u>I teatri</u>'s discussion of Pasta's "canto che è una continua lingua melodiosa del sentimento" (see above, note 12).
30. John Moore, M.D., <u>A View of Society and Manners in Italy</u>, fifth edition (London, 1790), II, 85-86.

For an understanding of the art of the bel canto of the castrato it is essential to realise that no virtue was put on that penetrating trumpet-like sound so often attributed to them. Any type of forcing of the voice was in particular to be avoided as it contradicted all the tenets of what writers chose to call 'purity of style'. Mancini says "forcing of the voice is always one of the greatest mistakes a singer can make".[31] A natural and easy manner of vocal delivery was praised, as discussed in Chapter 3; and this with the lack of any need to force the voice might well have militated against the type of 'vibrato' that afflicts singers today. Tosi connects these ideas himself in discussing the early education of singers:

> "Let him learn to hold out the Notes without a Shrillness like a Trumpet, or trembling; and if at the Beginning he made him hold out every Note the length of two Bars, the Improvement would be the greater; otherwise ... [he] will become subject to a Fluttering in the Manner of all those that sing in a very bad Taste". (32)

The reference to vibrato is not quite so clear in the Italian, but Tosi certainly regards wavering of the voice as in very bad taste. Both this and loudness are to be regarded as a "corruption of taste"[33] that would inhibit naturalness in vocal colouring and chiaroscuro. Vibrato is, however, something that is never referred to in reviews of early nineteenth century singers. It is hard to prove a negative, but there seems little evidence to suppose that the singers of Bellini's time suffered from "wobble".

This is something that it would be better not to be dogmatic

---

31. Mancini, p.132: "lo sforzare la voce è sempre uno dei maggiori errori che possa commettere un Cantante".
32. Tosi, Observations, translated by Galliard, p.27; the eighteenth century English translation is a rendering of Tosi, Opinioni, pp.16-17: "Gli faccia imparare di sostener le note senza, che la voce titubi, o vacilli, e se l'insegnamento comincia da quelle di due battute l'una, il profitto sarà maggiore, altramente ... avrà indubitamente il difetto di svolazzar sempre all' uso di chi canta di pessimo gusto".
33. Mancini, p.53: "corruzione del gusto".

about, but it may be that they benefited from a lack of any need to force the voice, frequently a cause of too much vibrato today. We have seen also how L'Omnibus reviewed the most forceful style of Donzelli in 1842, and the effect that this had on diction. Indeed, few things are more common in contemporary reviews than the injunction to singers not to shout or sing loudly. Since it was through poetic diction that singers succeeded in working those effects on the hearts of listeners it is not surprising that the two ideas are linked with a natural, unforced vocal delivery. Of Fanny Tacchardini-Persiani (1812-1867) who later created the role of Lucia in Donizetti's opera, the Milanese Eco describes her assumption of Beatrice in Bellini's, saying:

> "Her method and the manner in which she speaks the recitative, is all pure and beautiful. ... The voice of this singer is not very strong, but it goes to the heart, when she does not force it too much". (34)

A strong voice was not deemed a bad thing, but what was more important was one that, through purity of style, reached the heart. This could be done even by a relatively weak voice, particularly in an era before the orchestral forces were bolstered and introduced instrumental voices to compete with that of the singer. What was not looked for, as was true also in the bel canto theses of the previous century, was any effort on the part of the singer to make the voice any louder than was natural to it. Any such exertion was regarded as shouting and "who shouts, does not sing, and we are certain that [the singer] wants to sing and not shout". (35) In Naples it was a point of principle that singing rather than shouting was required whatever they might have

---

34. L'Eco, 22 July 1833: "Il suo metodo, il modo con cui dice i recitativi, tutto è bello e puro ... La voce di questa Artista non è molto forte, ma va al cuore, quando non sia di lei troppo sforzata". Later the paper adds that "è difficile il non accorgersi che Madama T-P ha, nelle sua parte, veduta e studiata Madama Pasta".
35. Il caffè del molo, number 22 (Naples, 1830), p.4: "chi grida non canta, e siam certi ch'ella vorrà cantare e non gridare".

been prepared to accept in countries further north (like Italy!). In this example of Neapolitan chauvinism the reviewer describes Giorgio Ronconi as Torquato Tasso in Donizetti's opera in 1835:

> "He was a great success, declaimed his passionate aria with great eloquence, but that cursed vice that afflicts all those that come down here from Italy was not absent in him, that is to say, he shouted too much, and in Naples one has to sing properly". (36)

The most famous, perhaps infamous, innovator of the new dramatic style was Gilbert-Louis Duprez (1806-1896) who created a sensation with a "ut de poitrine" in <u>Guillaume Tell</u> in 1837. This is a measure of the difference between the poetic expression involved in the singing style we have been discussing, with its roots in <u>bel canto</u>, and the new expressive requirements of the more modern dramatic opera. Duprez himself said the C from the chest was like any note "a means of the expression of an idea" and what was a note "without the emotion that it depicts and with which it is animated?".(37) In other words Duprez's new methods were a means of meeting new standards of expression required in the <u>melodramma</u> from the late 1830s onwards. But Duprez's expression of an idea was not one that writers trained in the proud traditions of Naples ("colonia di Atene") were likely to find too philosophical, at least not at first. Celletti regards Duprez as the tenor who provided for Donizetti what Giovanni Battista Rubini (1795-1854) did for Bellini.(38) This would have surprised their contemporaries considerably, as in this

---

36. L'Omnibus, 11 April 1835: "Ha piaciuto molto, dice il canto di passione con gran verità, ma non vi esente dal maladetto vizio di tutti coloro che scendono dall' Italia, cioè, grida troppo, ed in Napoli bisogna giustamente cantare". Giorgio Ronconi, a favourite singer of Donizetti, is not to be confused with Domenico Ronconi (1773-1839), "the last and most precious survivor of the Golden Age of Singing" (Stendhal, Life of Rossini, p.443).
37. Gilbert-Louis Duprez, Souvenirs d'un chanteur (Paris, 1880), pp. 75-76: "car, enfin, qu'est-ce qu'on son, sinon un moyen d'exprimer une pensée? Qu'est-ce qu'une note, sans le sentiment qu'elle colore et dont elle est animée ...?".
38. Celletti, in Analecta Musicologica VII (1969), pp.226-228.

view of the former's assumption of the latter's role of Gualtiero in
<u>Il pirata</u>:

> "<u>Duprez</u> has no talent for singing such music which he
> forces continuously, and the penny has not yet dropped
> that in Naples one has to sing and not shout to succeed:
> he would appear to be used to talking to the deaf". (39)

On this simple point there was an incompatibility between the old traditions and the new. To find out what
the virtues of good singing were before the modern style took root,
we will have to go back to search out those details of the <u>bel canto</u>
<u>spianato</u> that had poetic expression as their aim. The poetic rather
than the dramatic element was emphasized in the days of <u>bel canto</u> and,
through this, singing was supposed to strike the soul. Tosi distinguishes two clear musical styles as "l'espressiva" and "i passaggi",
translated by a contemporary Englishman as "the Pathetick" and "the
Allegro".(40) Of these, he emphasizes the 'Pathetick' over the
'Allegro' and stresses the importance of the poetic element that was
its major aim: "It is the most precious pleasure for the listener, the
sweetest sentiment of the soul and the strongest foundation for
music".(41) This is the didactic model for the vocal delights noticed
by <u>Italian Love</u>, Dr. John Moore, Stendhal and other writers. Tosi
makes it clear that it is rooted in the traditions of the ancients and
"that the Ancients were unequalled in singing directly to the heart".(42)

---

39. L'Omnibus, 22 November 1834: "<u>Duprez</u> non ha vocazione a cantare quella musica ch' egli forza eternamente, e non gli è ancora nato il sospetto che in Napoli fa d'uopo <u>cantare</u> non <u>gridare</u> per aver ragione: ei pare avvezzato a parlare a' sordi".
40. Tosi, <u>Opinioni</u>, p.70; Tosi, <u>Observations</u>, translated by Galliard, pp.109-110.
41. Tosi, <u>Opinioni</u>, p.68: "è la delizia più cara dell'udito, la passione più dolce dell'animo, e la base più forte dell'armonia".
42. Tosi, p.70: "che gli Antichi erano inimitabili per cantare al cuore".

Of course we have seen before the importance of this poetic singing that was able "to spark that fire in one's own heart that one claims to carry into the hearts of others".[43]

This 'Pathetick' style continued to be especially valued in Bellini's time in a way that obtained much less by the mid-nineteenth century. The broadly arched legato style of the canto spianato is referred to by Lichtenthal as "The so-called Canto Spianato or Cantabile". Its particular characteristics were "the perfect possession of the art of spinning out the voice, of realizing the phrases of the Song, the graces and passages with expression, with that nobility which distinguishes this style from all the others".[44]

This noble and uplifting style was regarded as a particular inheritance from the castrati. Lichtenthal's adumbration of contemporary values is therefore an echo of those that Stendhal saw in the old soprani:

> "The supreme qualities of the soprani and of their pupils were seen at their most resplendent in the execution of largo and cantabile spianato passages; and we have a beautiful example of this style of writing in the prayer-scene from Giulietta e Romeo". (45)

This was the practical demonstration of Tosi's 'Pathetick' style; and in it the voice spoke to the heart through the long pure phrases, where flexibility of voice also had an important part to play. Naturally the aim was to achieve a broad legato or "canto spianato" in which the singer was urged to "pass from one note to the next with a perfectly

---

43. Gervasoni, II, 210-211: "per commover gli altri ... accendere nel proprio cuore quel fuoco che nel cuore delgi altri portar si pretende".
44. Lichtenthal, I, 12: "il così detto Canto Spianato o sia il Cantabile (le di cui qualità particolari ... sono: di possedere perfettamente l'arte di filar i suoni, d'eseguire le frasi del Canto, le grazie ed i tratti con espressione, e con quella nobilità che distingue questo carattere da tutti gli altri".
45. Stendhal, Life of Rossini, p.351.

proportioned vocal legato".[46] The prayer scene referred to by Stendhal was "Ombra adorata" as sung by Crescentini in Zingarelli's opera. The famous castrato is reported by Spohr speaking rather nostalgically of "the former simple yet noble style of his time".[47] In his own Raccolta di essercizi he echoes Mancini in saying that he aims to teach the pupil "to bind one note to the next, to lead the voice forward, without dragging it too much, however, to take a breath if possible only where there are rests".[48] Marcello Perrino extends the emphasis on legato to refer not just to moves from one note to the next but also to include leaps.[49] The ultimate test of this largo canto spianato was seen after many years of study in the famous messa di voce.[50] According to Duey it was regarded as the ultimate test of breath control and its practice highly recommended.[51] Tosi, as we have seen, advised its use to ensure security of tone.[52] Faller, following Mancini, notes its use particularly at the start of cadenzas.[53] It is also incorporated in solfeggios such as those printed in Solfèges d'Italie from 1772 onwards, where it is described in the 'Agrements du Chant': "One swells the notes where there is one that is long or one that is held, one starts very softly and swells it imperceptibly as loud as the voice will manage, and leads it back to a faint sound through an again imperceptible diminuendo of the voice".[54]

---

46. Mancini, p.137: "passare, legando la voce, da una nota all'altra con perfetta proporzione".
47. Spohr, I, 311.
48. Crescentini, section 2: "di Legare una nota con l'altra, di portare la voce, senza però troppo strascinarla, di respirare soltanto se possibile fia, ove trovansi le pause".
49. Perrino, p.32.
50. Mancini, p.151.
51. Duey, p.89.
52. See above, note 32.
53. Hedwig Faller, Die Gesangskoloratur in Rossinis Opern und ihre Ausführung (Berlin, 1935), p.105.
54. Solfèges d'Italie (Paris, n.d. (c.1798)), p.xii ('Agrements du chant'): "Le son enflé se fait sur une note longue ou sur une tenue, on le commence très doux et on l'enfle imperceptiblement jusqu'au fort de la voix et l'on revient au faible en diminuant la voix aussi imperceptiblement".

Examples are then provided amongst the solfeggios as in the following by Leo (Example 1):

Example 1: <u>Solfèges d'Italie</u>. Pt.III

They appear marked in this way also by Crescentini in his <u>Raccolta di essercizi</u> of 1811 (Example 2):

Example 2: <u>Raccolta di essercizi</u> (1811), No.5

Bellini himself actually asks for a "messa di voce assai lunga" in the score of his opera Norma[55] (example 3):

Example 3: Bellini, Norma Act I, Aut. MS. F.84v

The messa di voce may have constituted some sort of ultimate test of the castrato's resources of lung power, but the true value of the canto spianato lay in its shading or chiaroscuro and in its ombreggiamento; in short, in the various devices of vocal flexibility advocated by Crescentini. According to Celentano the traditional singers' art concentrated on "the possession of chiaroscuro and vocal colouring",[56] echoing the three principal virtues stressed by Crescentini.

Of the earlier theorists, Tosi mentions this idea in introducing certain particular techniques of tonal embellishment, especially in the slower numbers, "in the cantabiles, in the sweetness of Portamento, in

---

55. Bellini, Norma, facsimile of the autograph manuscript, edited by Ottorino Respighi, 2 vols (Rome, 1935), I, f. 84v.
56. Celentano, p.12: "la proprietà del chiaroscuro e del colorito".

the Appoggiaturas, in art, in progressing through the piece intelligently, going from one note to the next with individual and unexpected rubato against the movement of the Bass", and that this rather than vocal virtuosity constituted true good taste in singing.[57]

The appoggiatura seems to have been very much part of the true Portamento, trained through the use of solfeggios.[58] Mancini devotes a whole chapter to the development of the "maniere di cavare, modulare e fermare la voce".[59] Its techniques are dealt with in more detail by Perrino in 1810, who shows the bel canto basis for the delicate and supple vocal line that was to be seen in many works by composers trained in Naples.

"The methods of vocal shading and legato apply to that type of melody, which is commonly called cantabile, that is, a broad and smooth melody that expresses a tender sentiment of the soul; in order for the voice to maintain its power in such cantilenas with a gentle expansiveness or cavata di tuono, and in that shading of piano and forte required by the sentiment, it requires a supple strength which supports and sustains it rather in the manner of a gentle spring".

"By vocal legato one does not just mean the method of joining two or more notes with the same breath without attacking them individually, but rather that constant even fluidity, and suppleness of the voice, with which it has to flow in the sounding and passing of the notes comprising the melody". [60]

---

57. Tosi, pp.81-82: "il buon gusto non risiede nella velocità continua ... ma nel cantabile, nella dolcezza del Portamento, nelle Appoggiature, nell'Arte, e nell'Intelligenza de' Passi, andando da una nota all'altra con singolari, e inaspettati inganni con rubamento di Tempo, e sul MOTO de' Bassi".
58. Mancini, p.137.
59. Mancini, 'Articolo VII', p.125.
60. Perrino, pp.41-42: "La maniera di ombreggiare e di legare la voce appartiene a quel genere di melodia, che comunemente dicesi cantabile, cioè ad una melodia larga e spianata esprimente un tenero affetto dell'animo: A sostenersi perciò la voce nelle cantilene di tal natura con una soave espansione, o sia cavata di tuono, e con quella gradazione di piano e forte che richiede l'espressione, ha ella bisogno di una forza flessibile, che a guisa di una molla gentile l'appoggi e la sostenga ... Per legatura della voce non deve intendersi soltanto la maniere di legare col medesimo fiato due o più tuoni senza batterli distintamente, ma bensì quella costante scorrevole eguaglianza, e flessibilità della voce, con cui fluir deve nell'attacco e passaggio de' tuoni componenti la melodia".

Much of this could be said to have been written with a type of supple vocal cantabile in mind that, expressing a tender sentiment of the soul, is not very different from Bellini's own. In fact the Neapolitan composers seem to have specialized in music of this type that we might well call sentimental. A classic model of the type comes from Paisiello's <u>Nina ossia la pazza per amore</u>, an opera that Bellini refers to a number of times in connection with <u>La sonnambula</u> and <u>I puritani</u>, as we have seen. Nina's famous cavatina (Example 4) shows the long breathed sentimental style with its very simple accompaniment, very open to possibilities of introduced appoggiaturas and <u>ombreggiamento</u> of the voice.

A further example (No.5) from the younger Guglielmi (1763-1817) will show the similar style in his <u>Paolo e Virginia</u> (Naples, 1817) still in evidence, with an effective use of appoggiatura. The <u>canto spianato</u> is very much in contrast to contemporary Rossinian examples.

Example 4: Paisiello Nina, Act I Cavatina for Nina
Vocal score (Paris, Carli, n.d. (after 1819)), p.36.

Example 5: P. C. Guglielmi, Paolo e Virginia Act III
Paolo's scena and aria
Naples, Conservatory, Rari Cornice 7, 9. f.273

There are also examples of more serious pieces where the inward rapture of the bel canto singer is caught in music in a more emotional vein. An opera such as Paër's Agnese (Parma, 1809), which was frequently performed in Naples, provides us with another simple accompaniment; incorporating gently see-sawing violins, and a vocal line that achieves its effects with more chromatic appoggiaturas.

Example 6: Paër, <u>Agnese di Fitzhenry</u>, Act I, Finale
Naples, Conservatory, XXIX, 2, 32, f.198

The full nobility of the old traditions of singing is realized in written out form when we come to Julia's prayer in <u>La Vestale</u> (Paris, 1807); as we have seen, very much a standard at Naples during the time Bellini was there. We cannot know precisely how it sounded in the voices of contemporary singers; but Spontini's Neapolitan inheritance seems evident. The expressive intent is achieved solely through vocal means, and that Bellini had a score of the opera perhaps suggests the impression it made on him.

Example 7: Spontini, <u>La Vestale</u>, Act II Finale, Vocal score
(Braunschweig, n.d.) p.117

These examples of the old Neapolitan styles of musical expression in the form of the <u>canto spianato</u> contrast very much with the impression of <u>bel canto</u> given by Rossinian <u>canto fiorito</u>. The vocal subtleties and nuances are well expressed in many Bellinian examples that hark back to them. Here is Norma's prayer which shows the same nobility of style. Even the flourish at the end of phrases, very characteristic of Bellini, and here marked "aspirato" can be seen in the earlier examples of Guglielmi and Spontini.

Example 8: Bellini, Norma, Act II, Finale, Vocal score
(Milan, n.d.) p.261

The evaluation of the most important aspects of good singing is an inheritance from the bel canto traditions and their conception of poetic opera. With regard to the examples and the theoretical writings discussed, it is worth pointing to one stylistic detail that has particular relevance in considering the roots of Bellinian melody itself: this is the emphasis given by writers to the appoggiatura, particularly in the canto spianato. These were originally a type of improvised embellishment, which may be why they often do not appear to be characteristic of late-eighteenth century composers. In performance they might well have been added; but this is, ultimately, an imponderable. Tosi considered that it was unnecessary to mark them.[61]

Their role as an improvised embellishment is significant because they were an expressive device, a measure of how wrong we are in assuming that bel canto concerned itself only with beauty of sound. Mancini draws attention to this expressive intent, particularly in accompanied recitative; where expressivity, unbound by formal conventions of recitative and aria, had more room to make itself felt, particularly in late-eighteenth century Neapolitan opera.[62] He says that "all the virtue of the recitative stands and depends on knowing where the appoggiaturas are best placed",[63] and particular expressive value was accorded the appoggiatura that attacked a note from below.[64]

As an embellishment the appoggiatura assumed great importance from early times, and Tosi devotes one of his first chapters to it alone. This continued to be so with later writers as well. To some extent it was regarded as the most basic form of ornament from which

---

61. Tosi, pp.22-23.
62. Robinson, p.83, notes that such recitatives tend to mark the expressive high-points in operas. There could be some support for the idea that this is paralleled in aria-like passages in Bellini's operas.
63. Mancini, p.239: "tutto il merito del recitativo consiste, e sta nel saper ben collacare l'appoggiature o sia accento Musicale".
64. Faller, p.99.

all others were derived. In his <u>Singers Preceptor</u>, Domenico Corri writes that it "is the most expressive ornament of Vocal music and appears to have been the origin of all other embellishments, as Turns, Shakes, &c.".(65) He translates the term as "the Grace".

Writers in the first part of the nineteenth century continued to stress the importance of this supple <u>canto spianato</u> style with its emphasis on the appoggiatura. This was true particularly of the teachers at Naples. Just as Tosi had done before him, Marcello Perrino associates the appoggiatura with the "canto spianato e sostenuto"; and says it can be combined to form a type of ornament much used by <u>bel canto</u> singers, the "gruppetti such as those formed from several appoggiaturas joined together".(66) Indeed he maintains that gruppetti cannot be talked of in any other way so that he has to explain the appoggiaturas first. As with Mancini, he also stresses its use in recitative: "the grace which is used most, and is almost indispensable in recitatives, is that called the <u>musical accent</u>; that is, the appoggiatura used over such a note".(67) The appoggiatura is thus a growth out of declamatory accentuation in recitatives, and other music.

Crescentini uses the same term for appoggiaturas, which he calls <u>L'Accento</u>. Together with <u>Flessibilità</u> and the <u>Colorito</u>, it is one of the most important features of a legato melody. He therefore sees it as a means of stressing important melodic points.(68) Other writers also consider it as part of a natural manner of stressing particular notes, so that it arises from the much sought-after <u>ondeggiamento</u> and <u>chiaroscuro</u> mentioned earlier. Giovanni Pacini therefore says it is

---

65. Domenico Corri, <u>The Singer's Preceptor; or, Corri's Treatise on Vocal Music</u> (London, 1810), p.32.
66. Perrino, p.38: "gruppetti, come quelli che si formano da più appoggiature unite insieme".
67. Perrino, p.62: "Lo abbellimento più usato, e quasi indispensibile ne' recitativi, è quel che chiamasi <u>accento musicale</u>, cioè l'appoggiatura praticata al disopra di quelle note".
68. Crescentini, section 1.

"nothing else than an alteration of the voice during the time that one has to hold a note suitable for it".[69] Lichtenthal describes the accento as "stronger or more clear vocal inflexion".[70]

What we have here is vocal embellishment growing out of what Italians would have called true declamation. In this the appoggiatura, developing from the musical accent, can be seen as a device that gives emphasis to the particular syllables so declaimed. This follows naturally enough from consideration of the singer as the declaimer of the poetry on the stage, and we too should be able to see its poetic basis, informed by our understanding of Italian operatic aesthetics of the time. That this has particular relevance for Bellini might escape immediate notice since the importance of the appoggiatura in his work has not been much discussed by the most modern writers, except briefly by Leslie Orrey.[71] But it is in fact one of the most obvious features of Bellinian melody for the listener, as the examples here will show. Manuel Garcίa the younger (1805-1906) considered that the appoggiatura was so much a part of Italian singing as to be hardly classed as an ornament,[72] and in these examples they have become an inherent part of the melodic construction.

---

69. Giovanni Pacini, Cenni storici sulla musica e trattato di contrapunto (Lucca, 1834), p.28: "non è altro che una modificazione della voce nel tempo in cui deve tenersi nel tuono conveniente".
70. Lichtenthal, I, 6: "Inflessione di voce più forte e più scolpita, un vigore più spiccato".
71. Leslie Orrey, Bellini (London, 1969), p.128.
72. Manuel Patricio Rodriguez Garcίa, A New Treatise on Singing (London, 1865), II, 59. By this time we read that the appoggiatura "placed on the inferior tone is seldom used in modern music" (Garcίa, 33).

Example 9: Bellini, La sonnambula, Act I, Amina's aria,
Vocal score (Milan, n.d.) p.22

Example 10: Bellini, Norma, Act I, Norma's aria, 'Casta Diva'
Vocal score (Milan, n.d.) p.63

Example 11: Bellini, <u>Il pirata</u>, Act I, duet for Gualtiero and Imogene, Vocal score (New York, n.d.) p.80

Many other similar examples can be found, including examples of notes struck from above and below. The type shown in Example 11, that involves a cross-relation, is by no means uncommon in Bellini, as a comparison with Example 8 will confirm. Their connexions with the old style of musical expression, rather than the new modes of dramatic expression, link Bellini with the traditional <u>bel canto</u> practices. After the 1830s, however, this style tended to diminish and such emphasis on melodic appoggiaturas is to be seen much less in Verdi's operas of the 1840s. The reason for this is quite simple and clearly contrasts the old and the new expressivity: emphasis through the sheer weight of sound proved to be much more dramatically effective than the fragile vocal emphasis of the appoggiatura. Eventually this led to an increasing dependence on the orchestra, but also on singers of the school of Duprez rather than <u>bel canto</u>.

Opposite to Tosi's 'Pathetick' classification was the "Allegro" style of <u>passaggi</u>. Perrino still seems to classify music into these two categories; between "canto spianato e sostenuto" (most of the examples given in this chapter have been designated "and$\frac{te}{}$ sos$\frac{to}{}$") on the one hand, and those "in tempo celere" on the other.[73] It is rather as if the task of composers was to manufacture these two contrasting types of vocal exercise. The distinction was in fact maintained in the two styles of solfeggio. Many of those in Solfèges d'Italie serve a didactic purpose and cultivate techniques of the canto spianato. No. 34 is thus called 'Pour apprendre a filer les sons', and others have a largo, adagio, or affettuoso designation. Contrasting with these are faster pieces; and sometimes the two are linked by key, so that one leads onto the other (through an imperfect cadence) in the manner of a cavatina and cabaletta.[74]

There were also the so-called gorgheggi vocalizzati which were technical exercises preparatory to the development of vocal ornamentation. The word "gorgheggiare" means to warble or "to trill" and is presumably connected with "gorgia" used as a generic term for vocal ornamentation in the early baroque, and explained by Caccini in his Nuove Musiche.

The distinction between these and the solfeggi can be seen still in Rossini's examples, where the vocal exercises called "gorgheggi" are considered in the explanatory note as "très necessaires pour rendre le voix agile".[75] As can be seen in these examples (Examples Nos. 12 and 13), the gorgheggi are characterized not by a broad smooth cantabile but by rhythmic accentuation with the notes falling into three and four-note groups marking the beats of the bar.

---

73. Perrino, p.63.
74. See for example in Solfèges d'Italie, part III, No. 197/198 by Hasse; No. 201/202 by Leo; No. 221/222 by Pasquale Cafaro.
75. Rossini, Gorgheggi e solfeggi (Paris, 1827).

Examples 12 and 13: Rossini: _Gorgheggi e solfeggi_ (Paris, 1827)

Rossini's 'solfeggi' are in a contrasting _canto spianato_ style; but, unlike Crescentini's examples, they are provided with a fully written out piano accompaniment.

Example 14: Rossini, _Gorgheggi e solfeggi_

The style of Rossinian vocal writing contrasts strongly with that of Bellini in a manner that parallels the distinction between solfeggio and gorgheggio. The use of reiterated semiquaver figurations is one of the sources of Rossini's characteristic rhythmic élan as in the following example from La donna del lago (Naples, 1819):

Example 15: Rossini, La donna del lago, Act II, terzetto for Rodrigo, Uberto, Elena, Vocal score (Paris, n.d.), p.174

The source of this in the gorgheggio style is plain enough, but in fact Rossini introduced this essentially rhythmic style into countless cavatinas as well; causing an articulation of the beats through reiterated note-groups, often emphasized by the chordal support or the use of appoggiaturas, as in this example from 1823:

Example 16: Rossini, *Semiramide*, Act II, Aria con Coro
for Arsace, Vocal score (London, n.d.) p.277

The strongly marked rhythmic style contrasts very clearly with the canto spianato style of Bellini and his bel canto predecessors, where appoggiaturas were designed as an expressive device rather than a rhythmical one. The old style was based on an approach to music that regarded its purpose as that of poetic declamation in which the rhythmic interest was less important. It could perhaps on occasion have become boring, but its best moments "could stir a man to the innermost recesses of his soul". This is the consistent achievement of Bellini's music as contemporaries saw. Rossini's style, however, "titillates the mind, and is never boring".[76] It would perhaps be more historically illuminating to point to the fact that purely musical rather than poetic considerations were important to Rossini, and in this respect he is more progressive than Bellini.

In conclusion it must be said that consideration of bel canto

---

76. Stendhal, *Life of Rossini*, p.352. Curiously enough, when Stendhal came to hear the music of Bellini, he was at first not enthusiastic (see Matteini, p.262), though he later preferred *Norma* to *La straniera* (see Matteini, p.273). Nevertheless, in most important respects "il est peut-être le musicien de l'avenir tel que l'a rêvé Stendhal - même si Stendhal ne l'a pas toujours aimé" (Pierre Brunel, *Vincenzo Bellini* (Paris, 1981), p.13).

aesthetics has suffered from a very superficial approach by writers. With the impressive example of Rossini to deal with, historians have tended to put a disproportionate stress on the element of vocal virtuosity, to an extent that seems promoted by motives more nosological than musicological. This attitude seems to be present even in the most up-to-date works. In The New Grove we are told that "The aspect of singing that became the main (and in some cases sole) concern of the 17th and 18th century writers on the voice was ornamentation".[77] In the light of the consideration given to vocal restraint, the cultivation of the legato and ombreggiatura of the voice, by all the theorists mentioned in this chapter (who include all of the most influential), this seems a gross misrepresentation of bel canto aesthetics. It has much to do with the theory that Italians could only be coaxed into the opera house by the promise of vocal pyrotechnics. One expects this of traditional musicology, based on the study of a predominantly instrumental repertory, but is surprised to find it accepted by writers on the Italian traditions. Thus even Michael Robinson talks of an eighteenth-century accent on vocal virtuosity, which he attributes to the inattentiveness of the audience.[78] So much has coloratura become a sort of musicological "dirty word" that writers now consider it a measure of a composer's musical integrity that he should distance himself from it. Thus Friedrich Lippmann counts Bellini's rejection of the canto fiorito of Rossini in La straniera as one of his most important advances, without considering what actually had been the tradition before Rossini.[79] Rodolfo Celletti similarly refers to the bel canto

---

77. Jander, 'Singing (Theory and Pedagogy)', in The New Grove, XVII, 345.
78. Robinson, p.64.
79. Lippmann, Vincenzo Bellini (1969), p.341. See also his assessment of La straniera: "con le melodie sillabiche di quest' opera Bellini rifiuta radicalmente il canto fiorito" (Lippmann, 'Vincenzo Bellini' (1981), p.509). Yet La straniera should not be taken as necessarily representative of his style as a whole, or even of the canto spianato as discussed in this chapter.

in terms of the <u>canto fiorito</u> and sees the individual styles of Donizetti and Bellini measured by the extent to which they freed themselves from Rossini's version of it.[80]

This has to be looked at anew: the <u>bel canto</u> was much more than a superficial interest in vocal virtuosity, and Rossini's codification only concerns one aspect of it. As we have seen, contemporary writers of the period were as likely to refer to the <u>canto spianato</u> as the <u>canto fiorito</u>, and tended to put more value on the former. The idea that Rossini incorporated the techniques of the <u>bel canto</u>[81] is misleading and tends to undervalue the seriousness with which Italians regarded the subject. Stendhal points out that "Rossini found himself compelled to turn his back even more completely upon the traditional <u>spianato</u> style of singing, and plunge ever more desperately into a welter of gorgheggi".[82] What this suggests is that, far from being a codification of <u>bel canto</u> practices, Rossinian coloratura accentuated the technique of <u>gorgheggio vocalizzato</u> which was a departure from the "former simple yet noble style" of Crescentini's time.[83]

Bellini's abnegation of the <u>canto fiorito</u> was therefore seen by contemporaries as a return to the "philosophical" practices of the old Italian school, rather than as something revolutionary.[84] His first biographers, who did not have to make Bellini live up to the example of Verdi, therefore sum up his place in music as "the restorer of the true Italian music",[85] by saying that he "brought back to the stage

---

80. Celletti, in <u>Analecta Musicologica</u> VII (1969), p.225.
81. Celletti, in <u>Analecta Musicologica</u> V (1968), p.269. See also Lippmann, <u>Vincenzo Bellini</u> (1969), p.164.
82. Stendhal, <u>Life of Rossini</u>, p.342.
83. See Spohr's report of his meeting with Crescentini in Naples in December 1816, in Spohr, <u>Autobiography</u>, I, 311-312.
84. See for example the cited article from <u>I teatri</u>, 19 March 1829, quoted in Cambi, p.206.
85. Filippo Gerardi, <u>Biografia di Vincenzo Bellini</u> (Rome, 1835), p.24: "Il <u>Bellini</u> in una parola sembrò fosse nato per essere il ristoratore della vera musica italiana". He tells us Bellini made a special study "del sommo <u>Durante</u>" (p.9).

the declamatory art" which had been lost since the days of "Zeno and Metastasio".[86]

The style of Bellini's own cantabiles certainly seems to have fulfilled the requirements of those writers that looked for a serious melodic opera even more clearly than some of his eighteenth-century forbears. Most of the aspects of operatic production that have been considered in this study ultimately serve the effectiveness of the poetically-inspired vocal melody. It has been pointed out that Bellini's concern for the words was by no means a new concept to Italian opera, even if he realized it more fully than other composers. But his interest in this should not be taken as a pre-echo of Verdian interest in drama which had little time for poetic niceties. Bellini's concern for the libretto was therefore different in kind rather than just different in extent.

With regard to more purely musical matters, the continuing Italian mistrust of music considered in isolation, bereft of words, had important implications for the orchestral setting, in which the texture was organized from the point of view of the basic accompanying line, called by Celentano the pedestal upon which the singer stood. Thus the lack of any interest in exploring the possibilities inherent in instrumental elaboration of the middle register. The operas of Bellini in particular, but also of many of his earlier contemporaries, therefore lack bolstering of the texture through brass instruments. The picture changes dramatically when we consider works such as Pacini's _Saffo_ (1840) or Mercadante's _Elena da Feltre_ (1838), or early Verdi.

---

86. Pietro Beltrame, _Biografia di Vincenzo Bellini_ (Venice, 1836), p.5: "Bellini ritornò a calcare il sentiero tracciato ai giorni di Zeno e di Metastasio ... richiamò sulle scene l'arte declamatoria". Of more modern writers only Fantoni has maintained that Bellini "fugge l'influenza di Rossini e s'ispira direttamente ai maestri del 18º secolo" (G. Fantoni, _Storia universale di canto_, 2 vols (Milan, 1873), II, 141).

The expression of the text in Italian opera before this change is therefore left to the singer. It is difficult to be sure how much earlier operas differed from Bellini's in matters of textual declamation in practice, because of the imponderable problems of ornamentation. It is impossible to say how much of the emphasis on the appoggiatura is peculiar to Bellini and how much would, under the influence of Tosi and Mancini, have been introduced before him. The same problem of course holds for Bellini's own music: reliable accounts of ornamentation are very rare.[87]

With regard to the close connexions between composition and performance entailed by any consideration of the possibilities of ornamentation, it is worth noting that Bellini worked intimately with singers of the old rather than the new schools: that is to say, that he was quite happy to write for <u>contralto musico</u> singers as in <u>I Capuleti e i Montecchi</u>, which took the place of the rapidly disappearing castratos. Great emphasis is put by Lippmann and Celletti on the fact that Bellini wrote for tenor rather than contralto male leads, and that the role of Gualtiero in <u>Il pirata</u> marks a watershed in the development of the Romantic tenor.[88] Such emphasis ignores the fact that Bellini and his contemporaries viewed such writing in a different context, and certainly did not see it as a revolutionary departure. Bellini was quite prepared to re-arrange this supposedly innovative work for the old voice-system with a contralto Gualtiero (for Brigida Lorenzani) and a tenor <u>antagonista</u> setting for Ernesto (Domenico Reina),

---

87. Very few contemporary prints of singers' embellishments exist from this era, and none that directly concern Bellini. Examples that have appeared in musicological works seem to lack adequate manuscript documentation. An exception lies in the notebooks of Laure Cinti-Damoreau discussed in Austin Caswell, 'Mme. Cinti-Damoreau and the Embellishment of Italian Opera in Paris 1820-1845', in <u>Journal of the American Musicological Society</u> XXVIII (1975), pp. 459-492.
88. Celletti, in <u>Analecta Musicologica</u> VII (1969), p.215; Lippmann, 'Vincenzo Bellini' (1981), p.456.

as his letters make clear.[89] Such a contralto-hero would have matched those already existing for Nerestano in <u>Zaira</u>, Romeo, and the title role in the unfinished setting of <u>Ernani</u>. Gualtiero was sung as a contralto role on a number of occasions.[90]

It is also curious that Bellini's attachment to the tenor voice was solely dependent on Rubini, for whom he wrote the roles of Gernando, Gualtiero, Elvino, and Arturo (in <u>I puritani</u>). These are the works where the tenor role is equal in prominence to that of the <u>prima donna</u>. In the other operas the tenor role tends to be, although a leading role, not one on a par with that of the leading lady. This is noticeably the case with Orombello in <u>Beatrice di Tenda</u>, and Pollione in <u>Norma</u>, if rather less so in <u>La straniera</u>. Rubini was a very different sort of tenor from Duprez, for example, and was particularly successful in "sweet and sentimental expression" and in "uniting the chest voice with the head voice" so that the hearer could not "notice this perilous passage of tonal register".[91] The latter point is a particular inheritance from the teachings of the <u>bel canto</u>. Tenors of this type, expert in flexible and supple vocalization, were hardly new to opera by this time; Rossini's <u>Otello</u> contains three large tenor roles, and his <u>Armida</u> parts for four tenor singers. Not surprisingly we find

---

89. Cambi, p.115 (16 June 1828). According to Barbaja, Bridiga Lorenzani was highly regarded in such roles: "occupa anch'essa il posto fra le prime ed è oggi il Contralto di maggior merito" (A/S, F.T. fascio 63, letter of 25th February 1826). It should be noted that the term <u>contralto</u> was at this time restricted to roles for a <u>contralto musico</u> male lead.
90. See for example reports of its assumption by Fodor-Mainville (<u>L'Indifferente</u>, fascicolo III (Naples, 1830), p.296) and particularly Malibran (<u>L'Omnibus</u>, 21 December 1833).
91. <u>Rivista teatrale</u>, 10 July 1824: "Riescegli specialmente l'espressione del dolce e sentimentale ... ad eccellenza sa egli unire la voce di petto a quella di testa ... senza farci accorgere questo passaggio pericoloso nel registro dei toni". Later mention is made of the fact that "ad un pubblico avezzo alle gride e voci forti, egli seppe far conoscere la naturalezza del canto". It is impossible to rely on reviews to give us an adequate picture of a singer. See, however, the discussion of this singer in Pleasants, p.133.

that Rubini regularly sang these Rossini roles as Duprez did not. For Duprez, even Elvino in La sonnambula was in an incompatible style.(92)

In the same way, Bellini's other great voice, the prima donna Giuditta Pasta, had assumed many of the old roles including several castrato roles. Amongst her more famous roles were Nina in Paisiello's opera, Tancredi, Curiazio in Cimarosa's Gli Orazi e i Curiazi, Romeo in Zingarelli's Giulietta e Romeo (the last two roles originally sung by Crescentini in 1796), Telemaco in Cimarosa's Penelope, Armando in Meyerbeer's Il Crociato in Egitto and so forth.(93) We have already seen that her singing embodied all the values of the bel canto spianato held dear by the old theorists.(94)

As sung by these practitioners of a lost vocal art, Bellini's vocal style might well have reminded listeners of all the values that they held dear. This is not to say that he was merely following in the old Neapolitan traditions: his style is informed with a Romantic sensibility that was definitely individual. There is no doubting either the strong influence it worked on Donizetti, Mercadante and early Verdi. For these reasons Lippmann's analyses of Bellini are usually correct.

To understand the operatic culture that gave birth to them, however, we have to dig deeper and credit contemporary Italians with more musical seriousness and artistic integrity than is usually done. That Bellini was constantly more serious than Rossini does not mean that he was therefore something entirely unheard of in Italy since the days of Monteverdi. Bellini would appear to have spoken to the hearts of the audiences in the manner in which contemporary writers thought that opera was always supposed to have done since the times of the Ancients. In Chapter 2 it was discussed how the Greeks were supposed

---

92. See above, note 39.
93. See Celletti, in Analecta Musicologica V, p.273; Stendhal, Life of Rossini, p.374 note 2.
94. See above, note 12.

to have gone to the theatre to be moved by the ravishing power of declamatory melody. In the early nineteenth century the _bel canto_ singer was still supposed to move audiences to tears as the modern representative of that ancient eloquence. In this respect the melodies of Bellini that worked such emotional effects on the listeners seem to fulfill all the requirements for the sentimental opera of his time. The testimony of Glinka at the first performance of _La sonnambula_ in 1831 is a famous expression of this.

> "in the second act the singers themselves wept and carried their audience along with them, so that in the happy days of Carnival, tears were continually being wiped away in boxes and parquet alike. Embracing Shterich in the Ambassador's box, I, too, shed tears of emotion and ecstasy". (95)

---

95. Mikhail I. Glinka, _Memoirs_, translated by Richard Mudge (Norman, 1963), p.63.

BIBLIOGRAPHY

The first three sections of this bibliography give details of the works referred to in the text. Sections 4 to 7 list sources that have contributed to this study as well as those referred to in the text. Library names have been abbreviated in the following manner:

A/S:	Naples, Archivio di Stato
BN:	Naples, Biblioteca Nazionale Vittorio Emanuele III
LP:	Naples, Biblioteca Lucchesi Palli
LR:	Naples, Biblioteca Nazionale Vittorio Emanuele III, Sezione Libri Rari
NC:	Naples, Conservatorio di Musica di San Pietro a Majella
RSC:	Rome, Conservatorio Santa Cecilia
SP:	Naples, Società Napolitana per la Storia Patria
VF:	Venice, Archivio del Teatro la Fenice

Other abbreviations have usually been avoided, except for the following:

AMZ:	Allgemeine musikalische Zeitung
ES:	Enciclopedia dello spettacolo, edited by S. d'Amico, 11 vols, Rome, Le Maschere, 1954-1966

1. Manuscript Music

Bellini, V., *I Capuleti e i Montecchi*, autograph full score, 2 vols, Catania, Museo Belliniano (no shelf-mark)

Bellini, V., *Ernani*, autograph sketches (unbound), Catania, Museo Belliniano

Bellini, V., *Il pirata*, autograph full score, 2 vols, NC, Rari 4.2.8/9

Bellini, V., *Zaira*, autograph full score, 2 vols, NC, Rari 4.2.10/11

Bellini, V., Solfeggios in autograph (unbound), Catania, Museo Belliniano

Bellini, V., 'Studi giornalieri' (unbound), Catania, Museo Belliniano

Guglielmi, P. C., *Paolo e Virginia*, NC, Rari Cornice 7.9.

Mercadante, G. S. R., *Elena da Feltre*, NC, III 3-5.11

Mercadante, G. S. R., *Zaira*, NC, Rari 3.6.9.

Pacini, G., *Saffo*, NC, XIV 4.15.

Paër, F., *Agnese di Fitzhenry*, NC, XXIX 2.32

Paisiello, G., *Nina; ossia, La pazza per amore*, NC, Rari 3.1.20/21

2. Printed Music

Bellini, V., Norma, facsimile autograph score, edited by Ottorino Respighi, 2 vols, Rome, Reale Accademia d'Italia, 1935

Bellini, V., Norma, vocal score, Milan, Ricordi, plate No. 41684

Bellini, V., Il pirata, vocal score, New York, Belwin Mills

Bellini, V., La sonnambula, facsimile autograph score, Milan, Ricordi, 1934

Bellini, V., La sonnambula, vocal score, Milan, Ricordi, plate No. 41686

Crescentini, G., Raccolta di essercizi per il canto all'uso del vocalizzo, Paris, Imbault, 1811, plate No. 962

Mercadante, G. S. R., Il giuramento, vocal score, Milan, Ricordi, plate No. 32281-32301

Paër, F., Agnese di Fitzhenry, vocal score, Paris, Janet et Cotelle, plate No. 314

Paisiello, G., Nina; ossia, La pazza per amore, vocal score, Paris, Carli, plate No. 459

Rossini, G. A., La donna del lago, vocal score, Paris, La Critique Musicale

Rossini, G. A., Gorgheggi e solfeggi, Paris, Pacini, 1827

Rossini, G. A., Semiramide, vocal score, London, Boosey

Solfèges d'Italie avec la basse chiffrée, edited by MM. Levèque e Bèche, Paris, Le Duc [c.1798]

Spontini, G., La Vestale, full orchestral score, Paris, Richault, plate No. 700

Spontini, G., Die Vestalin, vocal score, Braunschweig, Meyer

3. Librettos

Bellini (seniore), V. T., La vittoria di Gedeone, Catania, Pulejana, 1808 (NC, 5.12.24)

Bellini, V., Beatrice di Tenda, Venice, Casali, 1832-1833 (VF, libretto No. 160)

Bellini, V., Beatrice di Tenda, Naples, Tipografia dell'Omnibus, 1834 (RSC, G. libretti, N. XXIV 525)

Bellini, V., I Capuleti e i Montecchi, Venice, Casali, 1830 (RSC, G. libretti, XXIII 61)

Bellini, V., Norma, Milan, Truffi, 1831 (RSC, G. libretti, XXIII 35)

Bellini, V., Norma, Turin, 1834 (RSC, G. libretti, vol 130^{10})

Bellini, V., Norma, Venice, Molinari, 1844 (VF, libretto No. 268)

Bellini, V., Il pirata, Milan, Fontana, 1827 (RSC, G. libretti, XXIII 244)

Bellini, V., Il pirata, Venice, Casali, 1830 (VF, libretto No. 144)

Bellini, V., La straniera, Milan, Fontana, 1829 (RSC, G. libretti, XXIII 285)

Bellini, V., <u>La straniera</u>, Florence, 1830 (RSC, G. libretti, XXIII 286)
Bellini, V., <u>Zaira</u>, Parma, 1829 (RSC, G. libretti, XXIII 309)
Bellini, V., <u>Zaira</u>, Florence, Giachetti, 1836 (RSC, A. libretti, vol 18^2)
Donizetti, G., <u>Anna Bolena</u>, Venice, Casali, 1831 (VF, libretto No. 152)
Mercadante, G. S. R., <u>Elena da Feltre</u>, Naples, Flautina, 1838 (RSC, G. libretti, XXIV 144)
Mercadante, G. S. R., <u>Il giuramento</u>, Milan, Truffi, 1837 (NC, OE. 1.20)
Rossini, G. A., <u>Tancredi</u>, Florence, 1822 (RSC, G. libretti, XXIII 288)

4. Archival Sources: Mainly MSS

Naples, Archivio di Stato, Sezione Amministrativa, Fondo Teatri, Atti della Deputazione dei Teatri e spettacoli (1820-1827); della Sopraintendenza (1827+)

fascio 1	'Registro relativo al personale'
fascio 20	'Teatri e spettacoli, Regolamenti'
fascio 50	'Produzione in musica - Affari diversi'
fascio 53	'Collegio di musica: Cosegnamento de' spartiti ecc.'
fascio 63	'Artisti di canto e ballo dei R. Teatri'
fascio 113	'R. T. di San Carlo: Imprese diverse 1808-1858'
fascio 125	'R. T. di San Carlo: Personale degli artisti di canto 1807+'
fascio 127	'R. T. di San Carlo: Orchestra personale 1813+'

A/S, Sezione Amministrativa, Ministero dell'Interno: Terzo ripartimento: Istruzione pubblica, scienze e belle arti, Inventario primo

fascio 875   '1809-1842'
fascio 876   '1816'

5. Early Periodicals

As the great majority of the Neapolitan periodicals are not recorded elsewhere, the following dates of publication are offered. They should not be taken as final but indicate the years' issues traced in the libraries concerned. The libraries are indicated in brackets.

<u>Allgemeine musikalische Zeitung</u>, Leipzig, 1798-
<u>Il caffè del molo</u>: Giornale critico-letterario, Naples, Seguiri, 1829-1832 (BN)
<u>Collezione delle leggi e decreti reali del Regno di Napoli</u>, Naples, Stamperia Reale, 1815-1860
<u>I Curiosi</u>, Naples, 1836 (LP)

L'Eco: Giornale di scienze, lettere, arti, mode e teatri, Milan, Lampato, 1828-1835 (1834-1835 in SP)

La Farfalla: Giornale di letturatura, d'invenzione, scienze ed arti, Naples, 1830-1832 (BN) (LP)

Il Folletto: Foglio periodico, Naples, 1834 (BN)

Il Gagliano: Giornale di amena letteratura, Naples, Gargiulo, 1823-1824 (BN)

Giornale del Regno delle due Sicilie, Naples, 1816-

Giornale di commercio, arti, industrie, manufatture e varietà, Naples, 1834 (BN)

The Harmonicon, London, 1826-1833

L'Indifferente: Giornale di teatri, mode e varietà, Naples, Minerva, 1830-1831 (BN)

L'Indipendente: Giornale politico, letterario e commerciale, Naples, Tip. Francese, 1820-1821 (BN)

Monitore delle due Sicilie, Naples, 1811-1816

Monitore napolitano, Naples, 1806-1811 (BN)

L'Omnibus, Naples, Girard, 1833-(BN)

Rivista teatrale; [later] Rivista teatrale e giornale di mode, Naples, Biblioteca Analitica, 1824; Naples, Fernandes, 1824-1825; Naples, Zambraja, 1825 (LR) (LP)

Il Veritiero: Giornale periodico amena-letterario, Naples, Mosino, 1834 (BN)

Il Vesuvio: Giornale d'amena letteratura, scienze, belle arti, teatri, mode, e varietà, Naples, Borsini, 1834 (BN)

La Voce del secolo: Giornale politico letterario, Naples, Tip. strada Toledo, 1820-1821 (LR)

6. Books: Early and Other Primary Sources

Algarotti, F., An Essay on the Opera, London, Davis & Reymers, 1767

Algarotti, F., Saggio sopra l'opera in musica, Naples, 1756

Almanacco de' Reali Teatri S. Carlo e Fondo dell' annata teatrale 1834, Naples, Flautina, 1835 (SP)

Almanacco galante per l'anno 1827 (-1830), Venice, Orlandelli, 1827-1830 (VF)

Anderson, E., ed., The Letters of Mozart and His Family, 3 vols, London, Macmillan, 1938

Arteaga, S., Le rivoluzioni del teatro musicale italiano dalla sua origine fino al presente, second edition, 3 vols, Venice, Palese, 1785

Asioli, B., Trattato d'armonia e d'accompagnamento, Milan, 1813

Basevi, A., Studj sull'armonia, Florence, Guidi, 1865

Basevi, A., Studio sulle opere di Giuseppe Verdi, Florence, Tofani, 1859

Beltrame, P., Biografia di Vincenzo Bellini, Venice, 1836

Berlioz, H., *The Memoirs of Hector Berlioz*, translated and edited by D. Cairns, London, Gollancz, 1969

Brown, Dr. J. (1715-1766), *A Dissertation on the Rise, Union, and Power, the Progressions, Separations and Corruptions of Poetry and Music*, London, Davis & Reymers, 1763

Brown, J. (1752-1787), *Letters upon the Poetry and Music of the Italian Opera*, Edinburgh, Bell & Bradfute, 1789

Bürkli, G., *Biographie von Vincenz Bellini*, Zurich, 1841

Burney, C., *Music, Men and Manners in France and Italy 1770*, edited by H. E. Poole, London, Eulenburg, 1974

Burney, C., *The Present State of Music in France and Italy*, London, Becket, 1771

Cambi, L., ed., *Vincenzo Bellini, Epistolario*, Verona, Mondadori, 1943

Celentano, L., *Intorno all'arte del cantare in Italia nel secolo decimonono*, Naples, Ghio, 1867 (BN)

Choron, A. and Fayolle, F., *Dictionnaire historique des musiciens*, 2 vols, Paris, 1810-1811

Cicconetti, F., *Vita di Vincenzo Bellini*, Prato, Alberghetti, 1859

Colle, F., *Dissertazione sopra il quesito Dimostrare ... quanta parte avesse la musica nell'educazione de' Greci*, Mantua, 1775

Corri, D., *The Singer's Preceptor; or, Corri's Treatise on Vocal Music*, London, Silvester, 1810

Crescentini, G., *Raccolta di essercizi per il canto all'uso del vocalizzo*, Paris, Imbault, 1811

De la Fage, J., 'Zingarelli', in *La Revue Universelle*, Paris, 30 September 1837

Di Moiano, P. [attributed to], *Alcune osservazioni critiche intorno alla musica dell'opera 'La straniera' del sig. Maestro Vincenzo Bellini*, Milan, 1830

Dizionario portabile delle popolazioni del regno di Napoli con tavole interessanti e sua carta geografica, Naples, 1803

Duprez, G.-L., *Souvenirs d'un chanteur*, Paris, 1880

Edgcumbe, R., *Musical Reminiscences of an Old Amateur*, second edition, London, Clarke, 1827

Escudier, L., *Études biographiques sur les chanteurs contemporaine*, Paris, 1840

Eximeno, A., *Dell'origine e delle regole della musica colla storia del suo progresso, decadenza, e rinnovazione*, Rome, 1774

Ferri di S. Costante, Conte G., *Lo spettatore italiano*, 4 vols, Milan, Società tipografica de' classici italiani, 1822

Ferro e Ferro, Cav. G. di, *Delle belle arti dissertazioni*, 2 vols, Palermo, Solli, 1807-1808

Florimo, F., *Bellini, memorie e lettere*, Florence, Barbera, 1882

Florimo, F., *Breve metodo di canto*, composto e dedicato al Cav. Crescentini, third edition, Milan, Ricordi, n.d. [before 1864]

Florimo, F., *La scuola musicale di Napoli e i suoi conservatorii*, 4 vols, Naples, Morano, 1880-1881; reprinted Bologna, Forni, 1969

Garcia, M. P. R., New Treatise on the Art of Singing, London, Cramer, 1865

Gautier, T., Notice sur 'Norma', Paris, 1845

Gennaro Grossi, G. B., Le belle arti, 2 vols, Naples, Giornale enciclopedico, 1820

Gerardi, F., Biografia di Vincenzo Bellini, Rome, 1835

Gervasoni, C., La scuola della musica, 3 parts, Piacenza, 1800

I Giudizij dell'Europa intorno alla signora Catalani; ossia, articoli concernanti il merito di lei, tratti dalle più riputati opere periodiche di Londra, Parigi, Barlino, Amsterdam, Lipsia, Annover, Milano ecc., second edition, Milan, 1816

Glinka, M., Memoirs, translated by R. Mudge, Norman, University of Oklahoma Press, 1963

The Grace Book; or, Guide to the Science and Practice of Vocal Ornament, London, Chappell, n.d. [c.1835-1840]

Italian Love; or, Eunuchism Display'd, describing the different kinds of Eunuchs, London, Reason, 1758

The Italian Opera in 1839: Its latest improvements and existing defects impartially considered, London, Novello, 1840

Kotzebue, A. von, Travels through Italy in the years 1804 and 1805, English edition, 4 vols, London, Phillips, 1806

Lichtenthal, P., Dizionario e bibliografia della musica, 4 vols, Milan, Fontana, 1826

Majer, A., Discorso sulla origine progressi e stato attuale della musica italiana, Padua, 1821

Mancini, G. B., Pensieri e riflessioni pratiche sopra il canto figurato, Vienna, 1774; third edition, Milan, 1777 (NC)

Manfredini, V., Regole armoniche, second edition, Venice, 1797

Marchand, L., ed., Byrons Letters and Journals, 12 vols, London, 1976

Martuscelli, D., Biografia degli uomini illustri del regno di Napoli, 10 vols, Naples, 1813-1825

Mastriani, G., Il teatro e gli artisti, Naples, Androsio, 1849 (LP)

Mendelssohn-Bartholdy, P., ed., Reisebriefe aus den Jahren 1830 bis 1832 von Felix Mendelssohn-Bartholdy, Leipzig, Mendelssohn, 1865

Mercadante, G. S. R., 'Breve cenno storico sulla musica teatrale da Pergolesi a Cimarosa', in Atti della Reale Accademia di Archeologia, Lettere e Belle Arti, III, Naples, 1867, pp.33-37 (BN)

Metastasio, P., Opere dell'abbate Metastasio, edited by L. Nardini, third edition, 2 vols, London, Lackington, Hughes, Harding, Mavor & Lepard, 1821

Metastasio, P., Tutte le opere di Pietro Metastasio, edited by B. Brunelli, 5 vols, Milan, Mondadori, 1943-1954

Milizia, F., Trattato completo, formale e materiale del teatro, Venice, Pasquali, 1794

Momigny, J. J. de, La sola e vera teorica della musica, "versione dal francese", 2 vols, Bologna, 1823

Moore, Dr. J., *A View of Society and Manners in Italy*, fifth edition, 2 vols, London, 1790

Napoli-Signorelli, P., *Del gusto e del bello*, Naples, Orsini, 1807

Napoli-Signorelli, P., *Storia critica de' teatri musicali italiani*, 10 vols, Naples, Orsini, 1813

Napoli-Signorelli, P., *Vicende della coltura nelle due Sicilie dalla venuta delle colonie straniere sino a' nostri giorni*, second edition, 8 vols, Naples, Orsini, 1810-1811

Niccolini, A., *Alcune idee sulla risonanza del Teatro*, Naples, Masi [1811] (BN)

Niccolini, A., *Del Real Teatro di San Carlo*, cenno storico, Naples, 1817 (BN)

Niccolini, A., *Sulla nuova decorazione del Real Teatro S. Carlo*, Naples, n.d. [c.1817] (BN)

Opienski, H., ed., *Chopin's Letters*, translated and edited by E. Voynich, New York, Knopf, 1931; reprinted, New York, Vienna House, 1973

Pacini, G., *Cenni storici sulla musica e trattato di contrappunto*, Lucca, Giusti, 1834

Pacini, G., *Le mie memorie artistiche*, Florence, Guidi, 1865

Perrino, M., *Osservazioni sul canto*, Naples, Stamperia reale, 1810 (NC)

Philodemi [Philodemus], *De Musica*, Naples, 1793 (NC)

Planelli, A., *Dell'opera in musica*, Naples, Campo, 1772

Ritorni, C., *Ammaestramenti alla composizione d'ogni poema e d'ogni opera appartenente alla musica*, Milan, 1841

Rubini, G. B., *Twelve Lessons on the Modern Style of Singing*, London, Cramer, n.d. [1838]

Sabbatini, L. A., *Elementi teorici della musica*, 3 parts, Rome, 1789-1790; second edition, Rome, 1795

Scott, J., *Sketches of Manners, Scenery &c. in the French Provinces, Switzerland and Italy*, second edition, London, 1821

Simpson, A., *Secret Memoirs of Madame Catalani*, Bath, Gye, 1811

Spohr, L., *Louis Spohr's Autobiography*, translated from the German, 2 vols, London, Longman Green etc., 1865

Stabilmenti per l'interno regolamento del Real Conservatorio di musica San Sebastiano in Napoli, Naples, Trani, 1809

Stendhal [Henri Beyle], *Lives of Haydn, Mozart and Metastasio*, translated by R. N. Coe, London, Calder & Boyars, 1972

Stendhal, *Life of Rossini*, second edition, translated and annotated by R. N. Coe, London, Calder & Boyars, 1970

Stendhal, *Rome, Naples and Florence*, translated by R. N. Coe, London, Calder, 1959

Stendhal, *Vie de Rossini*, edited by H. Martineau, 2 vols, Paris, Le Divan, 1929

Tosi, P. F., *Observations on the Florid Song; or, Sentiments on the Ancient and Modern Singers*, translated by Mr. Galliard, London, Wilcox, 1743; reprinted London, Reeves, 1905; 1926; 1967

Tosi, P. F., Opinioni de' cantori antichi e moderni; o sieno, Osservazioni sopra il canto figurato, Bologna, Lelio dalla Volpe, 1723; reprinted in facsimile in J. F. Agricola, Anleitung zur Singkunst, edited by E. Jacobi, Celle, Moeck, 1966

Vallo, D., Compendio elementare di musica specolativo-practico, Naples, 1804 (NC)

Villarosa, Marchese di, Lettera biografica intorno alla patria ed alla vita di Gio. Battista Pergolese, Naples, Fibreno, 1831

7. Modern Studies and Other Secondary Sources

Adamo, M., 'Vincenzo Bellini, biografia', in M. Adamo and F. Lippmann, Vincenzo Bellini, Turin, Edizioni RAI Radiotelevisione Italiana, 1981, pp.9-311

Adler, G., ed., 'Die Oper im 19. Jahrhundert: Italien', in G. Adler, Handbuch der Musikgeschichte, second revised edition, Berlin, Keller, 1930, II, pp.904-916

Amore, A., Vincenzo Bellini, Arte (Studie e ricerche), Catania, Giannotta, 1892

Aniante, A., Vita di Vincenzo Bellini, Turin, 1925 (NC)

Ashbrook, W., Donizetti and his Operas, Cambridge, CUP, 1982

Barzun, J., ed., Pleasures of Music, London, Cassell, 1977

Bloch, E. H., 'Une soirée à Paris en 1835. Bellini, Musset et la principesse de Belgiogoso', in Feuilles d'histoire, I, No.6, Paris, Roger & Chernoriz, 1 June 1909, pp.495-499 (NC)

Boromé, J., 'Bellini and Beatrice di Tenda', in Music and Letters, XLII, 1961, pp.319-325

Branca, E., Felice Romani e i più reputati maestri del suo tempo, Turin, Loescher, 1882

Brauner, C., 'Textual Problems in Bellini's Norma and Beatrice di Tenda', in Journal of the American Musicological Society, XXIX, 1976, pp.99-118

Brauner, C., 'Vincenzo Bellini and the Aesthetics of Opera Seria in the First Third of the Nineteenth Century' (unpublished Ph.D. dissertation, Yale, 1972)

Brunel, P., Vincenzo Bellini, Paris, Fayard, 1981

Budden, J., The Operas of Verdi, 3 vols, London, Cassell, 1973-1981

Cambi, L., 'Un pacchetto di autografi', in Scritti in onore di Luigi Ronga, Milan and Naples, Ricciardi, 1973, pp.53-90

Carse, A., The Orchestra in the Eighteenth Century, Cambridge, Heffer, 1940; reprinted New York, Broude Bros., 1969

Carse, A., The Orchestra from Beethoven to Berlioz, Cambridge, Heffer, 1948

Caswell, A., 'Mme. Cinti-Damoreau and the Embellishment of Italian Opera in Paris 1820-1845', in Journal of the American Musicological Society, XXVIII, 1975, pp.459-492

Cavazzuti, P., Bellini a Londra, Florence, 1945

Celletti, R., 'Il vocalismo italiano da Rossini a Donizetti', in *Analecta Musicologica*, V, Cologne and Vienna, Böhlau, 1968, pp. 267-294; and VII, 1969, pp.214-247

Celletti, R., 'On Verdi's Vocal Writing', in W. Weaver and M. Chusid, eds., *The Verdi Companion*, London, Gollancz, 1980, pp.216-236

Collins, M., 'The Literary Background to Bellini's *I Capuleti e i Montecchi*', in *Journal of the American Musicological Society*, XXXV, 1982, pp.532-538

Commons, J., '*Maria Stuarda* and the Neapolitan Censorship', in *The Donizetti Society Journal*, III, 1977, pp.151-167

Conati, M. and M. Pavarani, eds., *Orchestre in Emilia-Romagna nell' Ottocento e Novecento*, Parma, Orchestra Sinfonica dell'Emilia-Romagna "Arturo Toscannini", 1982

Convegno di studi sull'opera "Bianca e Fernando" di Vincenzo Bellini 1978, Genoa, Amministrazione Provinciale di Genova: Assessorato alla Pubblica Istruzione e Cultura, 1980

Cottrau, G., *Lettres d'un mélomane pour servir de document à l'histoire musicale de Naples de 1829 à 1847*, Naples, Morano, 1885 (NC)

Croce, B., *I teatri di Napoli, secolo XV-XVIII*, fourth edition, Bari, Laterza, 1947

Dahlhaus, C., *Esthetics of Music*, translated by W. Austin, Cambridge, CUP, 1982

Dallapiccola, L., 'Words and Music in Italian Nineteenth-Century Opera', in W. Weaver and M. Chusid, *The Verdi Companion*, London, Gollancz, 1980, pp.193-215

Dalmonte, R., 'La canzone nel melodramma italiana del primo Ottocento. Ricerche di metodo strutturale', in *Rivista Italiana di Musicologia*, XI, 1976, pp.230-313

Damerini, A., 'Bellini e la critica del suo tempo', in I. Pizzetti, ed., *Vincenzo Bellini, l'uomo, le sue opere, la sua fama*, Milan, Treves, 1936, pp.215-250

Dannreuther, E., *Musical Ornamentation*, 2 vols, London and New York, Novello & Ewer, [1893]

De Filippis, F., and R. Arnese, *Cronache del Teatro di San Carlo (1737-1960)*, 2 vols, Naples, 1959

De Filippis, F., *Napoli teatrale*, dal teatro romano al S. Carlo, aneddoti e figure, Milan, Curci, 1962

Degrada, F., 'Prolegomeni a una lettura della *Sonnambula*', in *Il melodramma italiana dell'Ottocento. Studi e ricerche per Massimo Mila*, Turin, Einaudi, 1977, pp.319-350

Della Corte, A., *Canto e bel canto*, Turin, Paravia, 1933

Della Corte, A., and G. Pannain, *Vincenzo Bellini: Il carattere morale, i caratteri artistici*, Turin, Paravia, 1935

Della Libera, S., 'Teatro La Fenice, Cronologia degli spettacoli 1792-1866', unpublished typescript (VF)

Dent, E. J., 'Donizetti, an Italian Romantic', in *Fanfare for Ernest Newman*, edited by H. van Thal, London, Barker, 1955, pp.86-107

Dent, E. J., *The Rise of Romantic Opera*, edited by W. Dean, Cambridge, CUP, 1976

Dent, E. J., 'The Romantic Spirit in Music', in Papers of The Musical Association, LIX, 1932-1933, pp.85-102

Di Benedetto, R., 'Lineamenti di un teoria della melodia nella trattatistica italiana fra il 1790 e il 1830', in Analecta Musicologica, XXI, 1981, pp.421-434

Duey, P., Bel Canto in its Golden Age, New York, Columbia, 1951

Einstein, A., Music in the Romantic Era, New York, Norton, 1947

Einstein, A., A Short History of Music, fourth American edition, New York, Knopf, 1969

Einstein, A., 'Vincenzo Bellini', in Music and Letters, XVI, 1935, pp. 325-332

Faller, H., Die Gesangskoloratur in Rossinis Opern und ihre Ausführung, dissertation published, Berlin, Triltsch & Huther, 1935

Fantoni, G., Storia universale del canto, 2 vols, Milan, 1873

Fetis, F. J., Biographie Universelle des musiciens, 8 vols, Paris, 1860-1865; Supplement, ed. A. Pougin, 2 vols, Paris, Firman-Didot, 1878-1880

Freeman, J., 'Pietro Generali in Sicily', in Music Review, XXXIV, 1973, pp.231-240

Gasparini, G. and F. Gallo, Biblioteca del R. Conservatorio di Musica di S. Pietro a Majella, Parma, Fresching, 1934

Gatti, G., Il Teatro alla Scala nella storia e nell'arte 1778-1963, 2 vols, Milan, Ricordi, 1964

Geering, A., 'Gesangspädagogik', in Die Musik in Geschichte und Gegenwart, IV, 1955, cols 1908-1934; especially cols 1924-1925, and bibliography

Cataldo, G., Il teatro di Bellini - Guida critica a tutte le opere, Bologna, Bongiovanni, 1980

Gosset, P., 'Gioachino Rossini and the Conventions of Composition', in Acta Musicologica, XLII, 1970, pp.48-58

Gosset, P., 'The Operas of Rossini, Problems of Textual Criticism in Nineteenth-Century Opera' (unpublished Ph.D. dissertation, Princeton University, 1970)

Gray, C., 'Vincenzo Bellini', in Music and Letters, VII, 1926, pp.49-62

Greenspan, C., 'The Operas of Vincenzo Bellini' (unpublished Ph.D. dissertation, University of California, Berkeley, 1977)

Haböck, F., Die Gesangkunst der Kastraten: Erstes Notenbuch, Die Kunst des Cavaliere Carlo Broschi Farinelli, Vienna, Universal, 1923

Haböck, F., Die Kastraten und ihre Gesangskunst, Stuttgart, Deutsche Verlags-Anstalt, 1927

Hanslick, E., The Beautiful in Music, translated by G. Cohen, The Library of Liberal Arts, Indianapolis and New York, Bobbs-Merrill, 1957

Heriot, A., The Castrati in Opera, London, Secker & Warburg, 1956

Hucke, H., 'Die neapolitanische Tradition der Oper', in Report of the IMS Congress New York 1961, New York, Kassel, 1962, pp.253-277

Hucke, H., 'Verfassung und Entwicklung der alten neapolitanischen Konservatorien', in *Festschrift Helmut Osthoff*, edited by L. Hoffman-Erbrecht and H. Hucke, Tutzung, Schneider, 1961, pp.139-154

Hussey, D., *Verdi*, The Master Musicians, London, Dent, 1940

Kerman, J., *Opera as Drama*, London, OUP, 1957

Kimbell, D., *Verdi in the Age of Italian Romanticism*, Cambridge, CUP, 1981

Kümmel, W. F., 'Vincenzo Bellini nello specchio dell'*Allgemeine Musikalische Zeitung* di Lipsia 1827-1846', in *Nuova Rivista Musicale Italiana*, VII, 1973, pp.186-205

Le Huray, P. and J. Day, *Music and Aesthetics in the Eighteenth and Early Nineteenth Century*, Cambridge Readings in the Literature of Music, Cambridge, CUP, 1981

Lippmann, F., 'Belliniana', in *Il melodramma italiana dell'Ottocento. Studi e ricerche per Massimo Mila*, Turin, Einaudi, 1977, pp.281-317

Lippmann, F., 'Der italienische Vers und der musikalische Rhythmus. Zum Verhältnis von Vers und Musik in der italienische Oper des 19. Jahrhunderts, mit einem Rückblick auf die 2. Hälfte des 18. Jahrhunderts', in *Analecta Musicologica*, XII (1973), pp.253-369; XIV (1974), pp.324-410; XV (1975), pp.298-333

Lippmann, F., 'Mozart Aufführungen des frühen Ottocento in Neapel', in *Analecta Musicologica*, III, 1969, pp.164-179

Lippmann, F., 'Su *La Straniera* di Bellini', in *Nuova Rivista Musicale Italiana*, IV, 1971, pp.565-605

Lippmann, F., *Vincenzo Bellini und die italienische Opera seria seiner Zeit*. Studien über Libretto, Arienform und Melodik, *Analecta Musicologica* VI, Cologne and Vienna, Böhlau, 1969

Lippmann, F., 'Vincenzo Bellini e l'opera seria del suo tempo. Studi sul libretto, la forma delle arie e la melodia', new edition, in M. Adamo and F. Lippmann, *Vincenzo Bellini*, Turin, ERI, 1981, pp.313-576

Luschnat, O., *Zum Text von Philodems Schrift De Musica*, Berlin, Deutsche Akademie der Wissenschaft, 1953

Luin, E. J., *Fortuna e influenza della musica di Pergolesi in Europa*, Quaderni della Accademia Chigiana VI, Siena, 1943

Maccolini, G., *Della vita e dell'arte di Antonio Tamburini*, Faenza, Montanari & Marabini, 1842

Mastrigli, L., *La Sicilia musicale*, Bologna, 1891

Matteini, O., *Stendhal e la musica*, n.p. [published in Turin], EDA, 1981

Medicus, L., *Die Koloratur in der italienische Oper des 19. Jahrhunderts*, dissertation published Zürich, Wetzikon & Rüti, 1939

Mila, M., *Cent'anni di musica moderna*, Milan, 1944

Miragoli, L., *Il melodramma italiana nell'Ottocento*, Rome, Maglione & Strini, 1924

Monaldi, G., 'Orchestre e direttore del secolo XIX', in *Rivista Musicale Italiana* XVI, 1909, pp.123-142; 531-549

Mondolfi, A. and H. Hucke, 'Neapel', in Die Musik in Geschichte und Gegenwart, IX, 1961, cols 1307-1342; especially col.1337

Oehlmann, V., Vincenzo Bellini, Zürich and Freiburg, Atlantis, 1974

Oliver, A. R., The Encyclopedists as Critics of Music, New York, Columbia, 1947

Orrey, L., Bellini, The Master Musicians, London, Dent, 1969

Pannain, G., Ottocento musicale italiano, Saggi e note, Milan, Curci, 1952

Pastura, F., Bellini secondo la storia, Parma, Guanda, 1959

Petrobelli, P., 'Bellini e Paisiello. Altri documenti sulla nascita dei Puritani', in Il melodramma italiana dell'Ottocento. Studi e ricerche per Massimo Mila, Turin, Einaudi, 1977, pp.351-363

Petrobelli, P., 'Note sulla poetica di Bellini a proposito di I puritani', in Muzikološki Zbornik, VIII, Ljubljana, 1972, pp.70-85

Pirrotta, N. and G. Graziosi, 'Direzione e concertazione', in Enciclopedia dello spettacolo, IV, 1957, cols 738-746

Pizzetti, I., La musica di Vincenzo Bellini, Florence, La voce, 1915; also in Pizzetti, La musica italiana dell'Ottocento, Turin, Palatine, 1947

Pleasants, H., The Great Singers, London, Gollancz, 1974

Pollin, A., 'Towards an Understanding of Antonio Eximeno', in Journal of the American Musicological Society, X, 1957, pp.86-96

Pougin, A., Bellini. Sa vie, ses oeuvres, Paris, Hachette, 1868

Povoledo, E. and R. de Luca, 'Orchestra', in ES, VII, 1960, cols 1386-1396

Prota-Giurleo, U., La grande orchestra del Teatro S. Carlo nel Settecento, Naples, the author, 1927 (NC)

Radiciotti, G., Gioacchino Rossini. Vita documentata, Opere ed influenza su l'arte, 3 vols, Tivoli, Chicca, 1927-1929

Robinson, M., Naples and Neapolitan Opera, Oxford, OUP, 1972

Rognoni, L., Gioacchino Rossini, Turin, ERI, 1968

Rolandi, U., Il libretto per musica attraverso i tempi, Rome, Ateneo, 1951

Rosen, C., The Classical Style, London, Faber, 1971

Rosselli, J., 'Agenti teatrali nel mondo dell'opera lirica italiana dell'Ottocento', in Rivista Italiana di Musicologia, XVII, 1982, pp.134-154

Rossi, R., Appunti biografici intorno a Girolamo Crescentini, Udine, 1873 (BN)

Sartori, C., 'Girolamo Crescentini', in ES, III, 1956, cols 1705-1707

Saussine, H. de, 'L'Harmonie Bellinienne', in Rivista Musicale Italiana, XXVII, 1920, pp.477-482

Scherillo, M., Vincenzo Bellini, note anddotiche e critiche, Ancona, Morelli, 1882

Schlitzer, F., Tommaso Traetta, Leonardo Leo, Vincenzo Bellini, Siena, Accademia Musicale Chigiana, 1952

Schmidl, C., *Dizionario universale dei musicisti*, 2 vols, Milan, Sonzogno, 1926

Serafin, T. and A. Toni, *Stile, tradizioni e convenzioni del melodramma italiano del Settecento e dell'Ottocento*, Milan, Ricordi, 1958

Smiles, J., 'Directions for Improvised Ornamentation in Italian Method Books of the late Eighteenth Century', in *Journal of the American Musicological Society*, XXXI, 1978, pp.495-509

Sternfeld, F., *Goethe and Music*, New York, New York Publ. Lib., 1954

Strunk, O., *Source Readings in Music History*, London, Faber, 1952

Triani, C., *Giovanni Battista Rubini*, Bergamo, 1954 (NC)

Viola, O., *Bibliografia Belliniana*, second edition, Catania, 1923

Viola, O., 'Vincenzo Bellini seniore', in *Rivista del Comune di Catania*, Catania, January-February 1930

Visetti, A., 'Tendencies on the Operatic Stage in the Nineteenth Century', in *Papers of the Musical Association*, XXII, 1896, pp. 141-151

Voss, P., *Vincenzo Bellini*, Musiker-Biographien vol.23, Leipzig, Reclam 1901

Walker, F., 'Lettere disperse e inedite di Vincenzo Bellini', in *Rivista del Comune di Catania*, Catania, October-December 1960

Weinstock, H., *Donizetti and the World of Opera in Italy, Paris and Vienna in the First Half of the Nineteenth Century*, New York, Pantheon, 1963

Weinstock, H., *Vincenzo Bellini, his Life and his Operas*, London Weidenfeld & Nicolson, 1972

Winternitz, G., 'I cimeli belliniani della R. Accademia Filarmonica di Bologna', in *Rivista Musicale Italiana*, XL, 1936, pp.104-118

Witzenmann, W., 'Grundzüge der Instrumentation in italienischen Opern von 1770 bis 1830', in *Analecta Musicologica*, XXI, 1981, pp.276-332

INDEX

acting, 61-68, 99
Algarotti, F., 26, 35, 121
appearance of singers, 59-60, 64
appoggiaturas, 167-178, 182
Arteaga, S., 18, 26, 29-30, 48, 155-156
audience, 35-37, 158
ballets, 108, 130, 138
Barbaja, D., 112, 129-130, 138
basso continuo texture, 33, 115, 117, 121-123, 134, 144, 146, 149
bel canto, 22, 44, 47, 50, 53, 63, 151-154, 158, 174, 182-184
Bellini, V., 4, 63, 68-70, 75, 83, 89, 91-94, 100-106, 119, 142-143, 176-178, 182, 184-189

canto spianato, 152, 162-163, 166, 168-175, 184
castratos, 44, 153-158, 163, 186-188
censorship, 97, 100
chauvinism, 5-6, 8, 24, 138(n), 161
conducting, 111, 118, 129, 134-147
contraltos, 186-187
Crescentini, G., 45, 61, 103, 118, 155-156(n), 164, 165, 175

Donizetti, G., 96, 99-100, 102, 128, 133, 145-146
double basses, 121, 125, 135, 146
drama, 2-3, 25, 71-73, 75-78, 82-83, 94-95, 106, 178
Duprez, G.-L., 161-162, 187
edification, 18, 28, 49, 51, 59, 94-102
Eximeno, A., 5, 21, 43, 84, 116
expression, 32, 48, 53-54, 89, 108-109, 111, 150-151, 158, 161, 172, 178
Ferro, Cav. G. di, 18, 33, 67
Festa, G.M., 129, 136-137
filosofi, 14, 19, 29-30, 79, 109
Florimo, F., 11, 130

Glinka, M., 189
gorgheggi, 179
Greeks, Ancient, 13-22, 25, 27, 29, 46, 50, 67
Grossi, G.B. Gennaro, 14-17, 22-23
heart (and soul), 15, 18-20, 22, 26, 48, 89, 92, 94, 109, 158, 160, 162, 182
imitation, 27, 39, 48, 51, 93
instrumental music, 21, 32, 43, 72, 108
keyboard (orchestral), 33, 123, 127, 131, 146, 118-120
libretto, 4(n), 74, 79-81, 139-141
Lichtenthal, 14, 43, 120, 123a-124, 132, 135, 152
Lippmann, F., 2-3, 12, 76-78, 86b, 183

mad scenes, 98-99
Majer, A., 20, 52
Mancini, G.B., 47, 51, 115, 117, 159
Mercadante, G.S.R., 7, 81, 85(n), 113, 144, 185
messa di voce, 152-153, 157, 164-166
Metastasio, P., 84-91, 102, 185
Milan, 37, 128-129, 139
Milizia, F., 43, 49, 91, 93-94, 96
mouth position, 58-59
Mozart, W.A., 6, 59

Naples, 4, 7-10, 22-25, 112-114, 126-138, 153, 35-36
newspapers and periodicals, 9, 19, 27, 62-63, 79, 99, 192-193
opera, 25-28, 38
orchestras, 126-128, 130-133, 146
ornamentation, 22, 46, 174, 179, 183, 186

Pacini, G., 60, 103, 120, 175, 185
Paisiello, G., 8-9, 11, 98-99, 126, 168-169, 188
Pasta, G., 63, 103, 152, 188
Pergolesi, G.B., 5, 8, 10, 11, 23, 92(n)
Perrino, M., 46, 59, 164, 167, 175, 178
plots, 70, 75, 92-105
poetry, 3, 14, 29-32, 42, 48, 53, 73, 82-93, 105-106, 162, 176
preghiera, 86-87, 163
pronunciation, 45, 51-59, 150

recitative, 85-86a
Romani, F., 75, 86-92, 95, 104-105
Romani, P., 141-142
Rossini, G.A., 2, 78, 101, 108, 112, 118, 158, 179-182, 184
Rousseau, J.-J., 21, 40, 48, 120
Rubini, G.B., 58, 63, 104, 161, 187-188

solfeggios, 116-118, 164-165, 167, 179
spectacle, 34-38, 81, 113
Spohr, L., 5, 65, 121, 123a, 129, 155, 164
Spontini, G., 9, 23, 102-103(n), 136, 171-173
Stendhal, 10, 37, 64-66, 74, 92(n), 110, 152, 154

tenors, 56, 59, 62-63, 186-188
terrore, 96, 99-100
Tosi, A., 57, 60, 69
Tosi, P.F., 44, 47, 116, 154, 159, 162, 166
unification of the arts, 15, 25-32, 38, 42
Venice, 140-141
Verdi, G., 2, 83, 85, 91, 95, 104, 108, 178
vibrato, 159
vocal force, 54-57, 149, 159-161, 178
Weber, C.M. von, 125
Zingarelli, N.A., 5, 10, 47, 103, 164, 188

For Product Safety Concerns and Information please contact our EU representative GPSR@taylorandfrancis.com
Taylor & Francis Verlag GmbH, Kaufingerstraße 24, 80331 München, Germany

www.ingramcontent.com/pod-product-compliance
Lightning Source LLC
Chambersburg PA
CBHW071832300426
44116CB00009B/1518